BIBLICAL AND NON-BIBLICAL EVIDENCES FOR THE BOOK OF MORMON

BIBLICAL AND NON-BIBLICAL EVIDENCES FOR THE BOOK OF MORMON

THAT SHOW ITS VALIDITY AS SCRIPTURE

A Layman's Thesis

By Joseph Dean DeBarthe

Edited by Pat Elliott Winholtz and Faye Shaw

Kravitz & Sons
INNOVATORS IN PUBLISHING, MARKETING AND ADVERTISING

Kravitz and Sons LLC
1301 Farmville Blvd, Suite 104
Greenville, NC 27834

Published by Kravitz and Sons LLC.

ISBN: 979-8-89639-198-2 (sc)
ISBN: 979-8-89639-197-5 (e)

Library of Congress Control Number: 2025914870

ACKNOWLEDGEMENTS

My thanks go to my editor, Pat Elliott Winholtz, for understanding what I was trying to say and helping me to express it correctly. I am also indebted to Faye Shaw of the Christian Center for Book of Mormon Study and Research for the time and editorial skills she so generously provided. The helpful criticism and guidance of these two women has kept me on "the straight and narrow" path. However, sometimes, as you might suppose, we had to compromise. In the same context, I must also say thank you to the people who freely allowed me the use of their research. Their openness and willingness to share information was a great blessing. Not to be forgotten is the kind attention of the members of my Harvest Hills Sunday school class who reviewed my preliminary draft of this book. Finally, I thank Maria, my wife, for her patience throughout this lengthy undertaking and you, the reader, for going on this journey with me.

Joseph Dean DeBarthe
September, 2012

Table of Contents

INTRODUCTION

What about the Book of Mormon? That it is a controversial book cannot be denied. Many do not accept it as scripture. They believe that Joseph Smith, Jr., "wrote" it. They also believe that the Bible is the *only* scripture ever written, but nowhere does the Bible make that claim. This belief is not biblical. In fact, just the opposite is true. The Bible testifies to the existence of other written scriptures and specifically a second scripture written about the tribe of Joseph (Ezekiel 37:19). This Joseph is the same Joseph of the coat of many colors, the same Joseph sold into slavery in Egypt and the same Joseph that saved Egypt and all of the tribes of Israel from the seven-year famine that occurred.

Due to his lack of knowledge and education, if Joseph Smith, Jr., had written The Book of Mormon, it would have been disproven years ago. Instead, as time passes, more and more of it is proven to be correct. Joseph Smith could not have written it for many reasons, not the least of which is the fact that he was a barely literate man. He knew very little of the scriptures and no Hebrew at all. Yet The Book of Mormon is clearly written by highly educated men with a strong background in Hebrew customs and writing techniques, none of which were known by any American in the 1800s. More information on this subject will be explored on the following pages.

This book was begun by the direction of the Holy Spirit and written to the entire body of Christ. Some might ask why they should read it. Some will read it to try to refute it; others will read it to learn, and still others will use it to further their own agendas. However, you should read it and pray over it, asking God through His Holy Spirit to give you a witness as to its validity.

We need direction from the Holy Spirit because we are always vulnerable to error. Even prophets can be deceived (2 Chronicles, Chapter 18). Satan will do anything he can to prevent us from gaining unity in our fight against him. For years he has used the "divide and conquer" plan, and we have fallen prey to it. It is time we stopped fighting over our petty differences and start working together for the salvation of all mankind. The harvest is plentiful; it is time to bring it in, and we can do it! With the help of God through His Son Jesus Christ and His Holy Spirit, we can accomplish what would otherwise be impossible on our own.

My goal has not been to write a scholarly work, and since I do not have the expertise to do that, I therefore am writing from a layman's point of view. My intention is to give you, the reader, useful information. I hope to provide enough support from the Bible and other sources to create a preponderance of evidence to show that The Book of Mormon is authentic. What I have in mind is to create a "nuts and bolts" approach, a set of tools or a manual, which anyone can use in discussing The Book of Mormon with the broader Christian community. I am trying to help people understand what the book has to offer, and for those who already believe in it, a reference to help them support their point of view. For non-believers, who are well acquainted with the Bible, I would like to offer some new relationships between scriptures that they might not know. My approach is to provide a large number of biblical and non-biblical evidences to show that The Book of Mormon is scripture and was not written by Joseph Smith.

I take full responsibility for the opinions expressed herein and pray that the book will meet your needs. I do not know how God will use this book, but I am trusting that He will use it for His purposes. I wish you well and pray that you will allow God through the power of His Holy Spirit to determine your beliefs and not man, not even me. Nevertheless, as a beginning, can we agree that scripture is whatever the Holy Spirit witnesses that it is?

Joseph Dean DeBarthe
March 2012

CHAPTER 1

WHAT DOES THE BIBLE TELL US ABOUT GOD'S CHARACTER?

Do you think God's word is trustworthy? One of the best scriptures I have found about His reliability is:

Isaiah 55:11:

So shall my word be that goeth forth out of my mouth: it shall not return unto me void, but it shall accomplish that which I please, and it shall prosper in the thing whereto I sent it.

Remember, God is omnipresent; by definition that means that He exists in every second of time and in all places at the same time, throughout all of what He has created.

Psalms 139:7-10:

Whither shall I go from thy Spirit? Or whither shall I flee from thy presence? If I ascend up into heaven, thou art there; if I make my bed in hell, behold, thou art there. If I take the wings of the morning, and dwell in the uttermost parts of the sea; Even there shall thy hand lead me, and thy right hand shall hold me.

There are many examples of the word of God being fulfilled, starting with the creation of this world:

Genesis 1:2:

And the earth was without form, and void; and darkness was upon the face of the deep. And the Spirit of God moved upon the face of the waters.

Job 26:13:

By his Spirit he hath garnished the heavens; his hand hath formed the crooked serpent.

Genesis 1:3-5:

And God said, Let there be light: and there was light. And God saw the light, that it was good: and God divided the light from the darkness.

And God called the light day, and the darkness he called night. And the evening and the morning were the first day.

Throughout the entire creation process (Genesis 1-2), God's commands were fulfilled. These scriptures mean that any word spoken by God is ever present across all of what we see as time. Once it is spoken, it cannot be taken back, or changed, even by God. Further on in the Old Testament, we read:

2 Samuel 22:31:
As for God, his way is perfect; The word of the Lord is tried: He is a buckler to all them that trust in him.

Once again, the scripture tells us of God's truth and perfection. He is incorruptible. Consider what Isaiah says:

Isaiah 45:15-19 (The Living Bible Paraphrased):
Truly, O God of Israel, Savior, you work in strange, mysterious ways. All who worship idols shall be disappointed and ashamed. <u>But Israel shall be saved by Jehovah with eternal salvation; they shall never b   e disappointed in their God through all eternity.</u> For Jehovah created the heavens and the earth and put everything in place, and he made the world to be lived in, not chaos. I am Jehovah, He says, and there is no other! I publicly proclaim bold promises; I do not whisper obscurities in some dark corner so that no one can know what I mean. And I did not tell Israel to ask me for what I did not plan to give! <u>No, for I, Jehovah, speak only the truth and righteousness.</u> (Emphasis added)

Next:

Isaiah 45:22-23:
Look unto me, and be ye saved, all the ends of the earth: For I am God, there is none else. <u>I have sworn by myself, the word has gone out of my mouth in righteousness, and shall not return,</u> that unto me every knee shall bow, every tongue shall swear. (Emphasis added)

Since God always speaks the truth, and He never recants, new messages must always agree with everything He has previously stated. Why? Because He never changes; therefore, He never disagrees with Himself.

Malachi 3:6:
For I am the LORD, I change not;....

Deuteronomy 32:4:

He is the rock, his work is perfect: for all his ways are judgment: a God of truth and without iniquity, just and right is he.

Psalms 25:10:

All the paths of the Lord are mercy and truth unto such as keep his covenant and his testimonies.

Furthermore, we also know that God speaks the truth through His holy prophets:

1 Kings 17:24:

And the woman said to Elijah, Now by this I know that thou art a man of God, and that the word of the LORD in thy mouth is truth.

The New Testament also tells of God's faithfulness:

Matthew 24:35:

Heaven and earth shall pass away, but my words shall not pass away.

Everywhere in the Bible, God's character is one of honesty, righteousness and fulfillment. Throughout His word He makes many promises and covenants. While many were accomplished within the timeframe of the Bible, some have been completed between the end of the Bible and today, and, as we know, there are many yet to be realized. Can we honestly say that promises not fulfilled within the confines of the Bible cannot be believed or trusted in? I think not. The Bible is clear: God's word can be trusted and believed, no matter how long it takes because He is the Alpha and Omega of time. Whereas we are restricted by time, He is not. That is why He knows the answer *before we even know what the question is, let alone the answer.*

CHAPTER 2

WHAT PROMISES OR COVENANTS DID GOD MAKE WITH THE TWELVE TRIBES OF ISRAEL?

To Abraham

God made many covenants with the Twelve Tribes of Israel, but most of them were conditional. He required faithful obedience to His word for the fulfillment of those covenants. Even though His people failed Him, He was willing to return to them whenever they chose to obey Him. However, God's first covenant with Abram, when He gave land to him and his descendants, was unconditional (See Jeremiah 16:14-15):

Genesis 15:18:

> *In the same day the LORD made a covenant with Abram, saying, Unto thy seed have I given this land, from the river of Egypt unto the great river, the river Euphrates.*

Jeremiah 16:14-15:

> *Therefore, behold, the days come, saith the Lord, that it shall be no more said, The Lord liveth, that brought the children of Israel out of the land of Egypt; But the LORD liveth, that brought the children of Israel from the land of the north, and from all the lands whither he had driven them: and I will bring them again unto their land that I gave unto their fathers.*

Then God changed Abram's name (Exalted Father) to Abraham (Father of Nations):

Genesis 17:4-5:

> *As for me, behold, my covenant is with thee, And thou shalt be a father of many nations. Neither shall thy name be Abram, but thy name shall be Abraham; for a father of many nations have I made thee.*

Following that, God made another covenant with Abraham, the covenant of circumcision:

Genesis 17:6-11:

And I will make thee exceeding fruitful, and I will make Nations of thee, and Kings shall come out of thee. And I will establish my covenant between me and thee and thy seed after thee in their generations for an everlasting covenant, to be a God unto thee, and to thy seed after thee. And I will give unto thee, and to thy seed after thee, the land wherein thou art a stranger, all the land of Canaan, for an everlasting possession; and I will be their God. And God said unto Abraham, Thou shalt keep my covenant therefore, thou, and thy seed after thee, in their generations. This is my covenant, which ye shall keep, between me and you and thy seed after thee; Every man child among you shall be circumcised. And ye shall circumcise the flesh of your foreskin; and it shall be a token of the covenant betwixt me and you. And he that is eight days old shall be circumcised among you, every man child in your generations, he that is born in the house, or bought with money of any stranger, which is not of thy seed.

God also changed Abraham's wife's name:

Genesis 17:15:

And God said unto Abraham, as for Sarai your wife, thou shalt not call her name Sarai, but Sarah shall her name be.

Then God fulfilled His promise:

Genesis 21:1-4:

And the LORD visited Sarah as he had said, and the LORD did unto Sarah as he had spoken. For Sarah conceived, and bare Abraham a son in his old age, at the set time of which God had spoken to him. And Abraham called the name of his son that was born unto him, whom Sarah bare to him, Isaac. And Abraham circumcised his son Isaac being eight days old, as God had commanded him.

Later on in Isaac's youth, God tested Abraham, and he passed the test:

Genesis 22:1-14:

And it came to pass after these things, that God did tempt Abraham, and said unto him, Abraham: and he said, Behold, here I am. And he said, Take now thy son, thine only son Isaac, whom thou lovest, and get thee into the land of Moriah; and offer him there for a burnt offering upon one of the mountains which I will tell thee of. And Abraham rose up early in the morning, and saddled his ass, and took two of his young men with him, and Isaac his son, and clave the wood for the burnt offering, and rose up, and went unto the place of which God had told him. Then on the third day Abraham lifted up his eyes, and saw the place afar off. And Abraham said unto his young men, Abide ye here with the ass; and I and the lad will go yonder and worship, and come again to you. And Abraham took the wood of the burnt offering, and laid it upon Isaac his son; and he took the fire in his hand, and a knife; and they went both of them together. And Isaac spake unto Abraham his father, and said, My father: and he said, Here am I, my son. And he said, Behold the fire and the wood: but where is the lamb for a burnt offering? And Abraham said, My son, God will provide himself a lamb for a burnt offering: so they went both of them together. And they came to the place which God had told him of; and Abraham built an altar there, and laid the wood in order, and bound Isaac his son, and laid him on the altar upon the wood. And Abraham stretched forth his hand, and took the knife to slay his son. And the angel of the LORD called unto him out of heaven, and said, Abraham, Abraham: and he said, Here am I. And he said, Lay not thine hand upon the lad, neither do thou anything unto him: for now I know that thou fearest God, seeing thou hast not withheld thy son, thine only son from me. And Abraham lifted up his eyes, and looked, and behold behind him a ram caught in a thicket by his horns: and Abraham went and took the ram, and offered him up for a burnt offering in the stead of his son. And Abraham called the name of that place Jehovah-jireh: as it is said to this day, In the mount of the LORD it shall be seen.

Following this severe test, God made a covenant with Abraham:

Genesis 22:16-18:

And said, By myself have I sworn, saith the LORD, for because thou hast done this thing, and hast not withheld thy son, thine only son: That in blessing I will bless thee, and in multiplying I will multiply thy seed as the stars of the heaven, and as the sand which is upon the sea shore; and thy seed shall possess the gate of his enemies; And in thy seed shall all the nations of the earth be blessed; because thou hast obeyed my voice.

Abraham's obedience to God became a type and shadow portraying the sacrifice of His beloved Son Jesus for our sins. Prior to Sarah's having Isaac, Sarah gave her handmaiden (Hagar) to Abraham and she bore him a son, Ishmael. He also had twelve sons who became the twelve tribes that bore their names:

Genesis 25:12-16:

Now these are the generations of Ishmael, Abraham's son, whom Hagar the Egyptian, Sarah's handmaid, bare unto Abraham: And these are the names of the sons of Ishmael, by their names, according to their generations: the first born of Ishmael, Nebajoth; and Kedar, and Abdeel, and Mibsam, And Mishma, and Dumah, and Massa, Hadar, and Tema, Jetur, Naphish, and Kedemah: These are the sons of Ishmael, and these are their names, by their towns, and by their castles; twelve princes according unto their nations.

These twelve tribes became the Arabic nations of today as a fulfillment of God's promise to Abraham.

Genesis 21:12-13:

And God said unto Abraham, Let it not be grievous in thy sight because of the lad, and because of thy bond woman; in all that Sarah hath said unto thee, hearken unto her voice; for in Isaac shall thy seed be called. And also of the son of the bondwoman will I make a nation, because he is thy seed.

To Isaac

When Isaac was of age, and Abraham was well stricken in years, Abraham sent his servant to his kindred, where he found Rebekah and brought her back to be Isaac's wife. Rebekah became pregnant with twins, Esau and Jacob. Esau became a hunter and Jacob a farmer. One day Jacob talked Esau, the firstborn, into selling him his birthright for some food. This created much animosity between the brothers. When Isaac was about to die, Jacob pretended to be Esau, and received Esau's blessing from Isaac. (That blessing was to have been a double portion for Esau.) This angered Esau very much, and after Isaac died, Jacob traveled back to the land of his kindred because he feared Esau. After Jacob arrived at his uncle Laban's house, he fell in love with Rachel. He worked for seven years to marry her, but Laban gave him Leah instead. So Jacob had to work seven more years for Rachel, which he did. Rachel was jealous of Leah because Leah was fertile and she was not, so Rachel gave Jacob her servant girl Bilhah, and Leah gave her servant girl Zilpah to Jacob also.

The following are the children of Jacob's two wives and two concubines:

Jacob's Wives		Jacob's Concubines	
Leah	Rachel	Bilhah	Zilpah
Male Children			
Rueben	Joseph	Dan	Gad
Simeon	Benjamin	Naphtali	Asher
Levi			
Judah			
Issachar			
Zebulum			
Female Children			
Dinah			

In time, Jacob returned home and made peace with his brother Esau. Along the way God changed Jacob's name to Israel:

Genesis 32:22-28:

And he rose up that night, and took his two wives, and his two women servants, and his eleven sons, and passed over the ford Jabbok. And he took them, and sent them over the brook, and sent over that he had. And Jacob was left alone; and there wrestled a man with him until the breaking of the day. And when he saw that he prevailed not against him, he touched the hollow of his thigh; and the hollow of Jacob's thigh was out of joint, as he wrestled with him. And he said, let me go, for the day breaketh. And he said, I will not let thee go, except thou bless me. And he said unto him, what is your name? And he said, Jacob. And he said, Thy name shall be called no more Jacob, but Israel: for as a prince hast thou power with God and with men, and hast prevailed.

To Joseph

So Israel (Jacob) had thus found much favor with God. His favorite son was Joseph, whose mother was Rachel, his beloved wife. As part of God's promise to make a great nation from Isaac, God allowed Joseph to be sold into slavery in Egypt. Joseph prevailed through his many hardships to finally become the second most powerful man in Egypt. He thus saved Israel, Egypt and many other people in the countries surrounding Egypt from the seven-year famine that occurred just as the Pharaoh had dreamed and Joseph interpreted. Joseph was reunited with his family, including his father Israel, who promised Joseph that God would return them to Canaan.

Genesis 48:21:

And Israel said unto Joseph, Behold, I die: but God shall be with you, and bring you again unto the land of your fathers.

Genesis 50:26:

So Joseph died, being an hundred and ten years old: and they embalmed him, and he was put in a coffin in Egypt.

Eventually, a new king came to the throne of Egypt who was fearful of the Israelites because of their great numbers; therefore, he enslaved them, putting great burdens on them. The harder he oppressed them, the more they seemed to multiply and, in return, the greater he mistreated them. It was during this time that Moses was born, and through the grace of God, became a member of pharaoh's household. But he learned that he was an Israelite and hated the way his people were being abused. One day he saw an Egyptian beating a Hebrew slave. He lost his temper, killed the Egyptian and hid his body:

Exodus 2:12,15:

And he looked this way and that way, and when he saw that there was no man, he slew the Egyptian, and hid him in the sand. Now when Pharaoh heard this thing, he sought to slay Moses. But Moses fled from the face of Pharaoh, and dwelt in the land of Midian: and he sat down by a well.

So Moses escaped, and God remembered His promise:

Exodus 2:23-25:

And it came to pass in process of time, that the king of Egypt died: and the children of Israel sighed by reason of the bondage, and they cried, and their cry came up unto God by reason of the bondage. And God heard their groaning, and God remembered his covenant with Abraham, with Isaac, and with Jacob. And God looked upon the children of Israel, and God had respect unto them.

Again God kept His word to His people who had lived in Egypt for many years:

Exodus 12:41-42:

And it came to pass at the end of four hundred and thirty years, even the selfsame day it came to pass, that all the hosts of the LORD went out from the land of Egypt. It is a night to be much observed unto the LORD for bringing them out from the land of Egypt: this is that night of the LORD to be observed of all the children of Israel in their generations.

Exodus, chapters 1-14, has the complete story of God's freeing of the Israelites from the Egyptians.

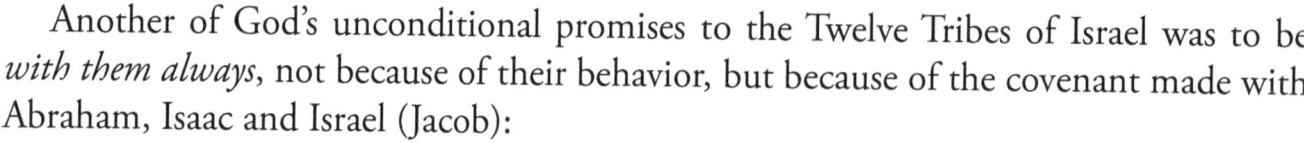

Another of God's unconditional promises to the Twelve Tribes of Israel was to be *with them always*, not because of their behavior, but because of the covenant made with Abraham, Isaac and Israel (Jacob):

Deuteronomy 4:31:

(For the LORD thy God is a merciful God;) he will not forsake thee, neither destroy thee, nor forget the covenant of thy fathers which he swear unto them.

While on their journey out of Egypt, Moses baptized the people:

Corinthians 10:1-2:

Moreover, brethren, I would not that ye should be ignorant, how that all our fathers were under the cloud, and all passed through the sea; And were all <u>baptized unto Moses</u> in the cloud and in the sea; And <u>did all eat the same spiritual meat;</u> And <u>did all drink the same spiritual drink: for they drank of that spiritual Rock</u> that followed them: <u>and that Rock was Christ.</u> (Emphasis added)

Moses took the Twelve Tribes of Israel through the cloud (God's Spirit) and baptized each one unto Christ. They also had communion, "**And all did eat the same spiritual meat**," the communion bread, and "**And all did drink the same spiritual drink**," the communion wine.

Moses also foretold the coming of Jesus Christ and said that He would be a prophet like unto himself:

Deuteronomy 18:15-18:

The LORD thy God will raise up unto thee a Prophet from the midst of thee, of thy brethren, like unto me; unto him ye shall hearken; According to all that thou desiredst of the LORD thy God in Horeb in the day of the assembly, saying, Let me not hear again the voice of the LORD my God, neither let me see this great fire any more, that I die not. And the LORD said unto me, They have well spoken that which they have spoken. I will raise them up a Prophet from among their brethren, like unto thee, and will put my words in his mouth; and he shall speak unto them all that I shall command him.

God's promise to the Israelites was:

Deuteronomy 30:16:

In that I command thee this day to love the LORD thy God, to walk in his ways, and to keep his commandments and statutes and his judgments,

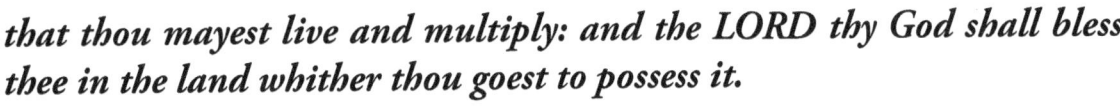

that thou mayest live and multiply: and the LORD thy God shall bless thee in the land whither thou goest to possess it.

But *this* promise was conditional, and if the people transgressed, God would depart from them, and they would be driven out of the land of their inheritance:

Deuteronomy 30:17-19:

But if thine heart turn away, so that thou wilt not hear, but shalt be drawn away, and worship other Gods, and serve them; I denounce unto you this day, that ye shall surely perish, and that ye shall not prolong your days upon the land, whither thou passest over Jordan to go to possess it. I call heaven and earth to record this day against you, that I have set before you life and death, blessing and cursing: therefore choose life, that both thou and thy seed may live.

God always knows what will happen; He knew the Israelites would forsake Him:

Deuteronomy 31:16:

And the LORD said unto Moses, Behold thou shalt sleep with thy fathers; and this people shall rise up, and go a whoring after the gods of the strangers of the land, whither they go to be among them, and will forsake me, and break my covenant which I have made with them.

God then told Moses to write a song that would testify to their seed; the song would be a witness against all Israel (Deuteronomy 31:19-21). The text of the song is in Deuteronomy 32:1-43. The Lord also promised to restore them in the last days, when Israel would remember its covenant with Him:

Deuteronomy 30:1-3:

And it shall come to pass, when all these things are come upon thee, the blessing and the curse, which I have set before thee, and thou shalt call them to mind among all the nations, whither the LORD thy God hath driven thee, And shalt return unto the LORD thy God, and shalt obey his voice according to all that I command thee this day, thou and thy children, with all thine heart, and with all thine soul; That then the Lord thy God will turn thy captivity, and have compassion upon thee, and will return and gather thee from all the nations, whither the LORD thy God hath scattered thee."

After this, Moses died and the authority passed to Joshua.

To Joshua

Joshua 1:5:

There shall not any man be able to stand before thee all the days of thy life: as I was with Moses, so I will be with thee: I will not fail thee, nor forsake thee.

Joshua had now become God's spokesman to the entire house of Israel. To prove to the people that Joshua was His choice to replace Moses, God performed another miracle. He allowed the Israelites to pass over the Jordan River on dry land, just like He had allowed them to cross the Red Sea under Moses, when they left Egypt:

Joshua 3:17:

And the priests that bare the ark of the covenant of the LORD stood firm on dry ground in the midst of Jordan, and all the Israelites passed over on dry ground, until all the people were passed clean over the Jordan.

As the children of Israel crossed over the Jordan, the Lord had one member from each tribe pick up a stone from the Jordan River bed and carry it to the other side of the river as a memorial to the crossing for future generations:

Joshua 4:5-7:

And Joshua said to them, Pass over before the ark of the LORD your God into the midst of the Jordan, and take ye up every man of you a stone upon his shoulder, according unto the number of the tribes of the children of Israel: That this may be a sign among you, that when your children ask their fathers in time to come, saying, What mean ye by these stones? Then ye shall answer them, that the waters of the Jordan were cut off before the ark of the covenant of the LORD; when it passed over the Jordan, the waters of the Jordan were cut off: and these stones shall be for a memorial unto the children of Israel forever.

Then came the challenge to capture the city of Jericho. The Lord sent a messenger to Joshua, telling him how to defeat Jericho. Joshua followed the messenger's direction and destroyed the inhabitants of the city, except Rahab and her household. (Joshua, Chapter 6) The Lord continued to bless the Israelites, allowing them to overcome all who lived in the land that He had given them. (Joshua, Chapters 12-13) Joshua then divided the land among the tribes of Israel. (Joshua, Chapters 14-19)

To The Prophets

For many years the Israelites lived and prospered in their Promised Land. However, in continuing to seek after His people, God raised up a prophet, Isaiah, who foretold the virgin birth of Christ. Writing in approximately 701 B.C., he said:

Isaiah 7:14:

Therefore the LORD himself shall give you a sign; Behold a virgin shall conceive, and bear a son, and shall call his name Immanuel.

Jesus Christ fulfilled this prophecy. Isaiah then goes even further in describing the coming Messiah:

Isaiah 9:6-7:

For unto us a child is born, unto us a son is given: and the government shall be upon his shoulder: and his name shall be called Wonderful, Councilor, The mighty God, The everlasting Father, and The Prince of Peace. Of the increase of his government and peace there shall be no end, upon the throne of David, and upon his kingdom, to order it, and to establish it with judgment and with justice from henceforth even forever. The zeal of the LORD of hosts will perform this.

Jeremiah also foresaw the coming of Jesus Christ and foresaw that He would be a descendant of King David:

Jeremiah 23:5:

Behold, the days come, saith the LORD, that I will raise unto David a righteous branch, and a King shall reign and prosper, and shall execute judgment and justice in the earth.

In 700 B.C., the prophet Micah named the tiny village of Bethlehem as the birthplace of Israel's Messiah (Micah 5:2). The fulfillment of this prophecy, the birth of Christ, is one of the most widely known and celebrated facts in history.

Isaiah also foretold of John the Baptist's ministry to prepare the way for Jesus Christ:

Isaiah 40:3-5:

The voice of him that crieth in the wilderness, Prepare ye the way of the LORD, make straight in the desert a highway for our God. Every valley shall be exalted, and every mountain and hill shall be made low: and the crooked shall be made straight, and the rough places plain: And the glory of the LORD shall be revealed, and all flesh shall see it together: for the mouth of the LORD hath spoken it.

Isaiah prophesied that Jesus Christ would perform many miracles:

Isaiah 35:4-6:

Say to them that are of a fearful heart, Be strong, fear not: behold, your God will come with vengeance, even God with a recompense; he will come and save you. Then the eyes of the blind shall be opened, and the ears of the deaf shall be unstopped. Then shall the lame man leap as an hart, and the tongue of the dumb sing: for in the wilderness shall waters break out, and streams in the desert.

Zechariah also foretold Jesus Christ's triumphant arrival riding on a colt into Jerusalem:

Zechariah 9:9:

Rejoice greatly, O daughter of Zion; shout, O daughter of Jerusalem: behold, thy King cometh unto thee: he is just, and having salvation; lowly, and riding upon an ass, and upon a colt the foal of an ass.

In the New Testament, Jesus, Himself, confirmed His identity to the Samaritan woman:

John 4:25-26:

The woman saith unto him, I know that the Messias cometh, which is called Christ: when he is come, he will tell us all things. Jesus said unto her, I that speak unto thee am he.

More than 600 years before crucifixion was invented, both Israel's King David and the prophet Zechariah described the Messiah's death in words that perfectly depict that mode of execution. Further, they said that His body would be pierced and that none of His bones would be broken, contrary to the customary procedure (Psalm 22 and 34:20; Zechariah 12:10). Again, historians and New Testament writers confirm the fulfillment: Jesus of Nazareth died on a Roman cross, and His extraordinarily quick death eliminated the need for the usual breaking of bones. A spear was thrust into His side to verify that He was, indeed, dead.

As we know, there are a great many more promises given and completed by God in the Bible, but there are also many prophecies which were not fulfilled within the timeframe of the Bible. However, one that has been accomplished, which was predicted by Jeremiah about 2600 years ago, is the exact location and construction sequence of Jerusalem's nine suburbs. The prophet referred to the time of this building project as "the last days," that is, the land of Israel's second rebirth as a nation in Palestine:

Jeremiah 31:38-40:

Behold, the days come, saith the LORD, that the city shall be built to the LORD from the tower of Hananeel unto the gate of the corner. And the measuring line shall yet go forth over against it upon the hill Gareb, and shall compass about to Goath. And the whole valley of the dead bodies, and of the ashes, and all the fields unto the brook of Kidron, unto the corner of the horse gate toward the east, shall be holy unto the LORD; it shall not be plucked up, nor thrown down any more forever.

This rebirth became history in 1948, and the construction of the nine suburbs went forward precisely in the locations and in the sequence predicted. (Ross 2)

Then we have the prophecy of Zachariah:

Zachariah 2:3-4:

And, behold, the angel that talked with me went forth, and another angel went out to meet him, And said unto him, Run, speak to this young man, saying, Jerusalem shall be inhabited as towns without walls for the multitude of men and cattle therein:

According to Roy Weldon in his book Other Sheep, this prophecy dealt with the future and told us that its message would be announced by an angel to a young man. When the angel came to Joseph Smith and directed him to the gold plates, he also gave him the above message. Therefore, this prophecy was fulfilled as it was only a short time later (1856) that for the first time in the history of Jerusalem, it began to be inhabited as a town without walls. (57)

As we have said, there are other prophecies that are not yet fulfilled. However, they will be, and we should not only believe in them but watch for them to be achieved.

Notice what Isaiah says:

Isaiah 66:23:

And it shall come to pass, that from one new moon to another, and from one Sabbath to another, shall all flesh come to worship before me, saith the LORD.

I have just finished a book, *The Heavenly Man* by Paul Hattaway, about God's presence and work in China. It tells how God is assisting individuals within the borders of that country, in spite of great persecution by the authorities. Hattaway shows that God can and will reach all nations, even if we do not. Today, there are many avenues available to spread the gospel of Jesus Christ, so what is stopping us from reaching the lost? Aren't we stopping ourselves, by our own argumentative attitudes and the contention over minor doctrinal issues between religious factions? God's prophetic word will be fulfilled with or without our help, so let's help!

To New Testament Writers

The most important unfulfilled prophecy is that of the return of Jesus Christ:

Matthew 24:29-31:

<u>Immediately after the tribulation</u> of those days shall the sun be darkened, and the moon shall not give her light, and the stars shall fall from heaven, and the powers of the heavens shall be shaken: <u>And then shall appear the sign of the Son of man in heaven</u>: and then shall all the tribes of the earth mourn, and they shall see the Son of man coming in the clouds of heaven with power and great glory. And he shall send his angels with a great sound of a trumpet, and they shall gather together his elect from the four winds, from one end of heaven to the other. (Emphasis added)

The time of this fulfillment is unknown to all but God himself:

Matthew 24:36:

But of that day and hour knoweth no man, no, not the angels of heaven, but my father only.

But there are signs of His imminent return, and we are directed to take heed and prepare for His coming:

Matthew 24:14:

And this gospel of the kingdom shall be preached in all the world for a witness unto all nations; then shall the end come.

How will we know when the time is near?

Matthew 24:32-34:

Now learn a parable of the fig tree; When his branch is yet tender, and putteth forth leaves, ye know that summer is nigh: So likewise ye, when ye shall see all these things, know that it is near, even at the doors. Verily I say unto you, This generation shall not pass, till all these things be fulfilled.

What are these signs that predict His imminent arrival? We are told that the times will be just like in the days of Noah:

Matthew 24:37:

But as the days of Noe were, so shall also the coming of the Son of man be.

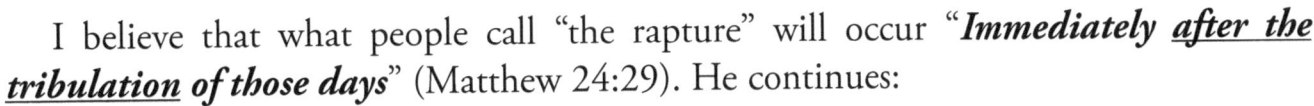

I believe that what people call "the rapture" will occur "*Immediately <u>after the tribulation</u> of those days*" (Matthew 24:29). He continues:

Matthew 24:40-41:

> *Then shall two be in the field; the one shall be taken, and the other left. Two women shall be grinding at the mill; the one shall be taken, and the other left.*

To me, the verses above affirm that the rapture comes after the tribulation, and at the time of Jesus Christ's return to earth. Other scriptures point out that His return will catch many people by surprise (2 Peter 3:1-18 and 1 Thessalonians 5:1-12).

After the return, John saw His throne surrounded by twenty-four smaller thrones. Who sits on those thrones?

Revelation 4:3-4:

> *And he that sat was to look upon like a jasper and a sardine stone: and there was a rainbow round about the throne, in sight like unto an emerald. And round about the throne were four and twenty seats: and upon the seats I saw four and twenty elders sitting, clothed in white raiment; and they had on their heads crowns of gold.*

The Bible tells us:

Matthew 19:28:

> *And Jesus said unto them, Verily I say unto you, That ye which have followed me, in the regeneration when the Son of man shall sit in the throne of his glory, ye also shall sit upon twelve thrones, judging the Twelve Tribes of Israel.*

Now think about this: Jesus explained that He came to visit only the lost sheep of Israel, not the Gentiles. So that would mean that He was sent to visit all Twelve Tribes of Israel, wherever they were located, which would include the Americas:

Matthew 15:24:

> *But he answered and said, "I am not sent but unto the lost sheep of the house of Israel."*

John 10:16:

> *And other sheep I have, which are not of this fold: them also I must bring, and they shall hear my voice; and there shall be one fold, and one shepherd.* (Emphasis added)

Christ was saying that He will visit *all* of Israel, even those that are not in Jerusalem or Israel ("*not of this fold*"). Although Judah and Benjamin, who were in the southern

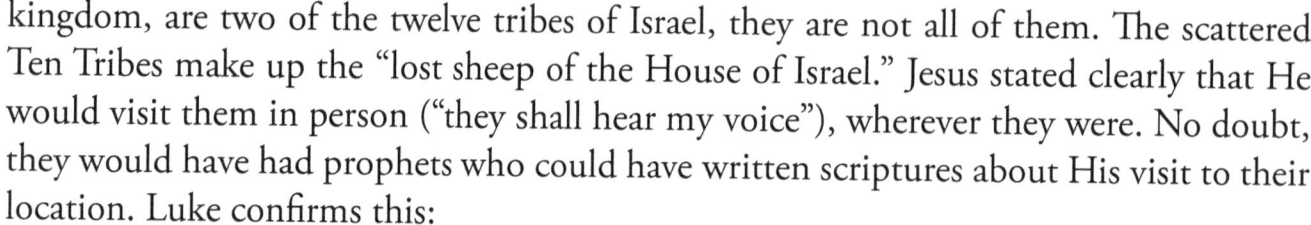

kingdom, are two of the twelve tribes of Israel, they are not all of them. The scattered Ten Tribes make up the "lost sheep of the House of Israel." Jesus stated clearly that He would visit them in person ("they shall hear my voice"), wherever they were. No doubt, they would have had prophets who could have written scriptures about His visit to their location. Luke confirms this:

Luke 11:49:

Therefore also said the wisdom of God, I will send them prophets and apostles, and some of them they shall slay and persecute.

God never does anything unless he tells his prophets beforehand, so He must have had prophets to direct His people. That applies to today as well!

Amos 3:7:

Surely the LORD God will do nothing but he revealeth his secret unto his servants the prophets.

God's covenant with Israel is that Jesus Christ will visit the entire house of Israel, *all Twelve Tribes*, wherever they are. This would include the Americas. The Book of Mormon tells us that Jesus also called twelve disciples in Bountiful (in the Americas). Will they fill the other twelve thrones that surround the throne of Christ? The Bible (from the scattering of the Northern Kingdom on) only tells us about two of the Twelve Tribes, Judah and Benjamin. Therefore, there should be additional scriptures that will tell us of Jesus Christ's visit to the other Ten Tribes of Israel.

One of the many things that the Bible tells us is that in the last days an angel will deliver the everlasting gospel to all the peoples of the earth. That could mean additional scripture. The Apostle John says:

Revelation 14:6:

And I saw another angel fly in the midst of heaven, having the everlasting gospel to preach unto them that dwell on the earth, and to every nation, and kindred, and tongue, and people,...

If we say that the Bible contains the complete, everlasting gospel (as believed by most Christians today), then why in the last days is this angel bringing the *"everlasting gospel to preach unto them that dwell on the earth"* if it is already here? The obvious answer is that it had been lost to mankind until it was returned by the angel. Could it be that the angel Moroni brought the fullness of the gospel by revelation to Joseph Smith, Jr., *just as God promised in the book of Revelation?*

CHAPTER 3

WHAT HAPPENED TO THE NORTHERN KINGDOM OF ISRAEL (THE TEN LOST TRIBES)? HOW WAS GOD INVOLVED?

Modern Day Israel

When people talk about modern-day Israel, most of them think that they are talking about all the descendants of Abraham through his son Isaac, and then through Jacob, that is, the Twelve Tribes of Israel, who they call the Jews. But the Bible teaches that the *House of Judah* is distinctly different from *all* of Israel. The Southern Kingdom was made up of the tribes of Judah, Benjamin and some of Levi. The Northern Kingdom consisted of the remaining Ten Tribes, which were taken into captivity and never restored to their homeland. From the time of the Dispersion of the northern tribes to the end of the Bible, any reference to the Jews is solely a reference to the Southern Kingdom. This concept has changed my understanding of scripture. Notice how the Bible refers to *the children of Israel* in the following passage from Hosea:

Hosea 1:10-11:

Yet the number of the <u>children of Israel</u> shall be as the sand of the sea, which cannot be measured nor numbered; and it shall come to pass, that in the place where it was said unto them, Ye <u>are</u> not my people, there it shall be said unto them, Ye are the sons of the living God. Then shall the <u>children of Judah</u> and the <u>children of Israel</u> be gathered together, and appoint themselves one head, and they shall come up out of the land: for great shall be the day of Jezreel [the gathering of all Israel, all Twelve Tribes, unto the Promised Land]. (Emphasis added)

For a better understanding of what happened to the northern tribes, we need to review some biblical history.

A Review Of Biblical History

Let's talk for a moment about the family of Joseph, the son of Israel (Jacob). You may remember that while he was in Egypt, Joseph had two sons, Ephraim and Manasseh, whose mother was an Egyptian woman. In his last days, Joseph's father, Israel, was visited

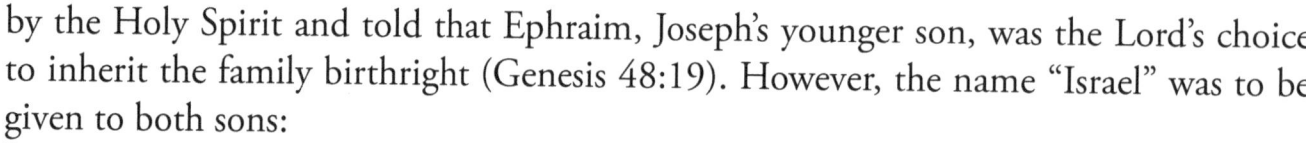

by the Holy Spirit and told that Ephraim, Joseph's younger son, was the Lord's choice to inherit the family birthright (Genesis 48:19). However, the name "Israel" was to be given to both sons:

Genesis 48:16:

> *...Let my name* [Israel] *be named on them,...* (Emphasis added)

Although Ephraim was given preference over Manasseh, they were to stay together until they outgrew their location. As the blessing explained:

Genesis 48:19:

> *And his father refused, and said, I know it, my son, I know it: he* [Manasseh] *also shall become a people, and he also shall be great: but truly his younger brother* [Ephraim] *shall be greater than he, and his seed shall become a <u>multitude of nations</u>.* (Emphasis added)

Deuteronomy 33:17:

> *...and they are the ten thousands of Ephraim, and they are the thousands of Manasseh.*

Around 1,000 B.C., Saul was removed as king, and David succeeded him. King David was ruthless, and because of the blood on his hands, the Lord would not allow him to build His temple. This task fell to his son Solomon, who followed him. Solomon built the temple in Jerusalem, and for many years he lived a righteous life. He was so righteous, in fact, that God granted him his wish for wisdom. This pleased the Lord greatly, so He rewarded Solomon with great wisdom and wealth. However, because King Solomon "loved many strange women" (he had 700 wives), he transgressed in his old age and set up idols for the gods of his foreign wives (1 Kings 11:1-12).

As a consequence, God removed control or kingship from Solomon's son Rehoboam. This resulted in the division of Israel into two kingdoms: the Northern Kingdom (House of Israel) led by the tribe of Ephraim, with Samaria as its capital; and the Southern Kingdom (House of Judah) with Jeroboam (son of Solomon) as its king, and Jerusalem as its capital. This breakup is recorded in 1 Kings 11-12.

The House of Judah, those we call the Jews, consists of the tribes of Judah, Benjamin and some of Levi that remained in the southern part of the original kingdom. The House of Israel, the Northern Kingdom, which was made up of the remainder of the Twelve Tribes, was later scattered by God and became known as the "Lost House of Israel." It is clear that they became two different houses, even though they are both part of the Twelve Tribes; so notwithstanding that they are from the same family, they are completely separate groups.

As a Christian, I was surprised by this revelation that "two houses" made up the Twelve Tribes of Israel. I did not know the number of scriptures that refer to each of them (Jeremiah 3:8, 11; 30:3-4; 32:30; 33:7, Hosea 1:11). Just consider these two:

Hosea 1:6,7:

> *I will no more have mercy upon the house of Israel;... but I will have mercy upon the house of Judah....*

Jeremiah 13:11:

> *For as a girdle cleaveth to the loins of a man, so have I caused to cleave unto me the whole house of Israel and the whole house of Judah,...*

The point I want to make is that the Bible narrative, from the Dispersion of the House of Israel and all the way through the New Testament, is the chronicle of the House of Judah (the Jews) and only that house. Changing our perception about that one thing helps us to distinguish between the people of Israel, the people of Judah, and the land of Israel.

But if we grant that there are two houses, then *where is the House of Israel?* Where did God send them and what happened to the promises He made to them? As Christians, we all have a stake in the answer to these questions. On one level, the answer is simple. The Bible states that they were dispersed over *all* the earth:

Deuteronomy 30:1-3:

> *...when all these things are come upon thee, the blessing and the curse, which I have set before thee, and thou shalt call them to mind <u>among all nations</u>, whither the LORD thy God hath driven thee, and shalt return unto the LORD thy God, and shalt obey his voice according to all that I command thee this day, thou and thy children, with all thine heart and with all thine soul; That then the LORD thy God will turn thy captivity, and have compassion upon thee, <u>and will return and gather thee from all the nations, whither the LORD thy God hath scattered thee</u>.* (Emphasis added)

We know that God scattered the Ten Tribes "***among all nations***" because He stated that He will gather them "***from all the nations***." *If we believe scripture, that would have to include the Americas.*

The Bible also gives us the details of the actual Dispersion:

2 Kings 17:6:

> *...In the ninth year of Hoshea the king of Assyria took Samaria, and carried Israel away into Assyria, and placed them in Halah and in Habor by the river of Gozan, and in the cities of the Medes.*

<u>2 Kings 17:23:</u>

> *...Israel carried away out of their own land to Assyria unto this day.*

We know that Israel was taken to Assyria and the House of Judah (Jews) was carried away about 130 years later into Babylon. The prophet Amos had prophesied concerning the captivity and dispersal of the House of Israel:

<u>Amos 5:27:</u>

> *Therefore will I cause you [House of Israel] to go into captivity beyond Damascus, saith the LORD, whose name is the God of hosts.*

<u>Amos 6:14:</u>

> *...behold, I will raise up against you a nation, O house of Israel, saith the LORD the God of hosts;...*

<u>Amos 7:17:</u>

> *...and thou shalt die in a polluted land: and Israel shall surely go into captivity forth of his land.*

Although none of the tribes of the Northern Kingdom ever returned to their former home, it is not correct to say that they ceased to exist as a people. The following articles, by Jack Flaws, and printed with his permission are backed up by scripture, and give us a clear explanation of where God sent them.

"THEY WENT THATTAWAY MIGRATIONS OF THE HOUSE OF ISRAEL

After being taken captive and relocated below the Black and Caspian Seas, the [ten] tribes of the House of Israel plus tens of thousands of Jews were used by their Assyrian conquerors as a buffer state to ward off any advances by the Medes. Soon, groups of Israelites started moving out to east, and north. The main body of people remained in the area for about a hundred years, during which time they fought as mercenaries for just about everyone. Their unique triangular arrow points were even found in the ruins of one of the burned gates of Jerusalem; meaning that some of them were in on the conquering of Jerusalem by Nebuchadnezzar! Soon after the power of the Assyrians was broken, vast numbers of the Israelites began several migrations, with the main two groups moving west under the Black Sea, and north through the Dariel pass of the Caucasus mountains into the steppes of south Russia. A large group also moved east. These were called Sakka (Saka) and Iskuza by the Medes and Persians. The Japanese name Sakai is but a step away from Saka. There are many strange customs of unknown origin in Japan that can only be explained by recognizing that some from the east Jordan tribes of Manasseh, Reuben and Gad, Manasseh being pre-eminent, made their way to that far eastern island, while their cousins headed west to populate northwest Europe and the far western island of Britain. Some of these migrations were undertaken all the way into the 17th century when, in the final migration, some from the tribe of Manasseh sailed the North Atlantic to Plymouth to fulfill Isaiah 49:20, which was prophesied to the hegemony of the House of Israel, Ephraim (England).

You see, the crux of the whole subject is that the names we want to look for to trace the Israelites are not the names that historical accounts and archeological finds give those same folks. To more confuse the issue, large groups of Israelites called themselves by different names. Some of them called themselves the House of Isaac, which is pronounced e-sahk with the emphasis on the last syllable. How natural for the Persians to call them the Sakka (Sacae in Greek), while the Assyrians called others, the House of Omri, after the sixth king of Israel. This name sounded like Khumri, and was variously pronounced Ghumri, Gimri, Gimira, Gammer, all of which turned into the Greek Kimmeroii, our English word Cimmerians.

The Israelites weren't lost, their name got lost. That fact coupled with the erroneous search for the Jews' fulfillment of the Old Testament prophesies has held the Lost Tribes teaching in virtual obscurity these millennia since 500 B.C.

At the end of the drawings I've included a list of many of the names given to the various groups of Israelites as they made their way to their new homes. I hope you'll be able to continue in this field of study. You'll probably discover that your own lineage goes back to those Bible people.

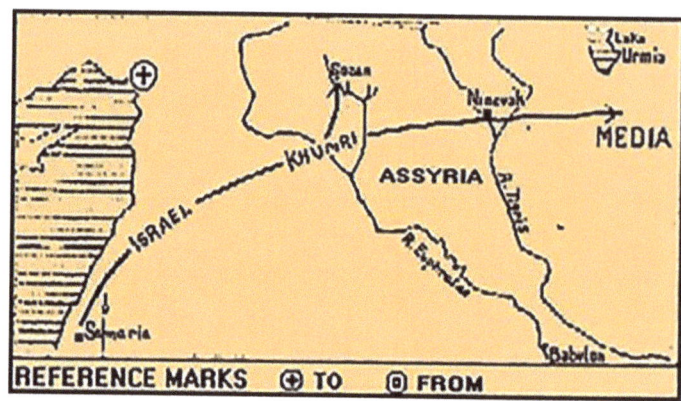

732-700 B C

Israel taken into exile by the Assyrians who called them Khumri, later corrupted to Gimira.

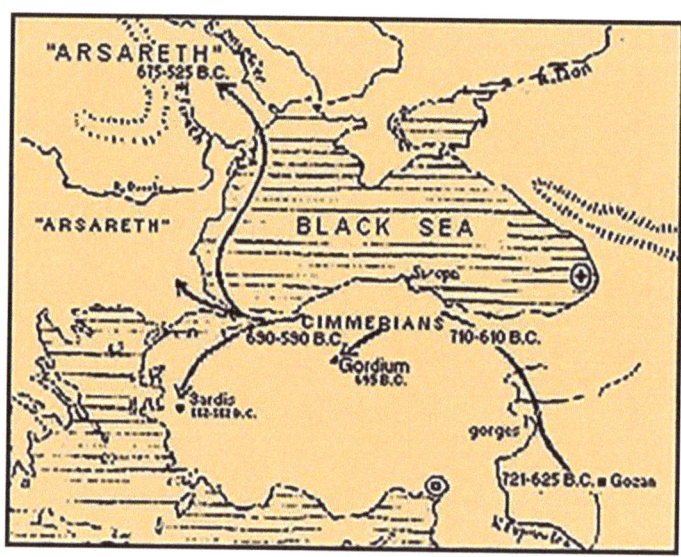

710-590 B C

Israelites, called Gimira by the Assyrians and Kimmeroii (Cimmerians) by the Greeks, established a reign of terror in Asia Minor. They finally migrated to Europe, to a place which they called Arsareth (2 Esdras 13:40-44 of the Apocrypha).

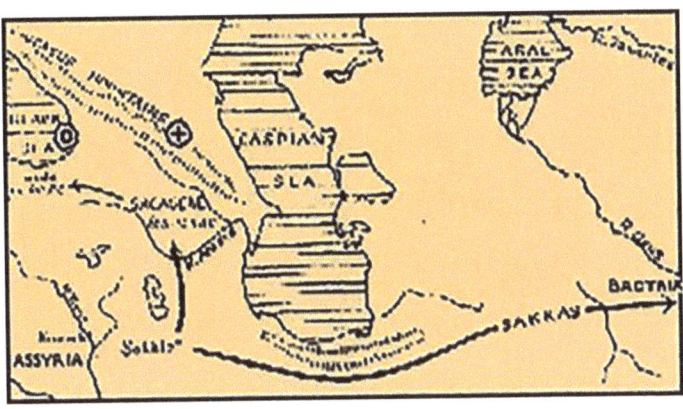

650-600 B C

Israelites in Media became known as Scythians. They fought as mercenaries, once with Babylon against Jerusalem.

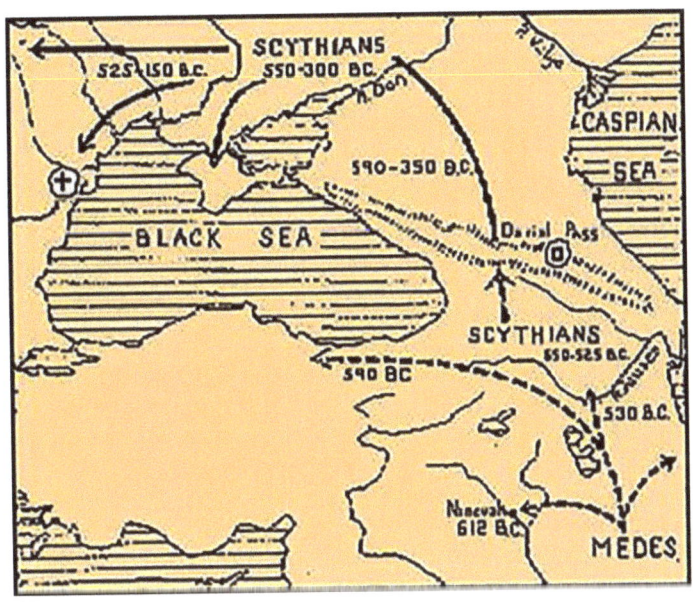

600-500 B C

Following the collapse of their Assyrian allies, the Scythians were driven north through the Caucasus by the Medes, and they settled in south Russia.

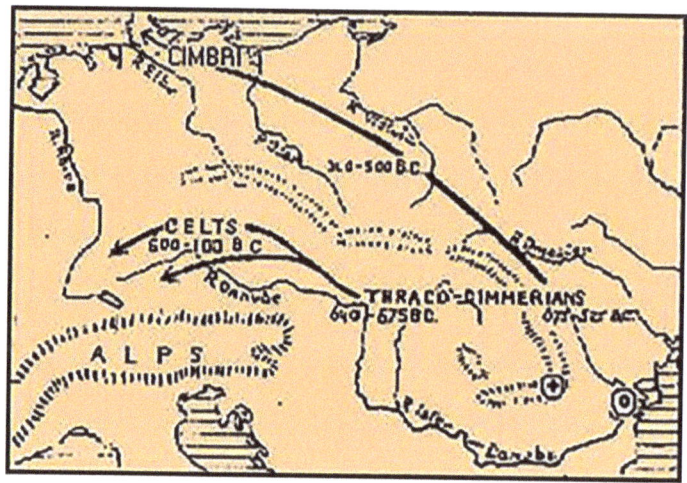

650-500 B C

Cimmerians in Europe moved up the Danube and became known as Celts, the English derivative of the Greek Keltoi.

525-300 B C

Others driven out of south Russia by the Scythians moved northwest between the rivers Oder and Vistula to the Baltic, where they later became known as Cimbri.

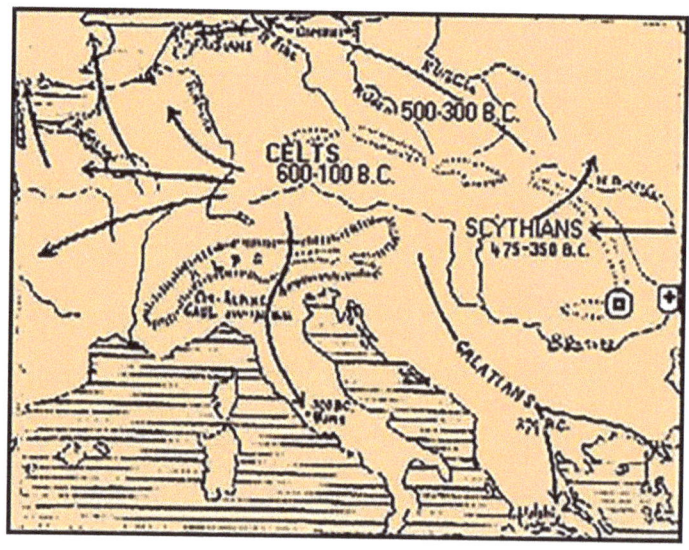

400-100 B C

The Celtic expansion from Central Europe: some attacked Rome in 390 B.C. and settled for 200 years in northern Italy; others known as Galatians, after invading Greece in 279 B.C., migrated to Asia Minor. Most of them moved west into France and later to Britain.

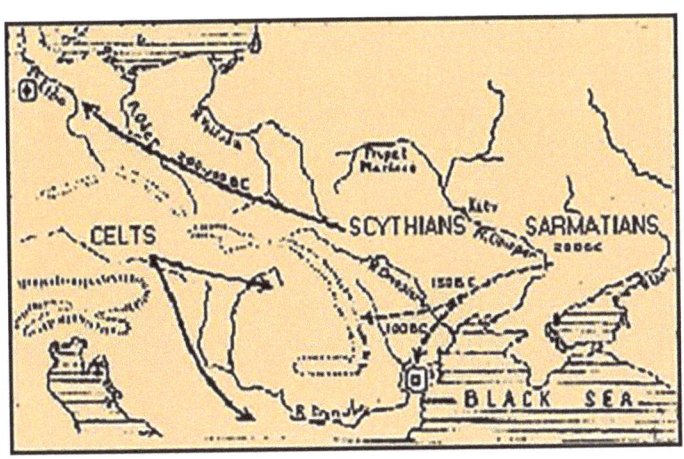

250-100 B C

South Russia was invaded from the east by the Sarmatians, who drove the Scythians northwest through Poland into Germany.

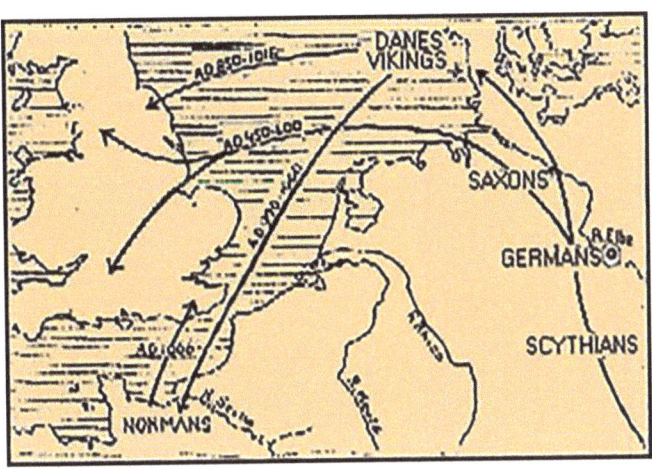

A D 450-1100

The Romans renamed the Scythians Germans ("genuine") to distinguish from the newly arrived Sarmatians in Scythia. Some of these came to Britain as Anglo-Saxons, AD 450-600; others, after moving north through Jutland, became known as Danes and Vikings. Some of these came directly to England, but others settled for a short time in France and were called Normans.

Even with all this evidence, some people still refuse to accept that this is valid. But wait, there is still more from the Ten Tribes themselves that provides a strong likelihood of them travelling as described above. Each has one or more emblems that represent its tribe, and the following chart by Mr. Flaws (http://asis.com/stag/symbols.html) explains what these symbols are and where we find them today:

THE SYMBOLS OF ISRAEL

Tribe	Sign	Color	Stone	Became	Emblem	Waiting
Rueben	Aquarius	Orange	Odem	France	Man /Water	Behold a son
Simeon	Pisces	Red/Orange	Sapphire	Silurian (Senones)	Sword/Gate	A hearing
Levi	Pisces	Red/Orange	Sapphire	(Jews)		Joining
Judah	Leo	Blue	Nophek	Juti (Jews)	Lion/3 Lions	Praise
Zebulum	Capricorn	Yellow/Orange	Pitdah-Topaz	Holland	Ship	A habitation
Issachar	Cancer	Blue/Violet	Bareket	Swiss/Dutch/Fins	Laden Ass	My hire
Dan	Scorpio	Yellow/Green	Leshem	Danes/Swedes/Norway	Serpent/Horse	Judge
Gad	Aries	Red	Yhalam/Ruby	Sweden	Troop	Good Fortune
Asher	Libra	Green	Shebo	Scots/Germans (orig)	Cup	Happy
Naphtali	Virgo	Blue-Green	Yashpeh (Jasper	Norwegians	Stag	My Wrestling
Benjamin	Gemini	Purple	Achelamah	Iceland/Norway Normans	Wolf	Sign of right hand
Ephraim	Taurus	Red-Purple	Tarshish	Britain	Ox, Unicorn	Double Fruit
Manasseh	Sagittatius	Yellow	Shoham/Onyx	United States	Olive Branch, Arrows	Forgetting
Zarah					Red Lion, Red Hand	Rising

http://asis.com/stag/symbols.html

To continue from the same website:

And now for those of you that like pictures," Flaws says, **"I have taken E. Raymond Capt's version of the heraldry of the Twelve Tribes and shown them below. These come from his excellent book, <u>Missing Links</u>**

<u>**Discovered in Assyrian Tablets.**</u> **It is a very complete study work on the Lost Tribes. I recommend you get a copy.**

A MAN

Gen 49:3-4 Rueben, thou art my firstborn.

WATER

Gen 49:3-4 Unstable as water, thou…

SIMEON

A SWORD

Gen 34:25, 26 Simeon and Levi, each man took his sword.

CASTLE GATE

Gen 33:18 [Establishes a relationship between a city gate and Simeon.]

JUDAH

A LION

Gen 49:9-11 Judah is a lion's whelp.

THREE LIONS

[The lion has been expanded to three lions in many Celto -Saxon countries. A sceptre and grapevine are Judah's other symbols.]

ZEBULUN

SHIP

Gen 49:13 Zebulun shall dwell in the haven of the sea, and be for a haven of ships.

ISSACHAR

LADEN ASS

Gen 49:14 Issachar is a strong ass couching down between two burdens.

DAN

A SERPENT

Gen 49:17 Dan shall be a serpent by the way

HORSE

Gen 49:17 …that biteth the horse's heels.

GAD

TROOP OF HORSEMEN

Gen 49:19 Gad, a troop…

ASHER

GOBLET

Gen 49:20 Out of Ash his bread shall be fat, and he shall yield royal dainties.

NAPHTALI

LEAPING HIND

Gen 49:21 Naphtali is a hind let loose.

BENJAMIN

WOLF

Gen 49:27 Benjamin shall raven as a wolf.

EPHRAIM

OX or BULL

The Ox or Bull plays an important part in the heraldry of Denmark, Netherlands, Scotland and England, where we can find "John Bull."

UNICORN

The Unicorn appears on both the Royal Arms of England and Scotland.

MANASSEH

OLIVE BRANCH

BUNDLE of ARROWS

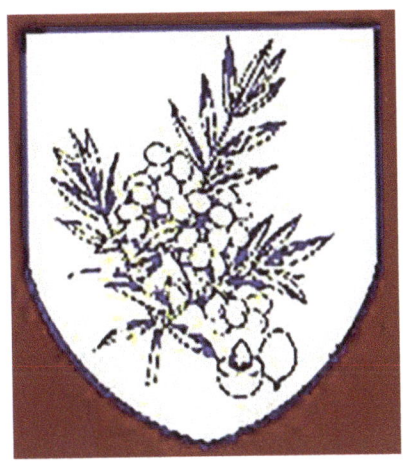 

Found on the Great Seal of the U.S. and the Netherlands and many arms in England and Scotland.

I know that some of you will say that this is just a fluke, and I would agree if only a few of the symbols showed up in today's societies. The problem is that all of them appear somewhere, either in contemporary Europe or America. This is too much to be a mere coincidence. Also, The Book of Mormon says:

2 Nephi 9:81 RCE, 2 Nephi 19:21 LDS:

> *Manasseh, Ephraim; and Ephraim, Manasseh—they together shall be against Judah.*

Nowhere in the Bible are we told that these two would be part of the fight against Judah during its Babylonian defeat, but here we are told that it would happen. For complete details, read all of Chapter 9 of 2 Nephi RCE (Chapters 16-22 of 2 Nephi LDS).

In Amos, God says that even though He has rejected His people Israel, not one of them will be lost. He will regather them to their Promised Land: These verses were written 199 years before the House of Judah went into captivity:

Amos 2:4-5:

> *Thus saith the LORD; for three transgressions of Judah, and for four, I will not turn away the punishment thereof; because they have despised the law of the LORD, and have not kept his commandments, and their lies caused them to err, after which their fathers have walked: But I will send a fire upon Judah, and it shall devour the palaces of Jerusalem.*

Amos 9:9:

For, lo, I will command, and I will sift the house of Israel among all nations, like as corn is sifted in a sieve, yet shall not the least grain fall upon the earth.

Amos 9:14:

And I will bring again the captivity of my people of Israel, and they shall build the waste cities, and inhabit them; and they shall plant vineyards, and drink the wine thereof; they shall also make gardens, and eat the fruit of them.

Remember, before the Jews were captured by the Babylonians, Amos prophesied that Israel would return from captivity. As you can see, he is talking about the Lost Ten Tribes (House of Israel), not the House of Judah. That means that the recent return of the Jews to the land of Israel does not fulfill this prophecy.

Then what has happened to the House of Israel? The answer is that they went north and west as described in the previous section. No doubt some went to England, and then some could have gone on to the Americas and beyond.

The Migratory Path

The people of the Northern Kingdom had failed to heed God's warnings or to return to worshiping only Him. As a result, they were carried away:

2 Kings 17:18:

Therefore the LORD was very angry with Israel, and removed them out of His sight: there was none left but the tribe of Judah only.

2 Kings 17:23:

...So was Israel carried away out of their own land to Assyria unto this day.

This started a time period when the House of Israel was without any formal structure as a nation:

Hosea 3:4:

For the children of Israel shall abide many days without a king, and without a prince, and without sacrifice, and without an image, and without an ephod, and without teraphim:

As an aside, but an interesting historical note:

2 Kings 17:24-25:

And the king of Assyria brought men from Babylon, and from Cuthah, and from Ava, and from Hamath, and from Sepharvaim, and placed them in the cities of Samaria instead of the children of Israel: and they possessed Samaria, and dwelt in the cities thereof. And so it was at the beginning of their dwelling there [Assyrians], *that they feared not the LORD: therefore the LORD sent lions among them, which slew some of them.*

The House of Israel had been warned by Moses in Deuteronomy that they would be forgotten as a people:

Deuteronomy 32:26:

I said, I would scatter thee into corners, I would make the remembrance of them to cease from among men:

Thereafter only part of Israel, the House of Judah and his fellows, remained in Judah (the Southern Kingdom) after the captivity of the Ten Tribes by Assyria. Nehemiah refers to them as the "*residue of Israel.*"

Nehemiah 11:20:

And the residue of Israel, of the priests, and the Levites, were in all the cities of Judah, everyone in his inheritance.

God then warned that He would start speaking to the House of Israel using another language.

Isaiah 28:11:

For with stammering lips and another tongue will He speak to this people. (Emphasis added)

This can only apply to the House of Israel because the House of Judah still uses Hebrew today.

The prophet Jeremiah played a special role in the dispersion of the House of Israel. As we know, he was destined to be a prophet like Moses and was told by God:

Jeremiah 1:5:

Before I formed thee in the belly I knew thee; and before thou camest forth out of the womb I sanctified thee, and I ordained thee a prophet unto the nations.

Jeremiah responded that he could not tell people what to do, that they would not listen to him:

Jeremiah 1:6:

Then said I, Ah, Lord GOD! Behold, I cannot speak: for I am but a child.

But God insisted. "Do not worry," He told Jeremiah, "I will see to it that they will listen." Then the Lord touched his lips and put His words into Jeremiah's mouth:

Jeremiah 1:7-9:

But the LORD said unto me, Say not, I am a child: for thou shalt go to all that I shall send thee, and whatsoever I command thee thou shall speak. Be not afraid of their faces: for I am with thee, to deliver thee saith the LORD. Then the LORD put forth his hand, and touched my mouth. And the LORD said unto me, Behold I have put my words in thy mouth.

Then He gave Jeremiah his commission:

Jeremiah 1:10:

See, I have this day set thee over the nations and over the kingdoms, to root out, to pull down, and to destroy, and to throw down, to build, and to plant.

As a result, Jeremiah told the Israelites:

Jeremiah 16:13:

Therefore will I cast you out of this land, into a land that ye know not, neither ye nor your fathers; and there shall ye serve other gods day and night; where I will not shew you favor.

There are five important claims made by Jeremiah in this prophecy:

1. **"Therefore will I cast you out of this land...."** They went to Assyria.

2. **"....into a land that ye know not...."** They knew Assyria, so they had to be going through Assyria to their final destination.

3. **"....neither ye nor your fathers...."** No one, except God, knew where they were going;

4. **"...there shall ye serve other gods day and night;"**

5. **"where I will not show you favor."**

Nevertheless, the Ten Tribes would find peace wherever God sent them.

Jeremiah 31:2:

Thus saith the LORD, The people which were left of the sword found grace in the wilderness; even [the House of] Israel, when I went to cause him to rest.

The above quotations from Jeremiah may show how they migrated to many different lands, unknown to their entire race, and a long way from their home. They were to move on through the nations, (sifting) into unknown areas, and unexplored wilderness.

Dariel Pass

Colonel R. G. Pearse in his article "Dariel Pass" informs us that the pass is located near the headwaters of the Euphrates River in the Caucasus mountains; it is also known as the "Pass of Israel." He states that the Lord led the Israelites through this narrow passageway. (Pearse 2) The following scriptures explore their migration:

Micah 2:13:
The breaker is come up before them: they have broken up, and have passed through the gate [Dariel Pass?], and are gone out by it: and their king shall pass before them, and the LORD on the head of them.

Hosea 12:1:
Ephraim feedeth on wind, and followeth after the east wind: he daily increaseth lies and desolation;... (Emphasis added)

Ezekiel 27:26:

> *Thy rowers have brought thee into great waters: the east wind hath broken thee in the midst of the seas.*

So, the tribes of Israel travelled north through the Caucasus mountains, then west over land and through "great waters," driven by the east wind. To continue:

Isaiah 11:11:

> *And it shall come to pass in that day, that <u>the LORD shall set his hand again the second time to recover the remnant of his people</u>, which shall be left, from Assyria, and from Egypt, and from Pathros, and from Cush, and from Elam, and from Shinar, and from Hamath, and <u>from the islands of the sea</u>.* (Emphasis added)

Isaiah 49:12:

> *Behold, these* [Israel in the islands] *shall come from far: and lo, these from the north and from the west;...*

If it is as Isaiah said, that they would be recovered from the north and the west including the isles of the sea, it is safe to say that God led them to a group of islands. However, Isaiah says once they arrive in the isles, possibly the British Isles, they are to:

Isaiah 41:1:

> *Keep silence before me, O islands; and let the people renew their strength:...*

Once they have had time to recover, according to the next scripture, they will seek someplace else to go for more space, which fulfilled prophecy."

Isaiah 49:20:

> *The children which thou shalt have, after thou hast lost the other, shall say again in thine ears, The place is too strait for me: give place to me that I may dwell.*

What if England was their primary base? We know that England colonized much of the world, some of it an uncivilized wilderness, including the Americas.

Amos 8:12:

> *And they shall wander from sea to sea, and from the north even to the east, they shall run to and fro to seek the word of the LORD, and shall not find it.*

In summary, Israel went through Assyria; and according to Amos, they wandered *"from sea to sea."* I would like to propose that the Israelites went as far as the British

Isles, where they were renewed. Later they colonized up to "a quarter of the earth's surface." (Meakin 14) Wouldn't it be fair to say that the Americas were a wilderness to the people of England and Europe? Eventually, Ephraim would become a "*multitude of nations.*"

Linguistics Links

To show the importance of linguistics in studying the migration of people, consider the following account recorded in Judges:

Judges 12:5-6:

> *And the Gileadites took the passages of Jordan before the Ephraimites: and it was so, that when those Ephraimites which were escaped said, Let me go over; that the men of Gilead said unto him, Art thou an Ephraimite? If he said, Nay; Then said they unto him, Say now Shibboleth: and he said Sibboleth: for he could not frame to pronounce it right. Then they took him, and slew him at the passages of Jordan: and there fell at that time of the Ephraimites forty and two thousand.*

In my research, I found a significant amount of documentation that connects the word "Saxon" to the Hebrew name "Isaac." Many references conclude that the Saxons are, in fact, the sons of Isaac, or in other words, the House of Israel.

These delicate nuances or shifts in language trace the movement of people for us. To explain, once the northern Ten Tribes of Israel were defeated by the Assyrians, they took on the name of *Isaac* or *House of Isaac*, but the Jews kept the name of *Jacob*. In time, the northern tribes stopped using the name "Israelite" altogether and took the name of "Saac," "Sacae," or "Saxae." This is a Latin derivative of the Hebrew name Isaac (Introduction to "They went Thattaway").

Isaiah 49:8:

> *Thus saith the LORD, In an acceptable time have I heard thee, and in a day of salvation have I helped thee: and I will preserve thee, and give thee for a covenant of the people, to establish the earth, to cause to inherit the desolate heritages;*

The House of Israel was also known as a "Covenant People." The word "British," when translated into Hebrew, means "Covenant Man." (Jones 1, 6) This is very likely a linguistic link between the House of Israel and Britain.

Jeremiah 51:20:

Thou art my battle axe and weapons of war: for with thee will I break in pieces the nations, and with thee will I destroy kingdoms;

God directs history. We have recently witnessed a modern miracle without realizing it. For the first time since the Twelve Tribes escaped from Egypt, they have fought together again. That is, Judah and Israel have battled as partners, this time against the prince of Persia, Iraq.

Not only did the Lord scatter the House of Israel, but He will also regather them in the last days (Jeremiah 16:14-15). What else does the Bible say about this latter-day gathering?

Deuteronomy 30:3:

...the LORD thy God will turn thy captivity, and have compassion upon thee, and will return and gather thee from all the nations, whither the LORD thy God hath scattered thee.

Ezekiel 37:21-22:

...Thus saith the Lord God; Behold, I will take the children of Israel from among the heathen, whither they be gone, and will gather them on every side, and bring them into their own land: And I will make them one nation in the land upon the mountains of Israel; and one king shall be king to them all: and they shall be no more two nations, neither shall they be divided into two kingdoms any more at all:

According to the above scripture, God will unite the houses of Judah and Israel under one king, who, I believe, will be Jesus Christ. I believe He will then combine the world-wide Christian community with the populace of Israel, thus leaving only one family of believers in God and Jesus Christ. (Wouldn't it be true that there would also be at least one community of non-believers?) This promised gathering will be so mind-boggling that everyone will know that it is the work of the Lord, much greater than the escape of Israel from Egypt! Not only that:

Jeremiah 50:4-5:

In those days, and in that time, saith the LORD, the children of Israel shall come, they and the children of Judah together, going and weeping: they shall go, and seek the LORD their God. They shall ask the way to Zion....

This has not yet happened, but we should be praying and watching closely because it could happen during our lifetimes.

As we know, Ephraim was to become a "*multitude of nations*" and Manasseh to become a great nation. I have discovered that many Christian scholars believe that the Commonwealth of Great Britain sprang from Ephraim while the United States came from Manasseh, but I wonder if it could be the other way around? Does it really matter? In either case, both countries are from the tribe of Joseph, and both countries have an Israelite heritage. To put it another way, in my opinion, if you are an Anglo-Saxon, you're an Israelite.

The Bible also tells us that in the places where the House of Israel settled, they would be told that they were not God's chosen people. However:

Hosea 1:10:

> *...and it shall come to pass, that in the place where it was said unto them, Ye are not my people, there it shall be said unto them, Ye are the sons of the living God.* (Emphasis added)

This prophecy is being fulfilled today! The Anglo-Saxons of America and Europe have for hundreds of years been told that they are Gentiles, and therefore, not God's chosen people. But recently and including this book, we are discovering that that is not true. We are now learning that we are from the Lost Ten Tribes of Israel, thus fulfilling Hosea's prophecy above.

CHAPTER 4

WHAT WAS THE POPULATION OF ALL OF ISRAEL WHEN THE LORD SCATTERED THE NORTHERN KINGDOM?

As previously mentioned, when the children of Israel left Egypt, there were a large number of men.

Exodus 12:37:

> *And the children of Israel journeyed from Rameses to Succoth, __about six hundred thousand__ on foot that were men, besides children.* (Emphasis added)

Now, before a man could be counted, he was required to be married. So, for every man there had to be at least one woman. That brings the total adult population to about 1.2 million. This could also be stated as 600,000 families, and if the average household had three children, then there would have been approximately 1.8 million children that escaped from Egypt, including all unmarried adult children. That would bring the total Israeli population to around 3 million at that time. Can you see the scope of the miracle? God not only freed that many people, but He fed them for forty years while they were in the desert. That was a lot of people and a lot of food!

When Israel crossed the Jordan, going into their Promised Land, Joshua tells us:

Joshua 4:13:

> *About forty thousand prepared for war passed over before the LORD unto battle, to the plains of Jericho.*

According to the numbers above, this would be nearly seven percent of the 600,000 men available. Much later, when the Ten Tribes rebelled against Judah, Judah prepared for war against Israel, but the prophet Shemaiah stopped them (See also 2 Chronicles 11:1-4):

1 Kings 12:21-24:

> *And when Rehoboam was come to Jerusalem, he assembled all the house of Judah, with the tribe of Benjamin, an hundred and four score thousand chosen men, which were warriors, to fight against the house of*

Israel, to bring the kingdom again to Rehoboam the son of Solomon. But the word of God came unto Shemaiah the man of God, saying, Speak unto Rehoboam, the son of Solomon, king of Judah, and unto all the house of Judah and Benjamin, and to the remnant of the people, saying, Thus saith the LORD, Ye shall not go up, nor fight against your brethren the children of Israel: return every man to his house; for this thing is from me. They harkened therefore to the word of the LORD, and returned to depart, according to the word of the LORD.

However, even though Judah obeyed the words of the prophet, there was continual warfare between Rehoboam and Jeroboam. Eighteen years later, after the death of Rehoboam, Israel decided to attack Judah.

2 Chronicles 13:3:

And Abijah [Rehoboam's son] set the battle in array with an army of valiant men of war, even four hundred thousand chosen men: Jeroboam also set the battle in array against him with eight hundred thousand chosen men, being mighty men of valor.

This was probably the height of their entire civilization. Using the percentage above (about 7%), that would make the total male population of all of Israel about eighteen million strong and the grand total (men, women and children) around ninety million shortly after the tribes became two kingdoms. (The Northern Kingdom would have been about 60 million, and the Southern Kingdom around 30 Million.) If only ten percent of the people still obeyed God's commandments, then the number of people led away from the Northern Kingdom would be about six million. According to God's word, He scattered them around the world; therefore, He would have had to have led away many different groups.

I realize that this might be a stretch, but here is a hypothetical scenario: If the average group size was 2,000 people, then God would have led 3,000 groups from the Northern Kingdom. This would mean there might have been around 3,000 prophets to lead the people. Each of them could have written scriptures about God's dealings with his group. That could add up to 3,000 scriptures other than the Bible, but, of course, they are lost to us. However, we do have one, the Book of Mormon.

Helaman 2:12-14 RCE, Helaman 3:13-15 LDS:

And now there are many records kept of the proceedings of this people— by many of this people—Which are particular and very large concerning them. But behold, a hundredth part of the proceedings of this people— Yea, the account of the Lamanites and the Nephites, And their wars and contentions and dissensions, And their preaching and their prophecies, And their shipping and their building of ships, And their building of temples and synagogues and their sanctuaries, And their righteousness and their wickedness and their murders and their robbings and their plunderings, And all manner of abominations and whoredoms—-Cannot be contained in this work. But behold, there are many books and many records of every kind, and they have been kept chiefly by the Nephites;...

The Book of Mormon is telling us that there are many historical accounts written about the Nephites and the Lamanites that we still do not have.

Yes, I have made some assumptions, but even today, as bad as our society is (some say today is worse than in the days of Noah), I would say more than ten percent of the people still try to live in accordance with their understanding of God's laws. By comparison, it is likely that God led away at least six-million people, maybe even more. It could also mean that there are thousands of additional records not yet revealed. The Book of Mormon is just one of them.

As a reminder, we also know that there are many scriptures missing from the Bible, just as Nephi stated:

1 Nephi 3:168, 174 RCE, 1 Nephi 13:26, 29 LDS:

For behold, they have taken away from the gospel of the Lamb many parts which are plain and most precious, And also many covenants of the Lord...which were plain unto the understanding of the children of men....

To illustrate, here are some of the books mentioned but missing from the Bible:

Missing Book	Referenced in:
1. Book of the Covenant	Exodus 24:7
2. Book of Wars of the Lord	Numbers 21:14
3. Book of the Manner of the Kingdom	1 Samuel 10:25
4. Book of Jasher	2 Samuel 1:18
	2 Samuel 10:25
	1 Kings 4:32
	Joshua 10:13
5. Acts of Solomon	1 Kings 11:41
6. The Chronicles of King David	1 Chronicles 27:24
7. Book of (Gad) the Seer	1 Chronicles 29:29
8. Book of (Samuel) the Seer	1 Chronicles 29:29
9. Book of Nathan the Prophet	1 Chronicles 29:29

10. Prophecy of Ahyah (Ahijah) the Shilonite	2 Chronicles 9:29
11. Vision and Story of Iddo, the Seer	2 Chronicles 9:29
	2 Chronicles 12:15
12. The Story of the Prophet Iddo	2 Chronicles 13:22
13. Book of Shemaiah, the Prophet	2 Chronicles 12:15
14. Book of Jehu	2 Chronicles 20:34
15. Book of Kings of Israel	2 Chronicles 20:34
16. Acts of Uzziah by Isaiah	2 Chronicles 26:22
17. Book of sayings of Seers (Acts and Prayers of Manasseh)	2 Chronicles 33:18-19
18. Book dictated by Jeremiah	Jeremiah 36:32
19. Sealed book of Daniel	Daniel 12:24
20. Book written to ephraim by hosea"	Hosea 8:11-12
21. Epistle to the Laodiceans	Colossians 4:16
22. Epistle from the Laodiceans	Colossians 4:16
23. Previous Epistle to the Corinthians	1 Corinthians 5:9
24. Second Epistle of Jude	Jude 3
25. Previous Epistle of Enoch	Jude 1:14
26. Second Epitle to the Ephesians	Ephesians 3:3-4
27. The Epistle of John to the church ruled by Diotrephes	3 John 1:9
28. Nazarene Prophecy Source	Matthew 2:23

(Richardson 1-4)
(www.answering-christianity 1-5)

CHAPTER 5

WHAT PROPHETIC WRITINGS IN THE BIBLE REFER TO THE BOOK OF MORMON?

In the ancient Holy Land, scrolls were often called sticks because the parchment was rolled up on sticks:

Ezekiel 37:19:

> *Say unto them, Thus saith the Lord GOD; Behold, I will take the stick of Joseph, which is in the hand of Ephraim, and the tribes of Israel his fellows, and will put them with him, even with the stick of Judah, and make them one stick, and they shall be one in mine hand.*

The necessity of at least two different records came about because of the division, of the Hebrew people, caused by their wickedness. Their separation and the subsequent destruction of the House of Israel signaled a major turning point in the history of the twelve tribes. Today, the "*stick of Judah*" is recognized as the Bible. This begs the questions: What is the other stick? Where is it?

Many Christians tell me that unless something is mentioned in the Bible, they will not believe it. I will show that the Bible points to leading people to the Americas and to the bringing forth of The Book of Mormon as the other stick. There are many biblical passages that talk about "*the stick of Joseph*" as we shall see, and they provide support for it being The Book of Mormon.

I've studied the Bible and Book of Mormon all of my life. I was raised in the Reorganized Church of Jesus Christ of Latter Day Saints. I've noticed that both books teach the same Christian beliefs. They include: salvation by God's grace, faith and repentance, God's forgiveness through Christ's sacrifice on the cross and the ideal of Christian community, Zion. The Book of Mormon also teaches the born-again experience and many other well-known Christian doctrines. But since most Christians have no personal experience with The Book of Mormon, it is therefore understandable why they deny its validity as scripture. To help you have some experience with it, we'll begin with a brief overview of what the Bible says.

The Testimony Of The Old Testament

Where is there evidence for The Book of Mormon in the Old Testament? To begin, venerated Bible prophets cited an unnamed distant land. Let's look first in Isaiah as there are some clues there:

When Isaiah blessed his son Joseph he stated the following about a land he stated, "Blessed of the Lord be his land":

Deuteronomy 33:13-16

> *And of Joseph he said, Blessed of the Lord be his Land, for the precious things of heaven, for the dew, and for the deep that coucheth beneath. And for the precious fruits brought forth by the sun, and for the precious things put forth by the moon, And for the chief things of the ancient mountains, and for the precious things of the lasting hills, And for the precious things of the earth and the fulness thereof, and for the good will of him that dwelt in the bush: let the blessing come upon the head of Joseph, and upon the top of the head of him that was separated from his brethren.*

Isaiah 18:1-2:

> *Woe to the land shadowing with wings, which is beyond the rivers of Ethiopia [Africa]; that sendeth ambassadors by the sea,...*

When seen from space, the outline of North, Central, and South America is shaped like a bird with its wings spread in flight. No other land mass compares to this description of a "**land shadowing with wings.**"

Ethiopia is a large country on the eastern bulge of Africa near the Red Sea and the Gulf of Aden. Isaiah's land that "**sendeth ambassadors by the sea**" would seem to imply that emissaries had sailed from a distant land into the Indian Ocean and Arabian Sea and then up the Red Sea to the Holy Land. The possibility of the land of the Americas sending such ambassadors can be inferred by connecting the two clues above. The prophet Zephaniah concluded that there were others who were sent beyond the same rivers that Isaiah saw:

Zephaniah 3:10:

> *From beyond the rivers of Ethiopia my supplicants, even the daughter of my dispersed, shall bring mine offering.*

The "*supplicants*" and "*daughter*" are the Israelites who were separated and traveled beyond these rivers.

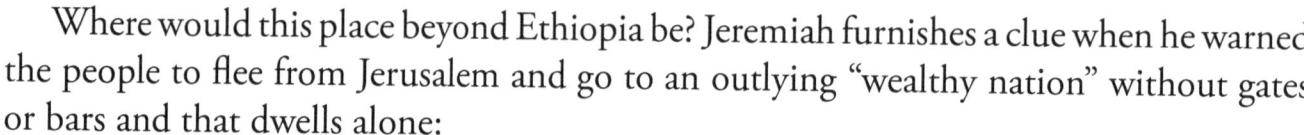

Where would this place beyond Ethiopia be? Jeremiah furnishes a clue when he warned the people to flee from Jerusalem and go to an outlying "wealthy nation" without gates or bars and that dwells alone:

Jeremiah 49: 30-31:

> *Flee, get you far off, dwell deep, O ye inhabitants of Hazar, saith the LORD; for Nebuchadnezzar king of Babylon hath taken counsel against you, and hath conceived a purpose against you. Arise, get you up unto the wealthy nation, that dwelleth without care, saith the LORD, which have neither gates nor bars, which dwell alone.*

In 600 B.C., most places in the world of Jeremiah and Isaiah would not fit that description; and even today they would not. Like other cities of that time, Jerusalem had defensive walls with gates, and the population of nearby towns was so plentiful that they were surrounded by inhabitants. In other words, the whole area was so populated that they did not "*dwell alone*." This distant location referenced in the prophecy more likely seems to fit the Americas, which had rich resources, was quite separate from the other historical cultures and lacked fortified cities with large populations.

Isaiah added more information about this place when he foretold that the Israelites who escaped from Jerusalem would be successful in establishing themselves in a new location and becoming firmly established under the blessings of the Lord.

Isaiah 37:31-32:

> *And the remnant that is escaped of the house of Judah shall again take root downward, and bear fruit upward: For out of Jerusalem shall go forth a remnant, and they that escape out of mount Zion: the zeal of the Lord of hosts shall do this.*

Who are these Israelites that escaped from Jerusalem? Could it be Lehi and his family? Israel (Jacob), a loving father, in providing his final blessings to his sons gave another hint. The following was directed to Joseph:

Genesis 49:22:

> *Joseph is a fruitful bough, even a fruitful bough by a well; whose branches run over the wall:*

Genesis 49:26:

> *The blessings of thy father have prevailed above the blessings of my progenitors unto the utmost bound of the everlasting hills: they shall be on the head of Joseph, and on the crown of the head of him that was separate from his brethren.*

Again, "branches [that] run over the wall" suggests extending beyond the boundaries of a given area. A thesaurus takes us even further than that, since synonyms for "utmost" enlarge our understanding to *"farthermost"* and *"remotest,"* "of the everlasting hills." Now where are *"the everlasting hills?"* We are told by archeologists that the longest mountain range on earth starts in Alaska and runs continuously to the southern tip of South America. Could this mountain range be the "everlasting hills?" If so, it only exists in the Americas.

To regress for a moment, when Lehi and his family crossed the sea to their Promised Land, they took with them the brass plates, which they had gotten from Laban. In reading those plates, Lehi found that Joseph was his forefather:

Where is this land of Joseph, when you read these quotes from the Bible, it is very clear that Josephs land is the Americas, nowhere else in this world agrees with these descriptions of Josephs land.

1 Nephi 1:158 RCE, 1 Nephi 5:10 LDS:

...my father Lehi took the records which were engraven upon the plates of brass and he did search them from the beginning;...

1 Nephi 164-165 RCE, 1 Nephi 5:14 LDS:

And it came to pass that my father Lehi also found upon the plates of brass a genealogy of his fathers; Wherefore, he knew that he was a descendant of Joseph, Yea, even that Joseph which was the son of Jacob which was sold into Egypt and which was preserved by the hand of the Lord, that he might preserve his father Jacob and all his household from perishing with famine;

Up to this point, the Old Testament supports their leaving Jerusalem, going *"over the wall,"* and being partakers of the blessings of Joseph. The Book of Mormon people were very aware that they had descended from Joseph because of the information on the brass plates taken from Laban.

As far as the plates which Lehi mentioned being made of brass, it may seem unusual to have writings on metal since those in the ancient Holy Land were usually written on parchment. However, there have been findings of writing on metal plates in that area.

As stated by Roy Weldon in his book *Other sheep*, he and his companion visited the Museo de Oro in Bogota Columbia in 1949. He said:

The Museo de Oro contains by far the largest and finest collection of ancient gold artifacts the author has seen in the Western Hemisphere [and probably the world]. Among the fabulous arrays of jewelry and golden artifacts, there is one showcase devoted to numerous rolls of thin gold

paper. On the wall of the showcase are a number of specimens of thin gold plates or paper on which there are inscriptions. (37)

In a more recent account (2002), Foster reports that in the Maya area of Mexico, "Some gold discs recovered from the Sacred Cenote at Chichen Itza were decorated with hieroglyphic texts that were embossed into the metal" (278).

The above information proves that the ancient Americans had the capability of making metal paper or plates, and of writing on them. Therefore, it is quite likely that the Brass Plates and the Gold Plates were actual ancient artifacts, made from metal, just as claimed. Therefore, from a technical point of view, it is perfectly believable that the record which Lehi and his descendants created, The Book of Mormon, could have been written on gold plates and could easily be the stick of Joseph that Ezekiel wrote about. When Lehi's family left Jerusalem, they then became part of the Lost Tribes of Israel. They kept a record of their travels and of their relationship with God in the Land of Joseph, the Americas.

The Book of Mormon also refers to the same groups as Ezekiel 37:19, where he talked about the books (testimonies) coming together at some future time. In other words, the Bible and The Book of Mormon reinforce each other. Nephi emphasized the importance of this by paraphrasing Ezekiel:

Nephi 12:61 RCE, 2 Nephi 29:8 LDS:

And when the two nations shall run together, The testimony of the two nations shall run together also;

Notice what Nephi said will happen when these two scriptures are joined:

2 Nephi 12:71-72 RCE; 29:13 LDS:

And it shall come to pass that the Jews shall have the words of the Nephites, and the Nephites shall have the words of the Jews; And the Nephites and the Jews shall have the words of the lost tribes of Israel; And the lost tribes of Israel shall have the words of the Nephites and the Jews.

Many people believe that has already transpired as the two books are held together in their hands. Through the gift and power of God, Joseph Smith was able to translate The Book of Mormon. This record has joined the Bible as a supplemental witness, providing additional evidence of the divinity of Christ and the divine nature of the Bible.

The voices of The Book of Mormon authors, which were buried in the earth for over 1,500 years, came forth "out of the dust" (or hiding):

Isaiah 29:4:

And thou shall be brought down, and shall speak out of the ground, and thy speech shall be low out of the dust, and thy voice shall be as one that hath a familiar spirit, out of the ground, and thy speech shall whisper out of the dust.

The testimonies of The Book of Mormon prophets strengthen and support the message of the Bible. Quite often its richness expands and further clarifies what the Bible has provided, for example, demystifying the term *"familiar spirit."* Is it not true that those of us who are familiar with the Holy Spirit are, in fact, dealing with a Spirit we know well? That *"familiar spirit,"* the Holy Spirit, leads us into all truth and verifies that these two testimonies are the same.

In so far as The Book of Mormon shows us the beauty and graciousness of the Lord Jesus, it should be welcomed and applauded. As Jesus said, "…Forbid him not: for he that is not against us is for us" (Luke 9:50). Wouldn't this apply to Joseph Smith and the Book of Mormon?

The Testimony Of The New Testament

John 3:16:

For God so loved the world, that he gave his only begotten Son, that whosoever believeth in him should not perish, but have everlasting life.

Sometimes we read a passage so often that we never really examine it closely. This verse affirms God's love for the whole world; do you think He would leave out the entire populace of the Americas? A favorite author of mine, Roy Weldon, states:

Did God give his Son to the Old World only? It is estimated that at the time of Christ the civilization of ancient America was in full bloom with a culture as great in some respects superior to the civilizations of Rome, Greece, Babylon, and Egypt. Estimates of the population in Mexico, Central America, and the Andean region at the time of Christ run as high as three hundred million people. (18) Did God respect the Old World above the New World that they should enjoy the priceless benefits of Christ's personal ministry while great civilized nations in America should be left to go it alone without a personal visitation and ministry of God's Son?

That number is similar to the population of the United States today. What kind of culture existed in the Americas at the time of Christ? Archeologists tell us that a great many people lived here during the lifetime of Jesus. Could they have had a highly cultured civilization? Could it have been just as great as those in the Mediterranean, like Rome, Greece, Babylon and Egypt?

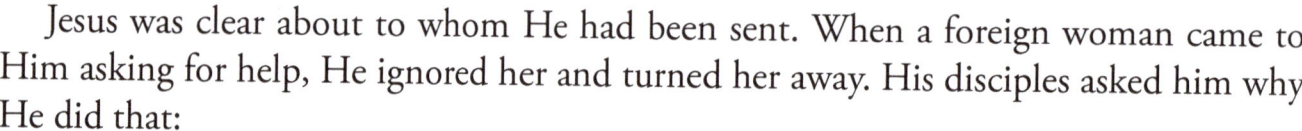
Jesus was clear about to whom He had been sent. When a foreign woman came to Him asking for help, He ignored her and turned her away. His disciples asked him why He did that:

Matthew 15:24:

...He answered and said, **I am not sent but unto the lost sheep of the house of Israel.**

He was saying that He was sent only to visit the tribes of Israel, that He did not come to tarry with the Gentiles (even though He did help the woman because of her great faith). The Word tells us further:

Matthew 10:5-6:

These twelve Jesus sent forth, and commanded them saying, **Go not into the way of the Gentiles, and into any city of the Samaritans enter ye not: But go rather to the lost sheep of the <u>House of Israel.</u>** (Emphasis added)

So where did Jesus tell them to go? At that point they were not being sent to the Gentiles or Samaritans. He was plainly directing them to go to the House of Israel. And who was the House of Israel and where were they at that time? They were the Scythians, and they were within traveling distance for the Apostles. (THEY WENT THATTAWAY)

As stated earlier in John, Jesus explained His mission:

John 10:16:

And other sheep I have, which are not of this fold: them also must I bring, and they shall hear my voice; and there shall be one fold, and one shepherd.

He was saying that there were Israelites not located in Jerusalem, "not of this fold," that He would visit, and "they shall hear My voice." Christians have pondered over these words of our Master, wondering, "Who were these people?" Many think that He was discussing the Gentiles, but the Bible and The Book of Mormon clearly refute that belief. After the massive earthquakes and storms here in the Americas following His death, Christ explained to the survivors why those in Jerusalem had no knowledge of them:

Nephi 7:15 RCE, 3 Nephi 15:14 LDS:

And not at any time hath the Father given Me commandment that I should tell it unto your brethren at Jerusalem, Neither at any time hath the Father given Me commandment that I should tell unto them concerning the other tribes of the house of Israel which the Father hath led away out of the land.

He continued by revealing to them who the "other sheep" were:

3 Nephi 7:20-23 RCE; 3 Nephi 15:21-24 LDS:

And Verily I say unto you that ye are they of which I said: 'Other sheep I have which are not of this fold; Them also I must bring, And they shall hear My voice, And there shall be one fold and one shepherd'--And they understood Me not; For they supposed it had been the Gentiles, For they understood not that the Gentiles should be converted through their preaching; And they understood Me not, that I said they shall hear My voice; And they understood Me not, that the Gentiles should not at any time hear my voice, That I should not manifest Myself unto them, save it were by the Holy Ghost. But behold, ye have both heard My voice and seen Me, and ye are My sheep, and ye are numbered among them which the Father hath given Me; (Emphasis added)

As I said, The Book of Mormon tells us that the *"other sheep."* mentioned in the New Testament are descendants of Joseph, the son of Israel, those who were separated by the Lord's command from the House of Israel.

I believe that the Book of Mormon is true and that it is an additional gospel upholding biblical prophesies about Jesus Christ being the Messiah, the Son of God. A portion of it is the eye-witness account in Third Nephi, by one of the *"other sheep,"* where Nephi described Christ's ministry in ancient America. It is quite possible that of the many details hinted at in the Bible, one was the uniquely American account of His *"other sheep."* The record of His visit to this hemisphere gives us a completely independent verification of Jesus Christ's divinity and further evidence that He is the Messiah of all people.

Summary

Frequently Christians will say something like, "Show it to me in the Word and I'll believe it." I feel that I have shown you in God's Word, and it *does* indeed point to The Book of Mormon.

We have explored scriptures from the Bible and The Book of Mormon, and both messages agree on His gathering of the Lost House of Israel.

It's my prayer you will ask God if these things are true. Remember, we are told in the Bible to **"Lean not unto thine own understanding"** (Proverbs 3:5). For that matter, do not lean on anyone else's understanding either, mine included. Only rely on the Holy Spirit.

CHAPTER 6

WHAT PROPHETIC WRITINGS IN THE BOOK OF MORMON REFER TO THE BIBLE?

Biblical Scriptures Quoted By The Book Of Mormon Prophets

Many people believe that Joseph Smith plagiarized the Bible because its verses are found in The Book of Mormon. They totally ignore the fact that prophets frequently cited previous scripture. This was a common practice that was continued throughout The Book of Mormon. Jesus Himself quoted from the Old Testament. Remember, Lehi sent Nephi and his brothers back to Jerusalem to get the "plates of brass" from Laban (1 Nephi 1: 61 RCE, 1 Nephi 3:3 LDS), which were in the treasury and contained all the inspired writings up to the reign of King Zedekiah. Therefore, it would be easy for any prophet after that to quote from those plates. Also, the Lord was directing the writers on both continents, so we should expect the texts to contain the same messages.

The Book of Mormon scriptures in this chapter are listed sequentially and are correlated to their counterparts in the Bible. For example, to show you a similarity in content between the Bible and The Book of Mormon, look at these three scriptures:

John 11:50:

> ...*it is expedient for us, that one man should die for the people, and that the whole nation perish not.*

John 18:14:

> *Now Caiaphas was he, which gave counsel to the Jews, that it was expedient that one man should die for the people.*

1 Nephi 1:115 RCE, 1 Nephi 4:13 LDS:

> *It is better that one man should perish than that a nation should dwindle and perish in unbelief.*

These are expressing similar thoughts, but from totally different circumstances. If you read on, the Bible states that Caiaphas (John 11:49) was prophesying *"that Jesus should die for that nation"* (John 11:51). Then, if you continue on from John 18:14, it is saying that Jesus should die. But in The Book of Mormon, the Holy Spirit explained to Nephi that God did not want Lehi's descendants to be without spiritual guidance. Therefore, He sent Nephi and his brothers back to obtain the plates which Laban controlled. Laban not only refused to give them the plates, but stole their parents' property, which they had offered in exchange for the plates, and tried to kill them as well. Later, God delivered Laban into the hands of Nephi.

The following sixty-five sets of quotes illustrate passages that were mentioned by Book of Mormon prophets. Some came from the plates of brass and some came by revelation from God. They cover a wide range of subjects.

1. John 20:31:

But these are written, that ye might believe that Jesus is the Christ, the Son of God; and that believing ye might have life through His name.

1 Nephi 2:4 RCE, 1 Nephi 6:4 LDS:

For the fullness of mine intent is that I may persuade men to come unto the God of Abraham and the God of Isaac and the God of Jacob and be saved;

The purpose of both the prophet Nephi and the Apostle John was the same: to bring people to the knowledge of Christ and be saved.

2. Jeremiah 32:2:

For then the king of Babylon's army besieged Jerusalem: and Jeremiah the prophet was shut up in the court of the prison, which was in the king of Judah's house.

Jeremiah 37:15:

Wherefore the princes were wroth with Jeremiah, and smote him, and put him in prison in the house of Jonathan the scribe: for they had made that the prison.

Jeremiah 38:6:

Then took they Jeremiah, and cast him into the dungeon of Malchiah the son of Hammelech, that was in the court of the prison: and they let down Jeremiah with cords. And in the dungeon there was no water, but mire: so Jeremiah sunk in the mire.

1 Nephi 2:22 RCE, 1 Nephi 7:14 LDS:

For behold, they have rejected the prophets and Jeremiah have they cast into prison,...

These scriptures show Jeremiah in prison in three different locations and obviously at three different times. Since Jeremiah's situation was a current event in Jerusalem, Nephi mentioned it to his older brothers when they rebelled against him. Shortly thereafter, they returned to their father's camp with the household of Ishmael.

3. First Nephi 3:2 RCE, 1 Nephi 10:2 LDS appears to paraphrase Jeremiah 52:4-7, 12-14. It is about the destruction of Jerusalem and the capture of most of its people by the Babylonians. This was shown to Lehi in a prophetic dream. I think we can agree that God provides prophetic dreams to His prophets. If we don't, aren't we denying the gifts and power of the Holy Spirit? Matthew 12:31 tells us that "*...but the blasphemy against the Holy Ghost shall not be forgiven unto men...*" and verse 32 "*...but whosoever speaketh against the Holy Ghost, it shall not be forgiven him, neither in this world, neither in the world to come.*"

This next set of verses about John the Baptist, were initially written by Isaiah and later quoted by both the Apostle John and Nephi:

4. Isaiah 40:3:

The voice of him that crieth in the wilderness, Prepare ye the way of the LORD, make straight in the desert a highway for our God.

John 1:6-8, 23, 27:

There was a man sent from God whose name was John. The same came for a witness, to bear witness of the Light, that all men through him might believe. He was not that Light, but was sent to bear witness of that Light.

He said, "I am the voice of one crying in the wilderness, Make straight the way of the Lord, as said the prophet Esaias [Isaiah].*"*

"He it is, who coming after me is preferred before me, whose shoe's latchet I am not worthy to unloose...."

1 Nephi 3:7-9 RCE, 1 Nephi 10:7-8LDS:

And he [Lehi] *spake also concerning a prophet which should come before the Messiah to prepare the way of the Lord; Yea, even he should go forth and cry in the wilderness: "Prepare ye the way of the Lord and make His paths straight, For there standeth One among you whom ye know not; And He is mightier than I, whose shoe's latchet I am not worthy to unloose."*

The above is a good example. Both John and Lehi had access to the writings of Isaiah, and both quoted him. This happened frequently in the Bible, so it should not be a surprise when it is also found in The Book of Mormon.

5. Romans 11:17-24:

And if some of the branches be broken off, and thou, being a wild olive tree, wert graffed in among them, and with them partakest of the root and fatness of the olive tree; Boast not against the branches. But if thou boast, thou bearest not the root, but the root thee. Thou wilt say then, The branches were broken off, that I might be graffed in. Well; because of unbelief they were broken off, and thou standest by faith. Be not highminded, but fear: For if God spared not the natural branches, take heed lest He also spare not thee. Behold therefore the goodness and severity of God: on them which fell, severity; but toward thee, goodness, if thou continue in his goodness: otherwise thou also shalt be cut off. And they also, if they abide not still in unbelief, shall be graffed in: for God is able to graff them in again. For if thou wert cut out of the olive tree which is wild by nature, and wert graffed contrary to nature into a good olive tree: how much more shall these, which be the natural branches, be graffed into their own olive tree?

1 Nephi 3:16-19 RCE, 1 Nephi 10:12-14 LDS:

Yea, even my father spake much concerning the Gentiles, and also concerning the house of Israel—That they should be compared like unto an olive tree whose branches should be broken off and should be scattered upon all the face of the earth; Wherefore, he said it must needs be that we should be led with one accord into the Land of Promise, unto the fulfilling of the word of the Lord that we should be scattered upon all the face of the earth; And after that the house of Israel should be scattered, they should be gathered together again; Or, in fine, that after the Gentiles had received the fullness of the gospel, the natural branches of the olive tree— or the remnants of the house of Israel—should be grafted in, or come to the knowledge of the true Messiah, their Lord and their Redeemer.

The above prophecy was given to Lehi at the river Laman in Arabia. These prophetic words helped convince the families to continue their journey to their Promised Land (America).

Nephi then requested to see the same vision that his father had seen. God granted his request and because of his faith, Nephi was allowed to see much more than his father saw. He was also given the interpretation of his father's dream, plus he saw Christ's birth, ministry and death upon the cross (1 Nephi 3:52-87 RCE, 1 Nephi 11:13-33 LDS). As with the rest of The Book of Mormon, this vision completely agreed with the biblical

account of the life of Jesus. Nephi then explained to his brothers the meaning of their father's vision:

1 Nephi 4:14-16 RCE, 1 Nephi 15:12-13 LDS:

Behold, I say unto you that the house of Israel was compared unto an olive tree by the Spirit of the Lord which was in our father. And behold, are we not broken off from the house of Israel? And are we not a branch of the house of Israel? And now the thing which our father meaneth concerning the grafting in of the natural branches through the fullness of the Gentiles is that in the latter days when our seed shall have dwindled in unbelief, Yea, for the space of many years and many generations after that the Messiah hath manifested Himself in body unto the children of men, Then shall the fullness of the gospel of the Messiah come unto the Gentiles, And from the Gentiles unto the remnant of our seed.

Here, we are given a deeper meaning of the scripture in Romans 11, for Nephi was stating that the remnant of his people are the natural branches that will be grafted back into the olive tree in the last days.

6. Revelation 17:6:

And I saw the woman drunken with the blood of the saints, and with the blood of the martyrs of Jesus: and when I saw her, I wondered with great admiration.

1 Nephi 3:140 RCE, 1 Nephi 13:5 LDS:

And the angel said unto me: "Behold the formation of a church which is most abominable above all other churches, Which slayeth the saints of God, yea, and tortureth them, and bindeth them down, and yoketh them with a yoke of iron, and bringeth them down into captivity."

These verses talk about the formation of the abominable church. Daniel 12:11 also stated that that church would start 1,290 days after the daily sacrifices were taken away. When was that? That is a good question, and I honestly do not know. It amounts to three years, six months and fifteen days and is when the offensive church would be formed. Which church is that? I will let you decide. Further on, Nephi witnessed the Bible being carried among the Gentiles. Nephi was also told that the abominable church had:

1 Nephi 3:168-169 RCE, 1 Nephi 5:16-17 LDS:

…taken away from the gospel of the Lamb many parts which are plain and most precious, And also many covenants of the Lord have they taken away.

Then Nephi sees other books brought forward by the power of the Lamb. These verify *"that the records of the prophets and of the twelve apostles of the Lamb are true"* (1 Nephi 3:191 RCE, 1 Nephi 11:35 LDS) and will convince the remnant of his people and the Gentiles of the truth of the Lamb. We are told in the Bible that God will provide witnesses as He deems necessary:

2 Corinthians 13:1:

> *This is the third time I am coming to you. In the mouth of two or three witnesses shall every word be established.*

The Bible is really one witness. Yes, it has four gospels concerning Christ's ministry, but all four witnesses are from one nation, therefore one witness. The Book of Mormon is the second witness of Jesus Christ's divinity; it provides an independent witness, one not contained within the Bible. Some people refer to 3 Nephi as the fifth gospel of Jesus Christ. You can read about His ministry for yourself; I have included chapters 5 thru 12:36 as Chapter 12 of this book.

7. Ezekiel 37:16-17:

> *Moreover, thou son of man, take thee one stick, and write upon it, For Judah, and for the children of Israel his companions: then take another stick, and write upon it, For Joseph, the stick of Ephraim, and for all the house of Israel his companions: And join them one to another into one stick; and they shall become one in thine hand.*

1 Nephi 3:192-197 RCE, 1 Nephi 13:40-41 LDS:

> *And the angel spake unto me saying: "These last records which thou hast seen among the Gentiles shall establish the truth of the first, which are of the twelve apostles of the Lamb, And shall make known the plain and precious things which have been taken away from them; And shall make known to all kindreds, tongues and people that the Lamb of God is the Eternal Father and the Savior of the world, And that all men must come unto Him or they cannot be saved; And they must come according to the words which shall be established by the mouth of the Lamb; And the words of the Lamb shall be made known in the records of thy seed, as well as in the records of the twelve apostles of the Lamb; Wherefore, they both shall be established in one; For there is one God and one Shepherd over all the earth;"*

While some people may claim that the New Testament is the second stick, the Bible gives directions to: *"take another stick, and write upon it, for Joseph, the stick of Ephraim, and for all the house of Israel his companions:"* Can you show me any

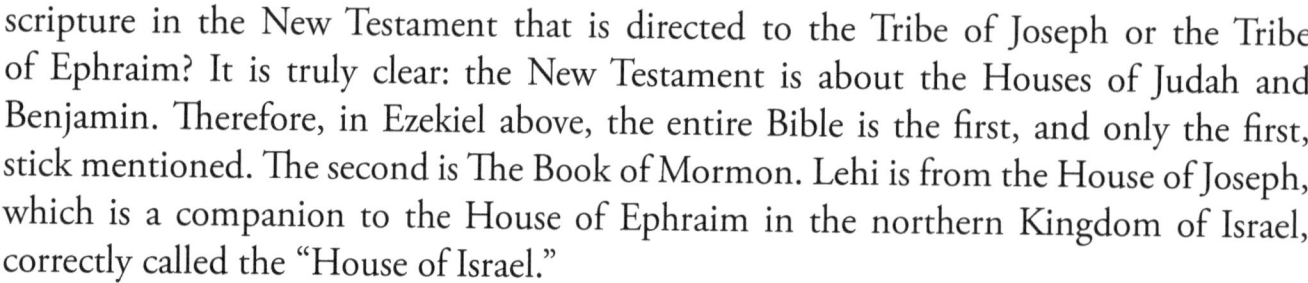

scripture in the New Testament that is directed to the Tribe of Joseph or the Tribe of Ephraim? It is truly clear: the New Testament is about the Houses of Judah and Benjamin. Therefore, in Ezekiel above, the entire Bible is the first, and only the first, stick mentioned. The second is The Book of Mormon. Lehi is from the House of Joseph, which is a companion to the House of Ephraim in the northern Kingdom of Israel, correctly called the "House of Israel."

<u>Mathew 19:30:</u>

But many that are first shall be last; and the last shall be first.

<u>Mathew 20:16:</u>

So the last shall be first, and the first last: for many be called, but few chosen.

<u>Mark 10:31:</u>

But many that are first shall be last; and the last first.

<u>Luke 13:30:</u>

And, behold, there are last which shall be first, and there are first which shall be last.

<u>1 Nephi 3:200 RCE, 1 Nephi 13:42 LDS:</u>

And the last shall be first, and the first shall be last.

I believe that the above scriptures reflect what God, through Jesus, did. First, He came to the Jews; second, he came to the Gentiles through the twelve apostles. The Jews rejected Jesus, but the Gentiles accepted Him. In the future, the Gentiles will bring the Jews to the knowledge of Jesus. So, the first to receive were the last to believe, and the last to receive were the first to believe. Can you say it more clearly?

Nephi loved to quote from Isaiah, so you will see lots of references to him in the next pages. Nephi told his people: ***And now the words which I shall read are they which Isaiah spake concerning all the house of Israel, Wherefore, they may be likened unto you, for ye are of the house of Israel*** (2 Nephi 5:13-14 RCE, 2 Nephi 16:11 LDS),…

<u>Isaiah 29:14:</u>

Therefore, behold, I will proceed to do a marvelous work among this people, even a marvelous work and a wonder: for the wisdom of the wise men shall perish, and the understanding of their prudent men shall be hid.

<u>1 Nephi 3:214 RCE, 1 Nephi 14:7 LDS:</u>

"For the time cometh." saith the Lamb of God, "that I will work a great and marvelous work among the children of men—"

1 Nephi 7:17 RCE, 1 Nephi 22:6 LDS:

And after that our seed is scattered, the Lord God will proceed to do a marvelous work among the Gentiles which shall be of great worth unto our seed;

2 Nephi 11:29 RCE, 2 Nephi 25:17:

Wherefore, He will proceed to do a marvelous work and a wonder among the children of men.

Many people believe these scriptures refer to Joseph Smith's translation of The Book of Mormon. It is indeed *a marvelous work and a wonder.*

10. Revelation 17:5:

And upon her forehead was a name written, MYSTERY, BABYLON THE GREAT, THE MOTHER OF HARLOTS AND ABOMINATIONS OF THE EARTH.

Revelation 17:15:

And he saith unto me, The waters which thou sawest, where the whore sitteth, are peoples, and multitudes, and nations, and tongues.

1 Nephi 3:223-225 RCE, 1 Nephi 14:10-11 LDS:

"And she is the whore of all the earth." And it came to pass that I looked and beheld the whore of all the earth; And she sat upon many waters; And she had dominion over all the earth among all nations, kindreds, tongues and people.

So, which church is that? But, seriously, could that be any single denomination? An angel explained there are only two churches, the church of the Lamb and the church of the devil (1 Nephi 3:220-221 RCE, 1 Nephi 14:10 LDS).

11. Ephesians 6:13:

Wherefore take unto you the whole armour of God, that ye may be able to withstand in the evil day, and having done all, to stand.

1 Nephi 3:231 RCE, 1 Nephi 14:14:

And they were armed with righteousness and with the power of God in great glory.

12. John 15:1:

I am the true vine, and my Father is the husbandman.

1 Nephi 4:21 RCE, 1 Nephi 15:25:

Yea, at that day will they not receive strength and nourishment from the True Vine?

We know that Jesus is "the True Vine".

13. Genesis 12:2-3:

And I will make of thee a great nation, and I will bless thee, and make thy name great; and thou shalt be a blessing: And I will bless them that bless thee, and curse him that curseth thee: and in thee shall all the families of the earth be blessed.

Genesis 22:18:

And in thy seed shall all the nations of the earth be blessed; because thou hast obeyed My voice.

Galatians 3:16:

Now to Abraham and his seed were the promises made. He saith not, And to seeds, as of many; but as one, And to thy seed, which is Christ.

1 Nephi 4:29 RCE, 1 Nephi 15:18 LDS:

Which covenant the Lord made to our father Abraham, saying: "In thy Seed shall all the kindreds of the earth be blessed."

Did you notice that this message from Genesis was quoted by both the New Testament and The Book of Mormon prophets?

14. Isaiah 45:18:

For thus sayeth the LORD that created the heavens; God himself that formed the earth and made it; He hath established it, He created it not in vain, He formed it to be inhabited: I am the LORD; and there is none else.

1 Nephi 5:126 RCE, 1 Nephi 17:36:

Behold, the Lord hath created the earth, that it should be inhabited;...

1.5 Numbers 21:9:

And Moses made a serpent of brass, and put it upon a pole, and it came to pass, that if a serpent had bitten any man, when he beheld the serpent of brass, he lived.

John 3:14-15:

And as Moses lifted up the serpent in the wilderness, even so must the Son of man be lifted up: That whosoever believeth in Him should not perish, but have eternal life.

1 Nephi 5:134-135 RCE, 1 Nephi 17:41:

He sent flying fiery serpents among them; And after they were bitten, He prepared a way that they might be healed; And the labor which they had to perform was to look; And because of the simpleness of the way, or the easiness of it, there were many which perished.

Here is another example of two writers referring to the same idea. Both are quoting from Numbers.

16. Philippians 4:13:

I can do all things through Christ which strengtheneth me.

1 Nephi 5:157 RCE, 1 Nephi 17:50 LDS:

And I saith unto them: "If God had commanded me to do all things, I could do it;…"

17. The next set of verses to compare is Isaiah 48:1-22 and 1 Nephi 6:8-29 RCE, 20:1-22 LDS. Here, Nephi quotes the entire 48th chapter of Isaiah.

Deuteronomy 6:13:

Thou shalt fear the LORD thy God, and serve him, and shalt swear by his name.

1 Nephi 6:8 RCE, 1 Nephi 20:1 LDS:

Hearken and hear this, O house of Jacob, which are called by the name Israel and are come forth out of the waters of Judah, Which swear by the name of the Lord and make mention of the God of Israel, yet they swear not in truth nor in righteousness;…

At first glance, this might look like a form of cursing, but it is not. This is like in court, when you swear to tell the truth. Nephi is pointing out the hypocrisy of the House of Judah. They were not being honest with God.

19. The verses in Isaiah 49:1-26 relate to 1 Nephi 6:31-56 RCE, 1 Nephi 21:1-26 LDS. This is long, quoting another entire chapter from Isaiah.

20. Amos 3:7:

Surely the LORD God will do nothing but he revealeth his secret unto his servants the prophets.

1 Nephi 7:4 RCE, 1 Nephi 22:2 LDS:

For by the Spirit are all things made known unto the prophets which shall come upon the children of men according to the flesh.

According to the Word, God always tells His prophets what He is going to do before He does anything. This is another place where the scriptures agree. Not only that, this also teaches us about the leadership role that prophets should have and why they should be found in churches today.

21. <u>Isaiah 49:22</u>:

Thus saith the LORD God, Behold, I will lift up mine hand to the Gentiles, and set up My standard to the people: and they shall bring thy sons in their arms, and thy daughters shall be carried upon their shoulders.

<u>1 Nephi 7:13 RCE, 1 Nephi 22:6 LDS</u>:

Nevertheless, after that they have been nursed by the Gentiles and the Lord hath lifted up His hand upon the Gentiles and set them up for a standard—And their children shall be carried in their arms, And their daughters shall be carried upon their shoulders; Behold, these things of which are spoken are temporal, For thus are the covenants of the Lord with our fathers;

<u>2 Nephi 5:17 RCE, 2 Nephi 6:6 LDS</u>:

"Thus saith the Lord God: 'Behold, I will lift up Mine hand to the Gentiles and set up My standard to the people;...'"

22. <u>Isaiah 52:10</u>:

The LORD hath made bare his holy arm in the eyes of all the nations; and all the ends of the earth shall see the salvation of our God.

<u>1 Nephi 7:22 RCE, 1 Nephi 22:11 LDS</u>:

Wherefore the Lord God will proceed to make bare His arm in the eyes of all the Nations in bringing about His covenants and His gospel unto they which are of the house of Israel.

God is faithful. He will show Himself to all the nations to fulfill His covenants.

23. <u>Deuteronomy 18:15, 18</u>:

The LORD thy God will raise up unto thee a Prophet from the midst of thee, of thy brethren, like unto me; unto him ye shall harken;...

I will raise them up a Prophet from among their brethren, like unto thee, and will put my words in his mouth; and he shall speak unto them all that I shall command him.

<u>1 Nephi 7:44 RCE, 1 Nephi 22:20 LDS</u>:

A Prophet shall the Lord your God raise up unto you like unto me; Him shall ye hear in all things whatsoever He shall say unto you;...

3 Nephi 9:60 RCE, 3 Nephi 20:23 LDS:

Behold, I Am He of whom Moses spake, saying: "A prophet shall the Lord your God raise up unto you of your brethren like unto me; Him shall ye hear in all things whatsoever He shall say unto you."

These are more prophetic words about the coming of Jesus Christ, as quoted by Jesus Himself.

24. Ephesians 6:11:

Put on the whole armour of God, that ye may be able to stand against the wiles of the devil.

2 Nephi 1:38 RCE, 2 Nephi 1:23 LDS:

Awake my sons! Put on the armour of righteousness;

Can we agree that we need the armour of God to protect us from evil?

25. Acts 4:24:

…and said, Lord, thou art God, which hast made heaven, and earth, and the sea, and all that in them is:…

2 Nephi 1:95 RCE, 2 Nephi 2:14 LDS:

For there is a God and He hath created all things—Both the heavens and the earth and all things that in them is,…

26. Genesis 49:22:

Joseph is a fruitful bough, even a fruitful bough by a well; whose branches run over the wall:…

2 Nephi 2:8 RCE, 2 Nephi 3:5 LDS:

Not the Messiah, but a branch which was to be broken off, Nevertheless, to be remembered in the covenants of the Lord—….

The references here are to the people of The Book of Mormon, the descendants of Joseph, who left Jerusalem and came to the Americas.

27. Proverbs 22:6:

Train up a child in the way he should go: and when he is old, he will not depart from it.

2 Nephi 3:11 RCE, 2 Nephi 4:5 LDS:

For behold, I know that if ye are brought up in the right way that ye should go, ye will not depart from it;…

It is the parents' responsibility to raise up their children to know God and Jesus so that society will not lead them astray.

28. <u>Isaiah 49:24-26</u>:

Shall the prey be taken from the mighty, or the lawful captive delivered? But thus sayeth the LORD, Even the captives of the mighty shall be taken away, and the prey of the terrible shall be delivered: for I will contend with him that contendeth with thee, and I will save thy children. And I will feed them that oppress thee with their own flesh; and they shall be drunken with their own blood, as with sweet wine: and all flesh shall know that I the LORD am thy Savior and thy Redeemer, the mighty One of Jacob.

<u>2 Nephi 5:41-45 RCE, 2 Nephi 5:25-29 LDS</u>:

"For shall the prey be taken from the mighty? Or the lawful captive delivered?" But thus saith the Lord: "Even the captives of the mighty shall be taken away, And the prey of the terrible shall be delivered." For the Mighty God shall deliver His covenant people. For thus saith the Lord: "I will contend with them that contendeth with thee, And I will feed them that oppress thee with their own flesh. And they shall be drunken with their own blood as with sweet wine. And all flesh shall know that I, the Lord, am thy Savior, And thy Redeemer, the Mighty One of Jacob."

No matter where His people are, God will set them free. He will also destroy those who try to stop Him.

The following two sets are too long to be quoted in this book:

29. Compare Isaiah 50:1-11 to 2 Nephi 5:47-69 RCE, 2 Nephi 7:1-11 LDS.
30. Compare Isaiah 51:1-23 to 2 Nephi 5:70-111 RCE, 2 Nephi 8:1-23 LDS.
31. <u>Isaiah 52:1-2</u>:

Awake, awake; put on thy strength, O Zion; put on thy beautiful garments, O Jerusalem, the holy city: for henceforth there shall no more come into thee the uncircumcised and the unclean. Shake thyself from the dust; arise, and sit down, O Jerusalem: loose thyself from the bands of thy neck, O captive daughter of Zion.

<u>2 Nephi 5:112-114 RCE, 2 Nephi 8:24-25 LDS</u>:

Awake, awake! put on thy strength, O Zion; Put on thy beautiful garments, O Jerusalem, the holy city! For henceforth, there shall no more come into thee the uncircumcised and the unclean. Shake thyself from the dust! Arise! Sit down, O Jerusalem! Loose thyself from the bands of thy neck, O captive daughter of Zion!

3 Nephi 9:74-76 RCE, 3 Nephi 20:36-38 LDS:

…Awake! Awake again; and put on thy strength, O Zion! Put on thy beautiful garments, O Jerusalem, the holy city! For henceforth there shall no more come into thee the uncircumcised and the unclean. Shake thyself from the dust—arise! Sit down, O Jerusalem! Loose thyself from the bands of thy neck, O captive daughter of Zion! For thus saith the Lord: "Ye have sold yourselves for nought; and ye shall be redeemed without money."

32. Isaiah 55:1-2:

Ho, every one that thirsteth, come ye to the waters, and he that hath no money; come ye, buy, and eat; yea, come, buy wine and milk without money and without price. Wherefore do ye spend money for that which is not bread? and your labor for that which satisfieth not? hearken diligently unto me, and eat ye that which is good, and let your soul delight itself in fatness.

2 Nephi 6:99-102 RCE, 2 Nephi 9:50-51 LDS:

Come, my brethren: "Every one that thirsteth, come ye to the waters; And he that hath no money, come, buy and eat. Yea, come, buy wine and milk without money and without price. Wherefore, do not spend money for that which is of no worth, Nor your labor for that which cannot satisfy." Hearken diligently unto me and remember the words which I have spoken, And come unto the Holy One of Israel and feast upon that which perisheth not, neither can be corrupted: "And let your soul delight in fatness."

2 Nephi 11:99 RCE, 2 Nephi 26:25 LDS:

… "Come unto Me, all ye ends of the earth, Buy milk and honey without money and without price."

Both the Bible and The Book of Mormon prophets are consistently calling people to Jesus Christ, always asking them to repent and accept Him as their Savior. They remind us that accepting Him is easy and free. If you have not done so, why not do so today? Simply tell God that you accept Jesus as your Savior, that you believe He died for your sins on the cross, and that God resurrected Him from the grave, so that you, too, can be resurrected and saved by the power of Jesus Christ.

33. Compare Isaiah 2:1-14:32 to 2 Nephi 8:17-10:54 RCE, 2 Nephi 12:1-24:32 LDS.

34. Isaiah 29:3-5:

And I will camp against thee round about, and will lay siege against thee with a mount, and I will raise forts against thee. And thou shalt be brought down, and shalt speak out of the ground, and thy speech shall be low out of the dust, and thy voice shall be, as one that hath a familiar spirit, out of the ground, and thy speech shall whisper out of the dust. Moreover the multitude of thy strangers shall be like small dust, and the multitude of the terrible ones shall be as chaff that passeth away: yea it shall be at an instant suddenly.

2 Nephi 11:82-88 RCE, 2 Nephi 26:15-18 LDS:

Yea, after that the Lord God shall have camped against them round about and shall have laid siege against them with a mount and raised forts against them; And after that they shall have been brought down low in the dust, even that they are not, Yet the words of the righteous shall be written, And the prayers of the faithful shall be heard, And all they which have dwindled in unbelief shall not be forgotten. For they which shall be destroyed shall speak unto them out of the ground, And their speech shall be low, out of the dust, And their voice shall be as one that hath a familiar spirit, For the Lord God will give unto him power that he may whisper concerning them, even as it were out of the ground; And their speech shall whisper out of the dust. For thus saith the Lord God: "They shall write the things which shall be done among them, And they shall be written and sealed up in a book; And they that have dwindled in unbelief shall not have them, for they seek to destroy the things of God; Wherefore, as they which have been destroyed have been destroyed speedily, And the multitude of their terrible ones shall be as chaff that passeth away, Yea", thus saith the Lord God, "it shall be at an instant, suddenly!"

There is a beautiful agreement of stories here. I believe both prophets were speaking about the Nephites, a remnant from Jerusalem, and their destruction. We are told how God would hide up the books of the righteous because the wicked would have destroyed them. Finally, they tell how their history (The Book of Mormon) will be brought forth in the last days "out of the ground, and thy speech shall whisper out of the dust."

35. Isaiah 29:6-10:

Thou shalt be visited of the LORD of hosts with thunder, and with earthquake, and great noise, with storm and tempest, and the flame of devouring fire. And the multitude of all nations that fight against Ariel, even all that fight against her and her munition, and that distress her, shall be as a dream of a night vision. It shall even be as when an hungry man dreameth, and, behold, he eateth; but he awaketh, and his soul is empty: or as when a thirsty man dreameth, and, behold, he drinketh; but he awaketh, and behold, he is faint, and his soul hath appetite: so shall the multitude of all the nations be, that fight against mount Zion. Stay yourselves, and wonder; cry ye out, and cry: they are drunken, but not with wine; they stagger, but not with strong drink. For the LORD hath poured out upon you the spirit of deep sleep, and hath closed your eyes: the prophets and your rulers, the seers hath he covered.

2 Nephi 11:117-124 RCE, 2 Nephi 27:2-5 LDS:

And when that day shall come, they shall be visited of the Lord of Hosts, With thunder and with earthquake, and with a great noise, and with storm and tempest, and with the flame of devouring fire; And all the nations that fight against Zion and that distress her shall be as a dream of a night vision; Yea, it shall be unto them even as unto a hungry man which dreameth, And behold—he eateth, But he awaketh, and his soul is empty; Or like unto a thirsty man which dreameth, And behold— he drinketh, But he awaketh, And behold he is faint, and his soul hath appetite; Yea, even so shall the multitude of all the nations be that fight against Mount Zion. For behold, all ye that do iniquity, stay yourself and wonder; For ye shall cry out and cry, Yea, ye shall be drunken, but not with wine; Ye shall stagger, but not with strong drink. For behold, the Lord hath poured out upon you the spirit of deep sleep, For behold, ye have closed your eyes; And ye have rejected the prophets, And your rulers and the seers hath He covered because of your iniquity.

36. Compare Isaiah 29:11-24 to 2 Nephi 11:125-160 RCE, 2 Nephi 27:6-35:

37. Isaiah 28:10:

For precept must be upon precept, precept upon precept; line upon line, line upon line; here a little, and there a little;...

Isaiah 28:13:

But the word of the LORD was unto them precept upon precept, precept upon precept; line upon line, line upon line; here a little, there a little; that they might go and fall backward, and be broken, and snared, and taken.

2 Nephi 12:36 RCE, 2 Nephi 28:30 LDS:

..."I will give unto the children of men, Line upon line and precept upon precept, Here a little and there a little;..."

38. Isaiah 9:12-13:

The Syrians before, and the Philistines behind; and they shall devour Israel with open mouth. For all this His anger is not turned away, but

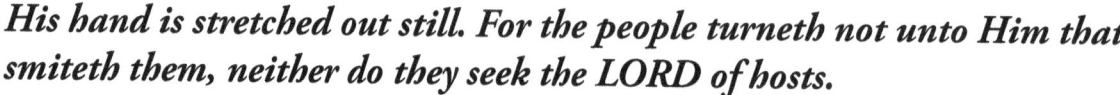

His hand is stretched out still. For the people turneth not unto Him that smiteth them, neither do they seek the LORD of hosts.

2 Nephi 12:40-41 RCE, 2 Nephi 28:32 LDS:

"Wo be unto the Gentiles!" saith the Lord God of Hosts; "For notwithstanding I shall lengthen out Mine arm unto them from day to day, they will deny Me; Nevertheless, I will be merciful unto them," saith the Lord God, "if they will repent and come unto Me, For Mine arm is lengthened out all the day long," saith the Lord God of Hosts.

39. Isaiah 11:11:

And it shall come to pass in that day, that the Lord shall set His hand again the second time to recover the remnant of His people, which shall be left, from Assyria, and from Egypt, and from Pathros, and from Cush, and from Elam, and from Shinar, and from Hamath, and from the islands of the sea.

2 Nephi 12:42 RCE, 2 Nephi 29:1 LDS:

But behold, there shall be many at that day when I shall proceed to do a marvelous work among them, That I may remember My covenants which I have made unto the children of men, That I may set My hand again the second time to recover My people which are of the house of Israel,…

40. Isaiah 11:4:

But with righteousness shall He judge the poor, and reprove with equity for the meek of the earth: and He shall smite the earth with the rod of His mouth, and with the breath of His lips shall He slay the wicked.

2 Nephi 12:88 RCE, 2 Nephi 30:9 LDS:

And with righteousness shall the Lord God judge the poor, And reprove with equity for the meek of the earth;…

41. Isaiah 11:5-9:

And righteousness shall be the girdle of His loins, and faithfulness the girdle of His reins. The wolf also shall dwell with the lamb, and the leopard shall lie down with the kid; and the calf and the young lion and the fatling together; and a little child shall lead them. And the cow and the bear shall feed; their young ones shall lie down together: and the lion shall eat straw like the ox. And the suckling child shall play on the hole of the asp, and the weaned child shall put his hand on the cocatrice' den. They shall not hurt nor destroy in all my holy mountain: for the earth shall be full of the knowledge of the LORD, as the waters cover the sea.

<u>2 Nephi 12:91-95 RCE, 2 Nephi 30:11-15:</u>

And righteousness shall be the girdle of His loins, And faithfulness the girdle of His reins. And then shall the wolf dwell with the lamb, And the leopard shall lie down with the kid, And the calf and the young lion and the fatling, together; And a little child shall lead them. And the cow and the bear shall feed; their young ones shall lie down together; And the lion shall eat straw like the ox. And the suckling child shall play on the hole of the asp, And the weaned child shall put his hand on the cockatrice's den. They shall not hurt nor destroy in all My holy mountain; For the earth shall be full of the knowledge of the Lord, as the waters cover the sea.

42. <u>Deuteronomy 8:18:</u>

But thou shalt remember the LORD thy God: for it is He that giveth thee power to get wealth, that He may establish His covenant which He sware unto thy fathers, as it is this day.

<u>Jacob 2:24 RCE, Jacob 2:19 LDS:</u>

And after that ye have obtained a hope in Christ, ye shall obtain riches—if ye seek them, And ye will seek them for the intent to do good: to clothe the naked, to feed the hungry, and to liberate the captive, and administer relief to the sick and the afflicted.

43. <u>Hebrews 6:8:</u>

But that which beareth thorns and briers is rejected, and is nigh unto cursing; whose end is to be burned.

<u>Jacob 4:11 RCE, Jacob 6:7 LDS:</u>

…Will ye bring forth evil fruit, that ye must be hewn down and cast into the fire?

44. <u>Psalms 37:4:</u>

…and He shall give thee the desires of thine heart.

<u>Enos 1:18 RCE, Enos 1:12 LDS:</u>

I will grant unto thee according to thy desires….

45. <u>Isaiah 52:7-10:</u>

How beautiful upon the mountains are the feet of him that bringeth good tidings, that publisheth peace; that bringeth good tidings of good, that publisheth salvation; that saith unto Zion, Thy God reigneth! Thy watchman shall lift up the voice; with the voice together shall they sing: for they shall see eye to eye, when the LORD shall bring again Zion. Break forth into joy, sing together, ye waste places of Jerusalem: for the LORD hath comforted his people, he hath redeemed Jerusalem. The LORD hath made bare his holy arm in the eyes of all the nations; and all the ends of the earth shall see the salvation of our God.

Mosiah 7:77-80 RCE, Mosiah 12:21-24 LDS:

"... 'How beautiful upon the mountains are the feet of him that bringeth good tidings, That publisheth peace, That bringeth good tidings of good, That publisheth salvation, That saith unto Zion, "Thy God reigneth!" Thy watchman shall lift up the voice; With the voice together shall they sing; For they shall see eye to eye, when the Lord shall bring again Zion. Break forth into joy! Sing together, ye waste places of Jerusalem! For the Lord hath comforted His people, He hath redeemed Jerusalem. The Lord hath made bare His holy arm in the eyes of all the nations; and all the ends of the earth shall see the salvation of our God!'?"

Mosiah 8:47-51 RCE, Mosiah 15:13-18 LDS:

... "And these are they which hath published peace, That hath brought good tidings of good, That hath published salvation, That saith unto Zion, 'Thy God reigneth!' "And, O how beautiful upon the mountains were their feet! "And again, how beautiful upon the mountains are the feet of those that are still publishing peace! "And again, how beautiful upon the mountains are the feet of those who shall hereafter publish peace, Yea, from this time henceforth and forever! "And behold, I say unto you, this is not all—For O how beautiful upon the mountains are the feet of him that bringeth good tidings, that is, the founder of peace!..."

Mosiah 8:67-69 RCE, Mosiah 15:29-31 LDS:

"... 'Thy watchman shall lift up their voice; With the voice together shall they sing; For they shall see eye to eye when the Lord shall bring again Zion. Break forth into joy! Sing together, ye waste places of Jerusalem! For the Lord hath comforted His people, He hath redeemed Jerusalem. The Lord hath made bare His holy arm in the eyes of all the nations, And all the ends of the earth shall see the salvation of our God!'"

3. Nephi 7:43-45 RCE, 3 Nephi 16:18 LDS:

"... 'Thy watchman shall lift up the voice, With the voice together shall they sing; For they shall see eye to eye when the Lord shall bring again Zion. Break forth into joy! Sing together, ye waste places of Jerusalem! For the Lord hath comforted His people, He hath redeemed Jerusalem. The Lord hath made bare his holy arm in the eyes of all the nations; And all the ends of the earth shall see the salvation of God!'"

3 Nephi 9:70-73 RCE, 3 Nephi 20:32:

'Then shall their watchmen lift up their voice, And with the voice together shall they sing; For they shall see eye to eye. Then will the Father gather them together again, And give unto them Jerusalem for the land of their inheritance. Then shall they break forth into joy! Sing together, ye waste places of Jerusalem! For the Father hath comforted His people, He hath redeemed Jerusalem. The Father hath made bare His holy arm in the eyes of all the nations; And all the ends of the earth shall see the salvation of the Father; And the Father and I are one.'

46. Exodus 20:2-4:

I am the LORD thy God, which have brought thee out of the land of Egypt, out of the house of bondage. Thou shalt have no other gods before Me. Thou shalt not make unto thee any graven image, or any likeness of any thing that is in heaven above, or that is in in the earth beneath, or that is in the water under the earth:...

Mosiah 7:95-97 RCE, Mosiah 15:34-36:

"... 'I Am the Lord thy God, which has brought thee out of the land of Egypt, out of the house of bondage; Thou shalt have no other god before Me! Thou shalt not make unto thee any graven image, or any likeness of anything in the heaven above, or things which are in the earth beneath.'"

The following three sets are too long to be quoted in this book:

47. Compare Exodus 20:4-17 to Mosiah 7:113-124 RCE, Mosiah 13:12-24 LDS.

48. Compare Isaiah 53:1-12, and 1 Peter 2:24 to Mosiah 8:16-27 RCE, Mosiah 14:1-12 LDS.

49. Compare Isaiah 53:7-11 to Mosiah 8:33-39, 44 RCE, Mosiah 15:6-10, 12 LDS.

50. Isaiah 25:8:

He will swallow up death in victory; and the LORD God will wipe away tears from off all faces; and the rebuke of His people shall He take away from off all the earth: for the LORD hath spoken it.

Mosiah 8:54 RCE, Mosiah 15:20:

But behold. the bands of death shall be broken; And the Son reigneth and hath power over the dead; Therefore, He bringeth to pass the resurrection of the dead.

51. 1 Thessalonians 5:18:

In everything give thanks: for this is the will of God in Christ Jesus concerning you.

Mosiah 11:149 RCE, Mosiah 26:39 LDS:

…Being commanded of God to pray without ceasing and to give thanks in all things.

52. 1 John 3:9:

Whosoever is born of God doth not commit sin; for His seed remaineth in him: and he cannot sin, because he is born of God.

1 John 4:7:

Beloved, let us love one another: for love is of God; and everyone that loveth is born of God, and knoweth God.

Alma 3:27 RCE, Alma 5:14 LDS:

…Have ye spiritually been born of God?

Alma 17:5 RCE, Alma 36:6 LDS:

…I say unto you, if I had not been born of God, I should not have known these things;…

John 3:3:

…Verily, verily, I say unto thee, Except a man be born again, he cannot see the kingdom of God.

1 Peter 1:23:

Being born again, not of corruptible seed, but of incorruptible, by the word of God, which liveth and abideth forever.

Alma 3:86 RCE, Alma 5:49 LDS:

…Yea, to cry unto them that they must repent and be born again.

Alma 5:24 RCE, Alma 7:14 LDS:

… "If ye are not born again, ye cannot inherit the kingdom of heaven."

The Bible and the Book of Mormon are in harmony: we must be born again to receive eternal salvation; that is, we must accept Christ as our Savior, ask for forgiveness, be baptized by water and the spirit, and live lives acceptable to Christ.

54. Luke 3:9:

And now also the axe is laid unto the root of the trees: every tree therefore which bringeth not forth good fruit is hewn down, and cast into the fire.

Alma 3:90 RCE, Alma 5:52 LDS:

… "Behold, the axe is laid at the root of the tree; Therefore, every tree that bringeth not forth good fruit shall be hewn down and cast into the fire,…"

55. Revelation 13:8:

...the lamb slain from the foundation of the world.

Alma 9:49 RCE, Alma 12:30 LDS:

...prepared from the foundation of the world;...

56. Philippians 4:13:

I can do all things through Christ which strengtheneth me.

Alma 14:92 RCE, Alma 26:12 LDS:

...For in His strength I can do all things....

57. Psalms 51:16-17:

For thou desirest not sacrifice; else would I give it: thou delightest not in burnt offering. The sacrifices of God are a broken spirit: a broken and a contrite heart, O God, thou will not despise.

3 Nephi 4:49 RCE, 3 Nephi 9:19 LDS:

...Yea, your sacrifices and your burnt offerings shall be done away, For I will accept none of your sacrifices and your burnt offerings; And ye shall offer for a sacrifice unto Me a broken heart and a contrite spirit;...

Many suggest that Joseph Smith simply copied the words of Christ from the New Testament. However, if Christ visited this continent, don't you think His message would be the same for everyone? Believing it could be different in another place or time is one of the fallacies of modern thinkers.

58. Compare the next lengthy set of verses in Matthew 5:1–7:29 to 3 Nephi 5:47–6:37 RCE, 3 Nephi 12:1-14:26 LDS.

59. Matthew 10:6:

But go rather to the lost sheep of the house of Israel.

Matthew 15:24:

But He answered and said, I am not sent but unto the lost sheep of the house of Israel.

John 10:16:

And other sheep I have, which are not of this fold: them also I must bring, and they shall hear my voice; and there shall be one fold, and one shepherd.

3 Nephi 7:16 RCE, 3 Nephi 15:7 LDS:

...That other sheep I have which are not of this fold; Them also must I bring, And they shall hear My voice, And there shall be one fold and one Shepard.

60. Isaiah 52:6-7:

"Therefore My people shall know My name: therefore they shall know in that day that I am He that doth speak: behold, it is I. How beautiful upon the mountains are the feet of him that bringeth good tidings, that publisheth peace; that bringeth good tidings of good, that publisheth salvation; that saith unto Zion, Thy God reigneth!"

3 Nephi 9:77-78 RCE, 3 Nephi 20:39-40 LDS:

'Verily, verily I say unto you that My people shall know My name— Yea, in that day they shall know that I Am He that doth speak. And then shall they say, "How beautiful upon the mountains are the feet of Him that bringeth good tidings unto them, that publisheth peace, That bringeth good tidings unto them of good, That publisheth salvation; That saith unto Zion, 'Thy God reigneth!'"

Notice Christ is quoting His own scriptures? Shouldn't we be familiar with sacred writings too? We have seen that prophets quote other prophets, and isn't Jesus the greatest prophet of all, as well as Lord and Savior?

61. Isaiah 52:11-15:

Depart ye, depart ye, go ye out from thence, touch no unclean thing; go ye out of the midst of her; be ye clean, that bear the vessels of the LORD. For ye shall not go out with haste, nor go by flight: for the LORD will go before you; and the God of Israel will be your rereward. Behold, my servant shall deal prudently, he shall be exalted and extolled, and be very high. As many were astonied at thee; his visage was so marred more than any man, and his form more than the sons of men: So shall He sprinkle many nations; the kings shall shut their mouths at Him; for that which had not been told them shall they see; and that which they had not heard shall they consider.

3 Nephi 9:79-83, RCE, 3 Nephi 20:41-45 LDS:

…'And then shall a cry go forth, Depart ye! Depart ye! Go ye out from thence. Touch not that which is unclean; Go ye out of the midst of her; Be ye clean that bear the vessels of the Lord. For ye shall not go out with haste, nor go by flight; For the Lord will go before you, And the God of Israel shall be your rearward. 'Behold, My servant shall deal prudently-- He shall be exalted and extolled and be very high. As many were astonied at thee; His visage was so marred---more than any man, And His form more than the sons of men; So shall He sprinkle many nations. The kings

shall shut their mouths at Him; For that which had not been told them shall they see, And that which they had not heard shall they consider.'

62. Micah 5:8-15:

And the remnant of Jacob shall be among the Gentiles in the midst of many people as a lion among the beasts of the forest, as a young lion among the flocks of sheep: who, if he go through, both treadeth down, and teareth into pieces, and none can deliver. Thine hand shall be lifted up upon thine adversaries, and all thine enemies shall be cut off. And it shall come to pass in that day, saith the LORD, that I will cut off thy horses out of the midst of thee, and I will destroy thy chariots: And I will cut off the cities of thy land, and throw down all thy strongholds: And I will cut off witchcrafts out of thine hand; and thou shalt have no more soothsayers:

Thy graven images also will I cut off, and thy standing images out of the midst of thee; and thou shalt no more worship the work of thy hands. And I will pluck up thy groves out of the midst of thee: so I will destroy thy cities. And I will execute vengeance in anger and fury upon the heathen, such as they have not heard.

3 Nephi 9:99-104, 106 RCE, 3 Nephi 21:12-18 LDS:

…'And My people which are a remnant of Jacob shall be among the Gentiles, Yea, in the midst of them, as a lion among the beasts of the forest, as a young lion among the flocks of sheep, Who, if he go through, both treadeth down and teareth into pieces, And none can deliver. Their hand shall be lifted up upon their adversaries, And all their enemies shall be cut off.' "Yea, wo be unto the Gentiles, except they repent! 'For it shall come to pass in that day,' saith the Father, 'That I will cut off thy horses out of the midst of thee, And I will destroy thy chariots, And I will cut off the cities of thy land, And throw down all thy strongholds. And I will cut off witchcrafts out of thy hand, And thou shalt have no more soothsayers. Thy graven images I will also cut off, And thy standing images out of the midst of thee; And thou shalt no more worship the works of thy hands; And I will pluck up thy groves out of the midst of thee--So will I destroy thy cities.

'…For it shall come to pass,' saith the Father, 'that at that day, whosoever will not repent and come unto My beloved Son, Them will I cut off from among My people, O House of Israel, And I will execute

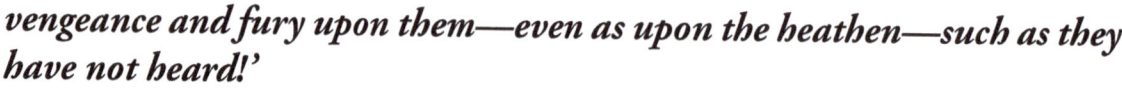

vengeance and fury upon them—even as upon the heathen—such as they have not heard!'

The following two sets are too long to be quoted in this book:

63. Compare Isaiah 54:1-17 to 3 Nephi 10:9-25 RCE, 3 Nephi 22:1-17 LDS: Also see Psalms 111:6, Proverbs 13:22 and James 5:1-3.

64. Compare Malachi 3:1–4:6 to 3 Nephi 11:4-27 RCE, 3 Nephi 24:1-25:6 LDS:

65. <u>Mark 16:17-18:</u>

And these signs shall follow them that believe; In My name shall they cast out devils; they shall speak with new tongues; They shall take up serpents; and if they drink any deadly thing, it shall not hurt them; They shall lay hands on the sick, and they shall recover.

<u>Mormon 4:87 RCE, Mormon 9:24 LDS:</u>

And these signs shall follow them that believe—In My name shall they cast out devils; they shall speak with new tongues; They shall take up serpents; And if they drink any deadly thing, it shall not hurt them; They shall lay hands on the sick and they shall recover.

Historical Accounts That Reflect The Bible

To begin, for many years biblical prophets, as well as Lehi of The Book of Mormon, had given warnings to the people of the House of Judah to repent and return to the Lord, or He would forsake them and allow the destruction of Jerusalem (Jeremiah 4:5-6, 6:1). About 130 years after the destruction of the Northern Kingdom by the Assyrians, the House of Judah failed to heed God's warnings. So, God allowed the complete destruction of Jerusalem, including the Temple, by the Babylonians in 588 B.C. Most of the House of Judah were killed or taken into captivity.

The Book of Mormon history begins here in Jerusalem, about ten years before that destruction. It details the accounts of three distinct groups of people, two of whom came from Jerusalem, one before and one after the destruction. The first, the Nephites, kept records, but the second group, people of Zarahemla, whom we call the Mulekites (although the Book of Mormon never used that term), did not. This second group, the Mulekites, were later discovered by the Nephites and assimilated into their culture around 200 B.C. The third, and much earlier migration, was the Jaredites, who came from the Great Tower around 3000 B.C. But back to our history: about 600 B.C. the events begin in Jerusalem, in the Southern Kingdom, with the prophet Lehi warning the

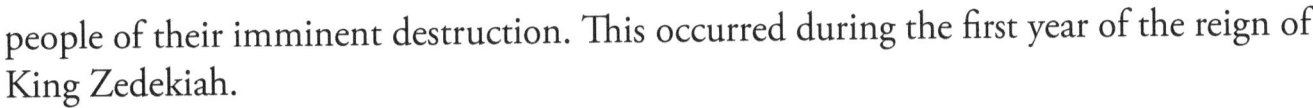

people of their imminent destruction. This occurred during the first year of the reign of King Zedekiah.

1 Nephi 1:3 RCE, 1 Nephi 1:4 LDS:

For it came to pass in the commencement of the first year of the reign of Zedekiah, king of Judah, my father Lehi having dwelt at Jerusalem in all his days, And in that same year there came many prophets prophesying unto the people that they must repent or that great City Jerusalem must be destroyed;

1 Nephi 1:18-22 RCE, 1 Nephi 1:18-20 LDS:

Therefore, I would that ye should know that after the Lord had shown so many marvelous things unto my father Lehi, yea, concerning the destruction of Jerusalem, Behold, he went forth among the people and began to prophesy and to declare unto them concerning the things which he had both seen and heard. And it came to pass that the Jews did mock him because of the things which he testified of them, for he truly testified of their wickedness and their abominations; And he testified that the things which he saw and heard--and also the things which he read in the book--manifested plainly of the coming of a Messiah and also the redemption of the world; And when the Jews heard these things, they were angry with him, Yea, even as with the prophets of old whom they had cast out and stoned and slain; And they also sought his life, that they might take it away.

1 Nephi 1:26 RCE, 1 Nephi 2:2 LDS:

And it came to pass that the Lord commanded my father, even in a dream, that he should take his family and depart into the wilderness.

Lehi then took his family and left Jerusalem, prior to the fall. Traveling south, they made their way to the Red Sea. Included in his household were his wife Sariah and his four sons: Laman, Lemuel, Sam and Nephi.

Lehi had a dream in which God told him to send his sons to get the brass plates which contained part of the Old Testament, up to the reign of King Zedekiah, including many prophecies which have been spoken by the mouth of Jeremiah. He was directed by God to ask the family of Ishmael to join them on their journey. Ishmael had two married sons and five daughters who provided wives for Lehi's sons and Zoram, Laban's slave whom Nephi freed. According to the brass plates, Lehi's family were descendants of Joseph through Josephs son Manasseh. These newly formed families gave birth to children, who eventually became the nations of Nephites and Lamanites.

The Lord directed Nephi to build a ship and gave him instructions on how to build it. This ship carried them to their "Land of Promise," in Central America. It is believed that they landed on the *west coast* of what is now Guatemala (Heater Center fold) and called it Joseph's Land. They arrived about 589 B.C. and settled in the *highlands* of Guatemala. A few years later, Lehi died, and Nephi, Sam and their families fled because they feared their brothers Laman and Lemuel. They and their families became the Lamanites, and Nephi and Sam and their group formed the Nephites. The Lamanites were the more wicked and kept no records while the Nephites were led by prophets of God and kept records. The Book of Mormon is, therefore, told from the perspective of the Nephites, and fourteen of the fifteen books composing it are about them and their struggles with the Lamanites. The third group led by profits of God was a group called the Jaredites that originated from the tower of Babble.

Around 269 B.C., the Nephites discovered the people of Zarahemla, who were led by Mulek, a son of King Zedekiah. They left Jerusalem around 586 B.C. shortly after its destruction by the direction of God. They also journeyed through the wilderness, crossed the Atlantic ocean and landed in the *lowlands* of Guatemala, on the east coast of Central America (Heater centerfold).

Taken as a whole, The Book of Mormon comes to us as a powerful witness of God's redeeming love for all mankind, including the people in the Americas.

In addition, unusual things happened in The Book of Mormon that coincide with the Bible. For instance, at Christ's birth a new star appeared, the same star that the wise men followed. At that same time, the Nephites had a day and a night and a day without darkness. (Could that have been caused by the brightness of the new star?)

3 Nephi 1:17 RCE, 3 Nephi 1:15 LDS:
> *For he beheld at the going down of the sun there was no darkness, And the people began to be astonished because there was no darkness when the night came.*

There were also many prophecies concerning Christ's life and His death upon the cross, burial in a tomb and resurrection on the third day. Beyond that, there were prophecies about the calamities that would follow His death. For example, the Book of Mormon people experienced tremendous volcanic eruptions and earthquakes when Christ died. (3 Nephi 4:6-16 RCE, 3 Nephi 8:5-19 LDS) In fact, the entire earth shook.

I believe that 3 Nephi is the most important book of The Book of Mormon. *It covers from Christ's birth until about 34 A.D. This* Nephi (others also had that name) was one of the twelve disciples ordained by CHRIST in America. He tells us about the ministry that Jesus brought to America. According to his record:

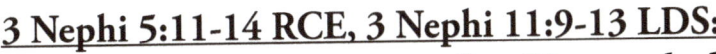

3 Nephi 5:11-14 RCE, 3 Nephi 11:9-13 LDS:

And it came to pass that He stretched forth His hand and spake unto the people, saying: *"Behold, I Am Jesus Christ of which the prophets testified that should come into the world; And behold, I Am the light and the life of the world; And I have drunk out of that bitter cup which the Father hath given Me, And have glorified the Father in taking upon Me the sins of the world, in the which I have suffered the will of the Father in all things from the beginning."* *And it came to pass that when Jesus had spake these words, the whole multitude fell to the earth, For they remembered that it had been prophesied among them that Christ should show Himself unto them after His ascension into heaven. And it came to pass that the Lord spake unto them, saying:* *"Arise and come forth unto Me, That ye may thrust your hands into My side, And also that ye may feel the prints of the nails in My hands and in my feet, That ye may know that I Am the God of Israel and the God of the whole earth and have been slain for the sins of the world."*

3 Nephi 8:27 RCE, 3 Nephi 17:25 LDS:

And they were in number about two thousand and five hundred souls; And they did consist of men, women and children.

Christ's arrival in Central America at the temple in the Land of Bountiful was witnessed by all, each of whom was allowed to feel the wounds in Jesus' side and the nail prints in His hands and feet. In speaking to the twelve He had chosen, Jesus said:

3 Nephi 7:13 RCE, 3 Nephi 15:12 LDS:

… 'Ye are My disciples: and ye are a light unto this people, which are a remnant of the house of Joseph.' (Emphasis added)

Within a short time of Christ's visit to the people of Bountiful, the twelve disciples went throughout the land baptizing the people and forming churches. This brought about both peace and prosperity between all the different nations.

4 Nephi 1:20 RCE, 4 Nephi 1:17 LDS:

There were no robbers, nor no murderers, Neither were there Lamanites, nor no manner of "ites"; But they were in one the children of Christ and heirs to the kingdom of God--

Peace reigned for more than 200 years. But then pride and other wickedness returned. The people had become wealthy and proud, putting aside God. (Are you listening, America?) As The Book of Mormon ends, great wars had broken out between the Nephites and Lamanites. In 385 A.D. about one million men, women and children were killed in one day! Of the Nephites, only twenty-four survived, including Mormon and his son, Moroni.

During that final battle, the surviving Nephites escaped into the land to the south, but were eventually all found and killed except for Moroni. He was tasked with recording the demise of the once-great Nephite nation and hiding the records for future retrieval. Thus ends The Book of Mormon, a history of events about a group of Israelites from the House of Israel who came to America from Jerusalem.

The prophet Mormon (310-385 A.D.) was the main editor of The Book of Mormon. It is my thinking that in his individual book, he named the entire book after himself:

Mormon 1:1:

And now I, Mormon, make a record of the things which I have both seen and heard, And call it The Book of Mormon. (Emphasis added)

None of the other books within The Book of Mormon make a statement like this. Another quote that might help in deciding how the book was titled comes from Omni:

Omni 1:54 RCE, Omni 1:30 LDS:

And I make an 1end of my speaking.

The marginal note says the quote refers to the "end of [the] small plates of Nephi," which Mormon did not abridge.

Take this quote in conjunction with the following quote:

Words of Mormon 1:13 RCE, Words of Mormon 1:9 LDS:

And now I, Mormon, proceed to 1finish out my record which I take from the plates of Nephi, ...

So, the margins say, "abridgement begins [here]; [and] ends Mn 3:33" with the conclusion of Mormon's writing. His son writes the last chapter in his book. Therefore, according to these notes, Mormon had made an abridgement of the first book, the book of Lehi, written on the small plates of Nephi. He also found six additional books that he inserted into his abridged, larger book, *The Book of Mormon*, as he explained in Words of Mormon 1:4-5 RCE, Words of Mormon 1:3 LDS.

Another option might have been that his son, Moroni, named it after him (Mormon) as he was writing the preface page, which says:

The Book of Mormon

An Account written by the hand of Mormon upon
plates taken from the plates of Nephi.

Some very knowledgeable people feel that the book is named after the Land of Mormon where Alma established covenant relationships by baptizing people into remembrance of and acceptance of Jesus Christ, who was to come.

Mosiah 9:41 RCE, Mosiah 18:10 LDS:

Now, I say unto you, if this be the desires of your hearts, What have you against being baptized in the name of the LORD as a witness before Him that ye have entered into a covenant with Him that ye will serve Him and keep His commandments, that He may pour out His spirit more abundantly upon you?

Mosiah 9:44 RCE, Mosiah 18:13 LDS:

And when he had said these words, the spirit of the LORD was upon him and he said: Helam, I baptize thee, having authority from the almighty God, as a testimony that ye have entered into a covenant to serve Him until you are dead, as to the mortal body; And may the spirit of the LORD be poured out upon you, And may He grant unto you eternal life through the redemption of Christ, which he hath prepared from the foundation of the world.

As one of the editors of the Restored Covenant Edition of The Book of Mormon, Ray Treat's personal testimony is that *"The land of Mormon to the Nephite believers meant the land where the covenant was restored; therefore, Mormon means (by inference) 'restoration of the covenant.'"* I feel this definition applies to both the land's name and the prophet's name because Mormon inserts the following in 3 Nephi:

3 Nephi 2:96 RCE, 3 Nephi 5:32 LDS:

And behold, I am called Mormon, being called after the Land of Mormon—The land in which Alma did establish the church...

Others feel that Mormon was not egotistical and would not have put his name on the book he mainly abridged. So, even if Mormon named the book after himself, or his son named it after him, since he was named after the Land of Mormon, you can still say that the book was named after the Land of Mormon. In other words, all three explanations could be true. Ray continues, *"And spiritually speaking, The Book of Mormon means the Book of the 'Restoration of the Covenant.'"* (Treat, Personal interview)

Further inquiry into the history and legends of the people of the American continents reveals similar stories. For example, Roy Weldon quotes Kathleen Romoli, a noted authority on the cultures of South America. She tells about the legend of the Chibchas Indians of Columbia, South America, who were visited by a white God. (18)

> **Bochica [Christ] must have really existed. He came to Cundinamarca from the east,…and when His mission was over He returned, alone as when He came….He leant upon a shepherd's crook and His long white beard fell to His waist. (This beard is one of the most curious features of the Bochica legend. It is extremely hard to imagine whiskers of which you have never heard, and the Chibchas were beardless.) The Messenger of God was dressed in long robes, and a mantle covered His shoulders; His skin was fair, and on His forehead was the sign of the cross. He went up and down the land, teaching, and wherever he stopped the people crowded to hear Him. He preached of the resurrection of the body and of the Last Judgement, of the afterlife and the immortality of the soul, and of the beneficent power of God; he enjoined his followers to practice good works and charity….The children of Bochue said *that Bochica lived with them fourteen centuries before the Conquistadores—whose coming He foretold;…(19)***

> *The last statement in this legend of Bochica is remarkable. Fourteen centuries before the arrival of the Spaniards in the New World puts us back to the very time when Jesus said, "Other sheep I have, which are not of this fold:…and they shall hear My voice." (19)*

Other Indian cultures have similar legends, the Aztecs have Quetzalcoatl (7), the Maya have Kukulcan (13), and there exist others from other Indian cultures. (16) In a more recent publication (2012), Diane Wirth informs us under the heading "Plausible Associations" of the following:

> *Many of the symbols associated with Christ also belong to Quetzalcoatl and the Maize God, symbols that may appear both in pre-Columbian art motifs and in some later colonial literatures that do not seem to be Christian interpolations. Thus it is quite possible that features of the God Quetzalcoatl may be derived, in part, from Mesoamericans' remembrance of Christ's visit to the Americas.*

To return to Roy Weldon in reference to Quetzalcoatl, he states:

> **The evidence that Quetzalcoatl was Jesus Christ is not complete until we add to the impact of His personality on prehistoric America the traditions**

which link and weld the history of Quetzalcoatl with the story of the Good Shepherd. (11)

Here I present further milestones in the life of Quetzalcoatl:

A. Quetzalcoatl's birth was accompanied by the appearance of a new star and mysterious omens and wonders in the heavens.

B. Tradition is silent as to his childhood years.

C. Manly P. Hall says, "we read of the temptations of Quetzalcoatl, how during his penance the spirits of evil came to him and tried to divert him from his course. In another place is the account of his fasting for forty days which later became a definite part of the Mexican ritual.

D. Quetzalcoatl had power of bidding the winds to be hushed, hence he is called "God of the Wind."

E. Quetzalcoatl destroys the death God (victory over death).

F. Of his many appllations in the ancient language signifies a vine or juice thereof.

G. The morning star is his symbol/

H. Spence says, that Quetzalcoatl died and was invisible for four days, after which he was resurrected and ascended his throne.

I. Between his death and his resurrection, Quetzalcoatl tarried in the underworld. (11)

How was the Book of Mormon brought to us?

Moroni hid the record sometime after 420 A.D., after which he said he was going to *"…rest in the paradise of God…"* (Moroni 10:31 RCE, Moroni 10:34 LDS). In 1827, the angel Moroni returned and directed Joseph Smith, Jr., to the gold plates. He translated them by the gift and power of God and then returned the plates to Moroni for their protection. It was a plan that was designed, prophesied and carried out by God.

Why is the Book of Mormon important to us?

The Book of Mormon itself has a response to this query. The Preface (verses 6 and 7), which was included on the gold plates and written by Moroni, gives us this insight:

> *…to show unto the remnant of the House of Israel how great things the Lord hath done for their fathers. And that they may know the covenants of the Lord, that they are not cast off forever. And also to the convincing of the Jew and Gentile that Jesus is the Christ, the eternal God, manifesting Himself unto all nations.*

The book also provides corroboration and authentication of the Bible as God's Holy Scripture.

Lehi, in his blessing to his son, Joseph, prophesied of the future importance of these scriptures when the Bible and The Book of Mormon would come together:

2 Nephi 2:19-23 RCE, 2 Nephi 3:12 LDS:

"Wherefore, the fruit of thy loins shall write, And the fruit of the loins of Judah shall write; And that which shall be written by the fruit of thy loins, And also that which shall be written by the fruit of the loins of Judah, Shall grow together

Unto the confounding of false doctrines, And laying down of contentions, And establishing peace among the fruit of thy loins, And bringing them to the knowledge of their fathers in the latter days,

And also to the knowledge of My covenants," saith the Lord;...

CHAPTER 7

WHAT CHRISTIAN DOCTRINES ARE FOUND IN THE BOOK OF MORMON?

In this chapter, we want to talk about the principles of the gospel and the blessings of the Lord and Savior that Christians should already know. They are faith, repentance, baptism, receiving the Holy Ghost, resurrection of the dead and eternal life. We will look at these topics through the lens of The Book of Mormon.

Faith

I Nephi 3:23-25 RCE, 1 Nephi 10:17 LDS:

And it came to pass that after I, Nephi--Having heard all the words of my father concerning the things which he saw in a vision; And also the things which he spake by the power of the Holy Ghost, which power he received by <u>faith on the Son of God</u>, And the Son of God was the Messiah which should come-- (Emphasis added)

I Nephi 3:117 RCE, 1 Nephi 12:10 LDS:

...Behold they are righteous forever, For because of their <u>faith in the Lamb of God, their garments are made white in His blood.</u> (Emphasis added)

2 Nephi 11:46 RCE, 2 Nephi 25:25 LDS:

...we are made alive in Christ because of our faith; (Emphasis added)

2 Nephi 13:28-29 RCE, 2 Nephi 31:19-20 LDS:

Behold, I say unto you, Nay; For ye have not come thus far save it were by the word of Christ, with <u>unshaken faith in Him, Relying wholly upon the merits of Him who is mighty to save.</u> Wherefore, ye must press forward with a steadfastness in Christ, Having a perfect brightness of hope and a love of God and of all men. (Emphasis added)

2 Nephi 15:8 RCE, 2 Nephi 33:7 LDS:

I have charity for my people, And great <u>faith in Christ</u> that I shall meet many souls spotless at His judgment seat. (Emphasis added)

Jacob 2:49 RCE, Jacob 3:1 LDS:

Look unto God with firmness of mind and pray unto Him with <u>exceeding faith</u>, And He will console you in your afflictions,... (Emphasis added)

Jacob 3:16-17 RCE, Jacob 4:11 LDS:

...beloved brethren, be reconciled unto Him, through the atonement of Christ, His only begotten Son, That ye may obtain a resurrection, according to the power of the resurrection which is in Christ, And be presented as the firstfruits of Christ unto God, <u>Having faith and obtained a good hope of glory in Him before He manifesteth Himself in the flesh.</u> (Emphasis added)

Enos 1:17-18 RCE, Enos 1:11-12 LDS:

And after that I, Enos, had heard these words, <u>my faith began to be unshaken</u> in the Lord, And I prayed unto Him with many long strugglings for my brethren the Lamanites. And it came to pass that after I had prayed and labored with all diligence, the Lord said unto me: '<u>I will grant unto thee according to thy desires, because of thy faith.</u>' (Emphasis added)

Enos 1:24-26 RCE, Enos 1:15-16 LDS:

For he had said unto me: "Whatsoever thing ye shall <u>ask in faith, believing that ye shall receive, in the name of Christ, ye shall receive it."</u> And I had faith, and I did cry unto God that he would preserve the records; And he covenanted with me that he would bring them forth unto the Lamanites in His own due time;... (Emphasis added)

Jarom 1:8-9 RCE, Jarom 1:4 LDS:

...there are many among us which have many revelations, for they are not all stiff-necked; <u>And as many as are not stiff-necked and have faith have communion with the Holy Spirit</u>, which maketh manifest unto the children of men <u>according to their faith.</u> (Emphasis added)

Mosiah 2:4-6 RCE, Mosiah 4:2-3 LDS:

*For we believe in Jesus Christ, the Son of God, who created heaven and earth, and all things, Who shall come down among the children of men. **And it came to pass that after they had spoken these words, the Spirit of the Lord came upon them, And they were filled with joy, <u>having received a remission of their sins and having peace of conscience because of the exceeding faith which they had in Jesus Christ</u>** which should come, according to the words which King Benjamin had spoken unto them.* (Emphasis added)

Mosiah 2:21 RCE, Mosiah 4:11 LDS:

And humble yourselves, even in the depths of humility, calling on the name of the Lord daily, And <u>standing steadfastly in the faith</u> of that which is to come which was spoken by the mouth of the angel. (Emphasis added)

Mosiah 3:9 RCE, Mosiah 5:7 LDS:

For behold, this day He hath spiritually begotten you, for ye say that <u>your hearts are changed through faith on His name</u>; Therefore, ye are born of Him and have become His sons and His daughters. (Emphasis added)

Alma 3:27-31 RCE, Alma 5:14-15 LDS:

*And now behold, I ask of you, my brethren of the church, Have ye spiritually been born of God? Have ye received His image in your own countenances? Have ye experienced this mighty change in your hearts? <u>**Do ye exercise faith in the redemption of Him who created you? Do you look forward with an eye of faith and view this mortal body raised in immortality? And this corruption raised in incorruption, to stand before God to be judged according to the deeds which hath been done in the mortal body?**</u>* (Emphasis added)

Alma 16:143 RCE, Alma 32:21 LDS:

And now as I said concerning faith, <u>Faith, is not to have a perfect knowledge of things; Therefore, if ye have faith, ye hope for things which are not seen, which are true.</u> (Emphasis added)

Ether 5:7 RCE, Ether 12:6-7 LDS:

Wherefore, dispute not because ye see not, <u>For ye receive no witness— not until after the trial of your faith.</u> For it was <u>by faith</u> that Christ showed Himself unto our fathers after that He had risen from the dead;... (Emphasis added)

Moroni 7:27-31 RCE, Moroni 7:27-30 LDS:

Wherefore, my beloved brethren, hath miracles ceased because that Christ hath ascended into heaven and hath sat down on the right hand of God to claim of the Father His rights of mercy which He hath upon the children of men?-

-For He hath answered the ends of the law, <u>And He claimeth all those that have faith in Him; And they that have faith in Him will cleave unto every good thing;</u> Wherefore, He advocateth the cause of the children of

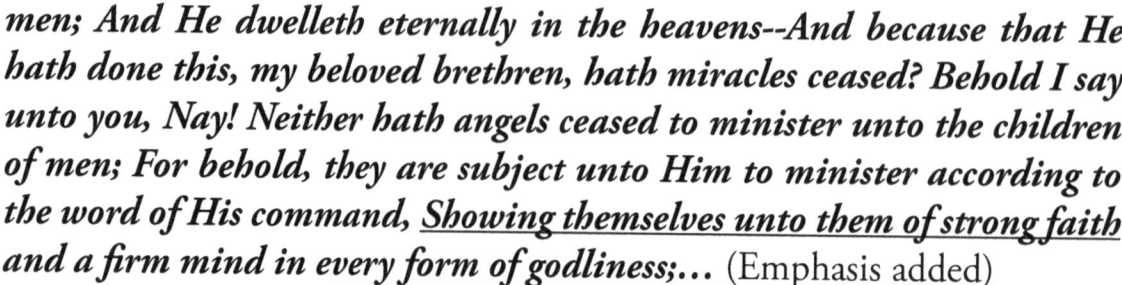

men; And He dwelleth eternally in the heavens--And because that He hath done this, my beloved brethren, hath miracles ceased? Behold I say unto you, Nay! Neither hath angels ceased to minister unto the children of men; For behold, they are subject unto Him to minister according to the word of His command, <u>Showing themselves unto them of strong faith and a firm mind in every form of godliness;</u>... (Emphasis added)

Repentance

2 Nephi 6:48-50 RCE, 2 Nephi 9:23-24 LDS:

And he commandeth all men that <u>they must repent</u> and be baptized in His name, having perfect faith in the Holy One of Israel, or they cannot be saved in the kingdom of God; And <u>if they will not repent</u> and believe in His name and be baptized in His name and endure to the end, <u>they must be damned,</u> For the Lord God, the Holy One of Israel, hath spoken it. (Emphasis added)

2 Nephi 12:77-78 RCE, 2 Nephi 30:2 LDS:

For behold I say unto you, As many of the Gentiles <u>as will repent are the covenant people of the Lord;</u> And as many of the Jews as <u>will not repent shall be cast off;</u> For the Lord covenanteth with none, Save it be <u>with them that repent</u> and believe in His Son, which is the Holy One of Israel. (Emphasis added)

2 Nephi 13:14 RCE, 2 Nephi 31:11 LDS:

And the Father saith: '<u>Repent ye! repent ye! And be baptized</u> in the name of My beloved Son.' (Emphasis added)

Mosiah 2:16 RCE, Mosiah 4:10 LDS:

And again, believe that ye must <u>repent of your sins and forsake them,</u> And humble yourselves before God and ask in sincerity of heart that He would forgive you. (Emphasis added)

Mosiah 7:32 RCE, Mosiah 11:21 LDS:

And <u>except they repent</u> and turn to the Lord their God, behold, <u>I will deliver them into the hands of their enemies,</u>... (Emphasis added)

Alma 3:55 RCE, Alma 5:31 LDS:

Wo unto such an one! For he is not prepared, And the time is at hand <u>that he must repent or he cannot be saved;</u>...(Emphasis added)

Alma 3:86-87 RCE, Alma 5:49-50 LDS:

Yea, to preach unto all--both old and young, both bond and free; Yea, I say unto you--the aged and also the middle aged, and the rising generation--Yea, to cry unto them that <u>they must repent</u> and be born again. Yea, thus saith the Spirit: <u>Repent</u> all ye ends of the earth, for the kingdom of heaven is soon at hand! Yea, the Son of God cometh in His glory, in His might, majesty, power and dominion;... (Emphasis added)

Alma 3:89 RCE, Alma 5:51 LDS:

And also the Spirit saith unto me, yea, crieth unto me with a mighty voice, saying: 'Go forth and say unto this people, <u>Repent!</u> For <u>except ye repent, ye can in no wise inherit the kingdom of heaven</u>.' (Emphasis added)

Alma 5:24 RCE, Alma 7:14 LDS:

Now I say unto you, that <u>ye must repent</u> and be <u>born again</u>: For the Spirit saith: "If ye <u>are not born again</u>, ye <u>cannot inherit the kingdom</u> of heaven." (Emphasis added)

Alma 10:12-13 RCE, Alma 13:18 LDS:

But Melchisedec, having exercised mighty faith and received the office of the high priesthood according to the holy order of God, did preach <u>repentance</u> unto his people. And behold, <u>they did repent</u>; And Melchisedec did establish peace in the land in his days. (Emphasis added)

Alma 10:18 RCE, Alma 13:21 LDS:

And now it came to pass that when Alma had said these words unto them, he stretched forth his hand unto them and cried with a mighty voice, saying: "Now is the time to repent! for the day of salvation draweth nigh." (Emphasis added)

Alma 12:180 RCE, Alma 19:36 LDS:

And we see that <u>His arm is extended to all people who will repent and believe on His name</u>. (Emphasis added)

Alma 13:37 RCE, Alma 22:6 LDS:

And also, what is this that Ammon said, "If <u>ye will repent</u>, ye shall <u>be saved</u>, And if ye will <u>not repent</u>, ye shall be <u>cast off</u> at the last day?" (Emphasis added)

Alma 19:84 RCE, Alma 42:4 LDS:

And thus we see that there was a time granted unto man to <u>repent</u>, Yea, a probationary time--<u>A time to repent and serve God</u>. (Emphasis added)

Helaman 2:49 RCE, Helaman 4:15 LDS:

And it came to pass that they did repent, And inasmuch as <u>they did repent, they did begin to prosper</u>;... (Emphasis added)

Helaman 4:70 RCE, Helaman 12:23 LDS:

Therefore, blessed are they who will <u>repent</u> and hearken unto the voice of the Lord their God, For <u>these are they that shall be saved</u>;... (Emphasis added)

3 Nephi 4:41-42 RCE, 3 Nephi 9:13-14 LDS:

O all ye that are spared because ye were more righteous than they! Will ye not now return unto Me and repent of your sins and be converted, that I may heal you? Yea, verily I say unto you, if ye will come unto Me, ye shall have eternal life;... (Emphasis added)

Alma 3:86 RCE, Alma 5:49 LDS:

Yea, to preach unto all--both old and young, both bond and free; Yea, I say unto you--the aged and also the middle aged, and the rising generation--Yea, to cry unto them <u>that they must repent and be born again</u>. (Emphasis added)

Can we agree that God wants everyone to accept Jesus as Savior.

Baptism

Nephi, in a vision, saw the baptism of Jesus Christ:

2 Nephi 13:10 RCE, 2 Nephi 31:8 LDS:

Wherefore, after that He <u>was baptized</u> with water, the Holy Ghost <u>descended upon</u> Him in the form of a dove. (Emphasis added)

He was given God's requirements for baptism:

2 Nephi 13:14-15 RCE, 2 Nephi 31:11-12 LDS:

And the father saith: 'Repent ye! Repent ye! And be <u>baptized in the name of My Beloved Son</u>!' And also the voice of the Son came unto me, saying: '<u>He that is baptized in My name, To him will the Father give the Holy Ghost</u>, like unto Me; Wherefore, follow Me and do the things which ye have seen Me do.' (Emphasis added)

These are the requirements of God:

1. Repent from your sins.
2. Be baptized by water as Christ was, by immersion.
3. Receive the baptism of the Spirit, as Christ promised.
4. Do it intentionally with singleness of heart.

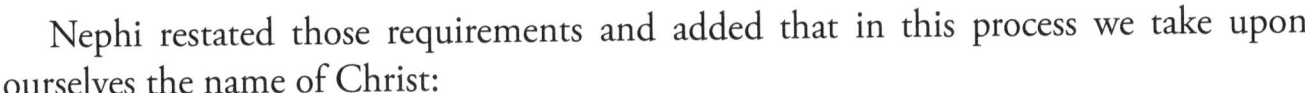

Nephi restated those requirements and added that in this process we take upon ourselves the name of Christ:

2 Nephi 13:16 RCE, 2 Nephi 31:13:

> *Wherefore my beloved brethren, I know that if ye shall follow the Son with full purpose of heart, Acting no hypocrisy and no deception before God, but with real intent, repenting of your sins, <u>Witnessing unto the Father that ye are willing to take upon you the name of Christ by baptism,</u> Yea, by following your Lord and <u>Savior down into the water</u> according to His word, Behold, then <u>shall ye receive the Holy Ghost;</u>...* (Emphasis added)

2 Nephi 13:23-24 RCE, 2 Nephi 31:17 LDS:

> *For, for this cause have they been shown unto me: That ye might know the gate by which ye should enter. <u>For the gate by which ye should enter is repentance and baptism by water,</u> And then cometh the remission of your sins by fire and by the Holy Ghost,...* (Emphasis added)

Mosiah, by way of explanation, tells us how Alma was given authority by God to baptize people after he repented of his sins:

Mosiah 9:41-45 RCE, Mosiah 18:10-14 LDS:

> *"...Now, I say unto you, if this be the desires of your hearts, What have you against being baptized in the name of the Lord as a witness before Him that <u>ye have entered into a covenant with Him</u> that ye will <u>serve Him</u> and <u>keep His commandments,</u> that He may pour out <u>His Spirit more abundantly upon you?</u>" And now when the people had heard these words, they clapped their hands for joy and exclaimed: "This is the desires of our hearts!" And now it came to pass that Alma took Helam, he being one of the first, and went and stood forth in the water and cried, saying: "O Lord, pour out Thy Spirit upon Thy servant, that he may do this work with holiness of heart!" And when he had said these words, <u>the Spirit of the Lord was upon him</u> and he said: "<u>Helam, I baptize thee, having authority from the Almighty God, as a testimony that ye have entered into a covenant to serve Him until you are dead, as to the mortal body;</u> And may the Spirit of the Lord be poured out upon you, And may He grant unto you eternal life <u>through the redemption of Christ</u> which He hath prepared from the foundation of the world." And after Alma had said these words, <u>both Alma and Helam were buried in the water;</u> And*

they arose and came forth out of the water rejoicing, being filled with the Spirit. (Emphasis added)

Mosiah also tells us that we:

Mosiah 9:54 RCE, Mosiah 18:21 LDS:

...should look forward with one eye, having one faith and one baptism,.... (Emphasis added)

Alma gives us insight that not only repentance, but also keeping His commandments, are part of the covenant created through baptism:

Alma 5:27 RCE, Alma 7:15 LDS:

Yea, come and go forth and show unto your God that ye are willing to repent of your sins and enter into a covenant with Him to keep His commandments, And witness it unto Him this day by going into the waters of baptism;... (Emphasis added)

Even Moroni tells us to approach baptism with a contrite spirit and a broken heart:

Moroni 6:1-4 RCE, Moroni 6:1-3 LDS:

And now I speak concerning baptism. BEHOLD, ELDERS, priests and teachers were baptized; And they were not baptized, save they brought forth fruit meet that they were worthy of it; Neither did they receive any unto baptism, save they came forth with a broken heart and a contrite spirit and witnessed unto the church that they truly repented of all their sins; And none were received unto baptism, save they took upon them the name of Christ, having a determination to serve Him unto the end. And after that they had been received unto baptism and were wrought upon and cleansed by the power of the Holy Ghost, they were numbered among the people of the church of Christ. (Emphasis added)

Moroni said that little children have no need for baptism and that Adam's curse was removed by Christ. Therefore, baptizing children is "solemn mockery before God:"

Moroni 8:5, 9-10 RCE, Moroni 8:5, 8-9 LDS:

For if I have learned the truth, there have been disputations among you concerning the baptizing of your little children."

'...Behold, I came into the world, not to call the righteous, but sinners to repentance; The whole need no physician, but they that are sick; Wherefore, little children are whole, for they are not capable of committing sin; Wherefore, the curse of Adam is taken from them in Me, that it hath no power over them; And the law of circumcision is done away in Me.'

And after this manner did the Holy Ghost manifest the word of God unto me; Wherefore, my beloved son, I know that it is <u>solemn mockery before God</u> that ye should baptize little children. (Emphasis added)

For more information about who needs baptism, read Moroni 8:11-29 RCE, Moroni 8:10-26 LDS.

Receiving The Holy Ghost

A person might say, "I read the scriptures but do not fully understand them. Can you explain further?" The Apostle Peter does this in Acts:

Acts 2:38-39:

Then Peter said unto them, Repent, and be baptized every one of you in the name of Jesus Christ for the remission of sins, and ye <u>shall receive the gift of the Holy Ghost</u>. For the promise is unto you, and to your children, and to all that are afar off, even as many as the Lord our God shall call. (Emphasis added)

Here is what Nephi said:

2 Nephi 13:23-25 RCE, 2 Nephi 31:17-18 LDS:

*For, for this cause have they been shown unto me: That ye might know the gate by which ye should enter. For the gate by which ye should enter is repentance and baptism by water,. **And then cometh the <u>remission of your sins by fire and by the Holy Ghost</u>,…And then are ye in this strait and narrow path which leads to eternal life; <u>Yea, ye have entered in by the gate</u>, Ye have done according to the commandments of the Father and the Son,…***
(Emphasis added)

If Nephi's steps are followed, disciples have a way to enter into God's kingdom by the gate, to receive the power of the Holy Ghost, and to be able to help others to do the same. Then they can heal the sick, cast out devils through the laying on of hands, speak in tongues, receive and give prophetic words through the interpretation of tongues. We will discuss these gifts later. However, they are for our benefit and to help us bring forth His kingdom:

2 Nephi 13:26 RCE, 2 Nephi 31:18 LDS:

And ye have received the <u>Holy Ghost which witnesses</u> of the Father and the Son <u>unto the fulfilling of the promise which He hath made</u>, that if ye entered in by the way [gate] ye should receive. (Emphasis added)

Mormon 4:87 RCE, Mormon 9:24 LDS:

And these signs shall follow them that believe—In My name shall they <u>cast out devils</u>; They shall speak with <u>new tongues</u>; They shall <u>take up serpents</u>; And if they drink <u>any deadly thing</u> it <u>shall not hurt</u> them; They shall <u>lay hands on the sick</u> and they <u>shall recover</u>. (Emphasis added)

1 Corinthians 12:8-11:

For to <u>one is given</u> by the Spirit the <u>word of wisdom</u>; to another the <u>word of knowledge</u> by the same Spirit; To another <u>faith</u> by the same Spirit; to another <u>the gifts of healing</u> by the same Spirit; To another the <u>working of miracles</u>; to another <u>prophecy</u>; to another <u>discerning of spirits</u>; to another divers kinds of <u>tongues</u>; to another the <u>interpretation of tongues</u>; But all these worketh that one and the selfsame Spirit, dividing to every man severally as he will. (Emphasis added)

Corinthians 12:28-31:

And God hath set some in the church, first apostles, secondarily prophets, thirdly teachers, after that miracles, then gifts of <u>healings, helps, governments, diversities of tongues</u>. Are all apostles? are all prophets? are all teachers? are all workers of miracles? Have all the gifts of healing? do all speak with tongues? do all interpret? But <u>covet earnestly</u> <u>the best gifts</u>: and yet shew I unto you a more excellent way. (Emphasis added)

Since there are many gifts of the Holy Spirit, and we do not all have the same endowments, how do we find out which ones God has given to each of us? We understand if we want to be a part of this end-time harvest, we need to know what gifts God has given us individually for Him to use. Until Christ comes, we need them. In order to find out what they are, as the Word says, we have to ask God, according to the counsel of James and Luke:

James 1:5:

If any of you lack wisdom, let him ask of God, that giveth to all men liberally, and upbraideth not; and it shall be given him.

Luke 11:9:

And I say unto you, Ask, and it shall be given you; seek and ye shall find; knock, and it shall be opened unto you.

Furthermore, Omni exhorts all of us to come unto God:

Omni 1:44 RCE, Omni 1:25 LDS:

And believe in <u>prophesying</u>, and in <u>revelations</u>, and in the <u>ministering of angels</u>, and in the gift of <u>speaking with tongues</u>, and in the gift of <u>interpreting languages</u>, and in all things which are good;... (Emphasis added)

Alma 7:31 RCE, Alma 9:21

And having the spirit of <u>prophecy</u> and the spirit of <u>revelation</u> and also many gifts—the gift of speaking with tongues and the gift of <u>preaching</u> and the gift of the <u>Holy Ghost</u> and the gift of translation,… (Emphasis added)

Moroni 8:8-10 RCE, Moroni 8:8-9 LDS:

And the <u>word of the Lord</u> came to me by the <u>power of the Holy Ghost</u>, saying: "Listen to the <u>words of Christ</u> your Redeemer, your Lord and your God…."…And after this manner did the <u>Holy Ghost</u> manifest the <u>word of God</u> unto me;… (Emphasis added)

Moroni 2:1-3 RCE, Moroni 2:1-3 LDS:

The words of Christ which He spake unto His disciples, the twelve whom He had chosen, as He laid His hands upon them. AND HE called them by name, saying: "Ye shall call on the Father in My name in mighty prayer; And after that ye have done this, ye shall have power that on him whom ye shall lay your hands, ye shall give the Holy Ghost; And in My name shall ye give it, For thus do Mine apostles." Now Christ spake these words unto them at the time of His first appearing; And the multitude heard it not; But the disciples heard it, and on as many as they laid their hands fell the Holy Ghost. (Emphasis added)

Moroni 7:42 RCE, Moroni 7:38 LDS:

Wherefore, <u>if these things have ceased, wo be unto the children of</u> men! For it is because of <u>unbelief,</u> And <u>all is in vain,</u> for no man can be saved, according to the words of Christ, save they shall have faith in His name;… (Emphasis added)

3 Nephi 13:59 RCE, 3 Nephi 29:6 LDS:

Yea, <u>wo unto him</u> that shall <u>deny the revelations</u> of the Lord! And that shall say: "The Lord no longer worketh by revelations, or by prophecy, or by gifts, or by tongues or by healings, or <u>by the power of the Holy Ghost</u>";… (Emphasis added)

If we deny the workings of the Holy Spirit, we are removing ourselves from His presence, denying the gospel of Christ, and replacing Him with a false god, not the God of the scriptures.

Mormon 4:66-68 RCE, Mormon 9:7-9 LDS:

And again, I speak unto you who deny the revelations of God and say that <u>they are done away,</u> That there are no revelations, nor prophecies, *nor gifts, nor healing, nor speaking with tongues, and the interpretation of tongues. Behold I say unto you, <u>he that denieth these things knoweth not the gospel of Christ</u>; Yea, they have not read the scriptures; If so, <u>they do not understand them</u>; For do we not read that God is the same yesterday, today and forever? And in Him there is no variableness, neither shadow of changing?* (Emphasis added)

Resurrection Of The Dead

The Book of Mormon tells us about Christ's sacrifice and resurrection and shares that He was the first to be resurrected:

2 Nephi 1:73-75 RCE, 2 Nephi 2:8 LDS:

Wherefore, how great the importance to make these things known unto the inhabitants of the earth, That they may know that there is no flesh that can dwell in the presence of God, save it be through the merits and mercy and grace of the Holy Messiah, Which layeth down His life, according to the flesh, and taketh it again, by the power of the spirit, <u>That He may bring to pass the resurrection of the dead</u>, being the <u>first that should rise</u>. (Emphasis added)

Nephi further clarifies this by telling us that the resurrection is needed to overcome the sin of Adam:

2 Nephi 6:10-12 RCE, 2 Nephi 9:5-6:

For it behooveth the great creator that He suffereth Himself to become subject unto man in the flesh and die for all men, that all men might become subject unto Him; For as death hath passed upon all men to fulfill the merciful plan of the great Creator, there must needs be a power of <u>resurrection</u>, And the <u>resurrection must needs come unto man by reason of the fall</u>,... (Emphasis added)

The resurrection of mankind will occur by the power of Jesus Christ:

2 Nephi 6:28-30 RCE, 2 Nephi 9:12 LDS:

Wherefore, death and <u>hell must deliver up its dead</u>; And hell must deliver up its captive spirits, And the <u>grave must deliver up its captive bodies</u>, And <u>the bodies and the spirits of men will be restored one to the other</u>, And it is by the <u>power of the resurrection of the Holy One of Israel</u>. (Emphasis added)

Jesus suffered for all of us so we could have a chance to be with Him in heaven. It is up to us to accept His sacrifice. Have you?

2 Nephi 6:46-47 RCE, 2 Nephi 9:21-22 LDS:

For behold, He suffereth the pains of all men, Yea, the pains of every living creature—both men and women and children—which belong to the family of Adam; And He suffereth this that the resurrection might pass upon all men, (and) that all might stand before Him at the great and judgement day. (Emphasis added)

In the following, Nephi explains that it is the power of Christ's resurrection that saves us from physical death and His atonement that saves us from spiritual death:

2 Nephi 7:43 RCE, 2 Nephi 10:24 LDS:

Wherefore, may God raise you from death by the power of the resurrection, And also from everlasting death by the power of the atonement,... (Emphasis added)

Nephi foretold of Christ's visit to his descendants after His resurrection:

2 Nephi 11: 58, 61 RCE, 2 Nephi 25: 26:1,3 LDS:

And after that Christ shall have risen from the dead, He shall show Himself unto you, my children and my beloved brethren,

And after that the Messiah shall come, there shall be signs given unto my people of His birth, and also of His death and resurrection;... (Emphasis added)

Jacob urged us to be reconciled to God through the atonement of Christ:

Jacob 3:16-18 RCE, Jacob 4:11-12 LDS:

Wherefore beloved brethren, be reconciled unto Him [God] through the atonement of Christ, His only Begotten Son, That ye may obtain a resurrection, according to the power of the resurrection which is in Christ, And be presented as the firstfruits of Christ unto God, Having faith and obtained a good hope of glory in Him before He manifesteth Himself in the flesh. And now beloved, marvel not that I tell you these things, For why not speak of the atonement of Christ and attain to a perfect knowledge of Him, as to attain to the knowledge of a resurrection and the world to come. (Emphasis added)

Jacob continued that if we reject the prophets and their words about Jesus Christ and the Holy Spirit, we will be ashamed of our actions on judgement day:

Jacob 4:12-14 RCE, Jacob 6:8-9 LDS:

Behold, will ye reject these words? Will ye reject the words of the prophets? And will ye reject all the words which have been spoken *concerning Christ, after that so many have spoken concerning Him? And deny the good word of Christ and the power of God and the Gift of the Holy Ghost? And quench the Holy Spirit and make mock of the great <u>plan of redemption</u> which hath been laid for you? Know ye not that if ye will do these things, that the <u>power of the redemption and the resurrection which is in Christ will bring you to stand with shame and awful guilt before the bar of God?</u>* (Emphasis added)

Mosiah 8:14 RCE, Mosiah 13:35 LDS:

Yea, and have they not said also that He should bring to pass the resurrection of the dead and that He, Himself, should be oppressed and afflicted?

Mosiah explained how Christ broke the bands of death and about the first resurrection at the time of His resurrection:

Mosiah 8:54-56, 58-59, 62 RCE, Mosiah 15:20-26 LDS:

But behold the bands of death shall be broken; And the Son reigneth and hath power over the dead; Therefore, He bringeth to pass the resurrection of the dead. And there cometh a resurrection, even a first resurrection; Yea, even a resurrection of those that have been, and which are, and which shall be, <u>Even until the resurrection of Christ</u>, for so <u>shall He be called</u>. And now, <u>the resurrection of all the prophets and all those that have believed</u> in their words, <u>or all those that have kept the commandments of God</u>, These shall come forth <u>in the first resurrection</u>;... And there are those who have part in the first resurrection; And these are they that <u>have died before Christ came, in their ignorance, not having salvation declared unto them</u>; And thus the Lord bringeth about <u>the restoration of these</u>; And <u>they have a part in the first resurrection, or hath eternal life, being redeemed by the Lord</u>....Yea, even all those that have perished in their sins ever since the world began, that have willfully rebelled against God, that have known the commandments of God and would not keep them; <u>These are they that have no part in the first resurrection</u>. (Emphasis added)

If Christ had failed, there could not have been a resurrection. Thank God He triumphed:

Mosiah 8:80, 81, 84 RCE, Mosiah 16:7-11 LDS:

And if Christ had not risen from the dead, or have broken the bands of death that the grave should have no victory and that death should have no sting, there could have been no resurrection. <u>But there is a resurrection;</u>

Therefore, the grave hath no victory, And the sting of death is swallowed up in Christ....If they be good, to the resurrection of endless life and happiness; And if they be evil, to the resurrection of endless damnation,... (Emphasis added)

Mosiah 9:29 RCE, Mosiah 18:2 LDS:

Yea, concerning that which was to come, And also concerning the resurrection of the dead and the redemption of the people, which was to be brought to pass through the power and sufferings and death of Christ, And His resurrection and ascension into heaven. (Emphasis added)

Mosiah continued to direct his people toward Christ:

Mosiah 9:40 RCE, Mosiah 18:9:

...That ye may be redeemed of God and be numbered with those of the first resurrection, that ye may have eternal life--.... (Emphasis added)

Eternal Life

Alma spoke to Helam before he baptized him:

Mosiah 9:44 RCE, Mosiah18:13 LDS:

...And may He grant unto you eternal life through the redemption of Christ which He hath prepared from the foundation of the world. (Emphasis added)

In this next verse, God told Alma that he would receive eternal life:

Mosiah 11:127 RCE, Mosiah 26:20 LDS:

Thou [Alma] art My servant and I covenant with thee that thou shalt have eternal life; And thou shalt serve Me and go forth in My name and shall gather together My sheep;... (Emphasis added)

King Mosiah inquired of the Lord about allowing his sons to go preach to the Lamanites; he was afraid that they would be killed:

Mosiah 12:11 RCE, Mosiah 28:7 LDS:

And the Lord said unto Mosiah: "Let them go up, for many shall believe on their words and they shall have eternal life; And I will deliver thy sons out of the hands of the Lamanites." (Emphasis added)

In view of the fact that the Lamanites were constantly attacking the Nephites and many were killed, Alma shared the following:

Alma 1:127-128 RCE. Alma 3:26 LDS:

And in one year were thousands and tens of thousands of souls sent to the eternal world, That they might reap their rewards according to their works—whether they were good or whether they were bad, to reap <u>eternal happiness or eternal misery according to the spirit which he listed to obey</u>—whether it be a good spirit or a bad one;... (Emphasis added)

Alma continued to speak to the Nephites, so they would be ready to meet God:

Alma 3:50-51 RCE, Alma 5:28 LDS:

"Behold, are ye stripped of <u>pride</u>? I say unto you, if ye are not, ye are not prepared to meet God.

"Behold, ye must prepare quickly, for the kingdom of heaven is soon at hand, and <u>such an one hath not eternal life</u>...." (Emphasis added)

Here Alma was trying to bring some of his people to salvation by asking them to repent, be baptized and obey God's laws. In preaching to the people of Gideon, he said if they would respond, they would receive eternal life:

Alma 5:27-28 RCE, Alma 7:15-16 LDS:

Yea, come and go forth and show unto your God that ye are willing to <u>repent of your sins</u> and enter into a <u>covenant with Him</u> to keep His commandments, And witness it unto Him this day by going into the <u>waters of baptism</u>; And whosoever doeth this and keepeth the commandments of God from thenceforth, The same will remember that I say unto him, yea, he will remember that I have said unto him, <u>he shall have eternal life</u> according to the testimony of the Holy Spirit which testifieth in me. (Emphasis added)

Again, Alma was giving direction to his people about how to fulfill the requirements for eternal life:

Alma 10:28-29 RCE, Alma 13:29 LDS:

But that ye would <u>humble yourselves</u> before the Lord <u>and call on His holy name</u> and watch and <u>pray continually</u>, That ye may not be tempted above that which ye can bear; And thus be <u>led by the Holy Spirit</u>, becoming <u>humble, meek, submissive, patient, full of love and all longsuffering</u>, having <u>faith on the Lord</u>, having a hope that ye shall receive <u>eternal life</u>, having the <u>love of God</u> always in your hearts, That ye may be lifted up at the last day and enter <u>into His rest</u>. (Emphasis added)

In this next verse, King Lamoni is asking Aaron how he could be saved:

Alma 13:48 RCE, Alma 22:15 LDS:

> *And it came to pass that after Aaron had expounded these things unto him, the king saith: "What shall I do that I may have this eternal life of which thou hast spoken?"* (Emphasis added)

And Aaron answered:

Alma 13:51 RCE, Alma 22:16 LDS:

> *… "If thou desirest this thing, if thou will bow down before God, Yea, if <u>thou repent</u> of all thy sins and will <u>bow down before God</u> and <u>call on His name in faith, believing</u> that ye shall receive, Then shalt thou receive the hope [of eternal life]which thou desirest."* (Emphasis added)

In another place, Helaman counseled his sons, advising them to do what was right by the Lord, so they could receive eternal life:

Helaman 2:70 RCE, Helaman 5:8 LDS:

> *…But that ye may do these things to lay up for yourselves a treasure in heaven, Yea, which is <u>eternal</u> and which fadeth not away; Yea, that ye may have that precious gift of <u>eternal life</u>, which ye have reason to suppose hath been given to our fathers.* (Emphasis added)

A later Nephi reminded those who had wanted to kill him of the time God sent flying serpents into the camps of Israel. All the people had to do to be healed was look up at Moses' serpent. Many, because of unbelief, refused to look and therefore died:

Helaman 3:47-48 RCE, Helaman 8:14-15 LDS:

> *"Yea, did He [Moses] not bear record that the Son of God should come? And as he lifted up the brazen serpent in the wilderness, even so should He be lifted up which should come; And as many as should look upon that serpent should live, Even so, as many as should <u>look upon the Son of God with faith</u>, having a <u>contrite spirit, might live</u>, even unto that <u>life which is eternal</u>…."* (Emphasis added)

In the following quote, Jesus Christ was speaking to the remnant of the people after the destruction which came at His death but before He descended from the heavens. At this time, they only heard His voice:

3 Nephi 4:42 RCE, 3 Nephi 9:14 LDS:

> *Yea, verily I say unto you, if ye will come unto Me, ye shall have eternal life;…* (Emphasis added)

He then addressed the people in person after He had descended from the heavens, as He had prophesied in both the Bible and The Book of Mormon:

3 Nephi 7:10 RCE, 3 Nephi 15:9 LDS:

Behold, I am the law and the light; Look unto Me and endure to the end and ye shall live, For unto him that endureth to the end will I give eternal life. (Emphasis added)

As Christians our belief in the core principles stated above are based on our acceptance of:

- The divinity of Jesus.
- The sufficiency of His atonement.
- His loving and undeserved grace towards us.
- His plan for our redemption and salvation.

Attributes Of Christ

His Divinity

What does the Book of Mormon say about this?

2 Nephi 11:36 RCE, 2 Nephi 25:19 LDS:

And according to the words of the prophets, and also the word of the angel of God, His name should be <u>Jesus Christ, the Son of God</u>. (Emphasis added)

2 Nephi 11:39 RCE, 2 Nephi 25:20LDS:

Yea, behold I say unto you that as these things are true, And as the Lord God liveth, There is <u>none other name</u> given under heaven, <u>save it be this Jesus Christ</u> of which I have spoken, whereby man can be saved. (Emphasis added)

2 Nephi 11:78 RCE, 2 Nephi 26:12-13 LDS:

And as I spake concerning the convincing of the Jews that <u>Jesus is the very Christ</u>, It must needs be that the Gentiles be convinced also that <u>Jesus is the Christ, the Eternal God</u>, And that He manifesteth Himself unto all they that believe in Him by the power of the Holy Ghost,... (Emphasis added)

2 Nephi 15:7 RCE, 2 Nephi 33:6 LDS:

I glory in plainness! I glory in truth! I glory in <u>my Jesus</u>, for he hath <u>redeemed my soul</u> from hell! (Emphasis added)

Jacob 3:7 RCE, Jacob 4:6 LDS:

Wherefore, we search the prophets, And we have many revelations, and the spirit of prophecy, And having all these witnesses, we obtain a hope, And our faith becometh unshaken, insomuch that we truly can <u>command</u>

in the name of Jesus, And the very trees obey us, or the mountains, or the waves of the sea;... (Emphasis added)

Mosiah 1:102-103 RCE, Mosiah 3:8-9 LDS:

'And He shall be called <u>Jesus Christ, the Son of God, the Father of heaven and earth, the Creator</u> of all things from the beginning; And His mother shall be called Mary; And lo, He cometh unto His own that salvation might come unto the children of men, even through faith on His name....'
(Emphasis added)

Mosiah 2:4 RCE, Mosiah 4:2 LDS:

We believe in <u>Jesus Christ, the Son of God,</u> who created heaven and earth and all things, Who shall come down among the children of men.
(Emphasis added)

Alma 3:83-84 RCE, Alma 5:48 LDS:

...I know that <u>Jesus Christ</u> shall come, Yea, <u>the Son of--the Only Begotten of--the Father,</u> full <u>of grace and mercy</u> and truth. And behold, it is He that cometh to take away the sins of the world; Yea, the sins of every man which steadfastly believeth on His name. (Emphasis added)

Alma 4:10 RCE, Alma 6:8 LDS:

And according to the spirit of prophecy which was in Him, according to the testimony of <u>Jesus Christ, the Son of God,</u> which should come for to redeem His people from their sins,... (Emphasis added)

Alma's people were confident of the Lord's power to save their souls:

Alma 21:74 RCE, Alma 46:39 LDS:

And it came to pass that there were many who died, firmly believing that their souls were redeemed by the <u>Lord Jesus Christ;</u> thus they went out of the world rejoicing. (Emphasis added)

Helaman 2:71 RCE, Helaman 5:9 LDS:

O remember, remember, my sons, the words which King Benjamin spake unto his people; Yea, remember that there is no other way nor means whereby man can be saved, Only through <u>the atoning blood of Jesus Christ,</u> which shall come; Yea, remember that he cometh to redeem the world. (Emphasis added)

3 Nephi 2:103 RCE, 3 Nephi 5:20 LDS:

I have reason to bless <u>my God and my Savior Jesus Christ</u>—That He brought our fathers out of the land of Jerusalem—and no one knew it, save it were Himself and those which He brought out of that land—

And that He hath given me and my people so much knowledge unto the salvation of our souls. (Emphasis added)

3 Nephi 2:109 RCE, 3 Nephi 5:26 LDS:

And then shall they know their Redeemer, which is <u>Jesus Christ, the Son of God</u>;... (Emphasis added)

3 Nephi 3:63 RCE, 3 Nephi 7:21 LDS:

But as many as were converted did truly signify unto the people that they had been visited by the power and <u>Spirit of God which was in Jesus Christ</u> in whom they believed. (Emphasis added)

3 Nephi 4:44-45 RCE, 3 Nephi 9:15 LDS:

Behold I am Jesus Christ, the son of God; I created the heavens and the earth and all things that in them is; I was with the Father from the beginning; I Am in the Father and the Father in Me, And in Me hath the Father glorified His name. (Emphasis added)

His Atonement

Jesus shed His blood for us on the cross of Calvary, and His atonement is sufficient for the worst of us. We must accept His sacrifice and believe that He died for our sins and was resurrected by His Father, thereby defeating death. The Book of Mormon attests to this.

Mosiah 1:118 RCE, Mosiah 3:18 LDS:

But men drinketh damnation to their own souls, except they humble themselves and become as little children, And believeth that <u>salvation was and is and is to come, in and through the atoning blood of Christ</u>, the Lord Omnipotent. (Emphasis added)

God's love is shown by His grace given toward us:

2 Nephi 7:42 RCE, 2 Nephi 10:24 LDS:

And remember, that after ye are <u>reconciled unto God</u>, That it is only in and through the <u>grace of God that ye are saved</u>;... (Emphasis added)

If we know Jesus, knowingly rebel against Him, and die in our rebellion, we will not receive salvation:

Mosiah 1:113 RCE, Mosiah 3:15 LDS:

And yet they hardened their hearts and understood not that <u>the law of Moses availeth nothing, except it were through the atonement of His blood</u>. (Emphasis added)

We are to accept Jesus and become His sons and daughters:

Mosiah 2:10-11 RCE, Mosiah 4:6-7 LDS:

And also <u>the atonement which hath been prepared from the foundation of the world, that thereby salvation might come to him that should put his trust in the Lord</u>, And should be diligent in keeping His commandments and continue in the faith, even unto the end of his life—I mean the life of the mortal body—I say that this is the man that receiveth salvation through the atonement which was prepared from the foundation of the world for all mankind, Which ever was, ever since the fall of Adam, or which is or which ever shall be, even unto the end of the world. (Emphasis added)

We must understand that even now there is only one way to stand in the presence of God, through the atonement of Jesus Christ:

Alma 16:208–209, 213 RCE, Alma 34:9, 13 LDS:

For it is expedient that an atonement should be made; For according to the great plans of the Eternal God, there must be an atonement made, or else <u>all mankind must unavoidably perish</u>—Yea, all are hardened, Yea, all are fallen and are lost and must perish, <u>except it be through the atonement</u> which it is expedient should be made. (Emphasis added)

But the law requireth the life of him who hath murdered; Therefore, <u>there is nothing which is short of an infinite atonement which will suffice for the sins of the world</u>, Therefore, it is expedient that there should be a great and last sacrifice. (Emphasis added)

Jacob 5:21 RCE, Jacob 7:13 LDS:

Wherefore, I know <u>if there should be no atonement made, all mankind must be lost</u>. (Emphasis added)

Mosiah 1:115-116 RCE, Mosiah 3:16-17 LDS:

For behold, as in Adam, or by nature, they fall, even so the <u>blood of Christ atoneth for their sins</u>. And moreover, I say unto you that there shall be no other name given, nor no other way nor means whereby salvation can come unto the children of men--Only in and through the name of Christ, the Lord Omnipotent. (Emphasis added)

Mosiah 1:118-120 RCE, Mosiah 3:18-19 LDS:

But men drinketh damnation to their own souls, except they humble themselves and become as little children, And believe that salvation was, and is, and is to come, in and through <u>the atoning blood of Christ</u>, the

Lord Omnipotent. For the natural man is an enemy to God and has been from the fall of Adam and will be for ever and ever, But if he yieldeth to the enticings of the Holy Spirit and putteth off the natural man--And becometh a saint through the <u>atonement of Christ</u> the Lord, and becometh as a child--submissive, meek, humble, patient, full of love, Willing to submit to all things which the Lord seeth fit to inflict upon him, even as a child doth submit to his father. (Emphasis added)

These prophets are speaking to us "out of the dust." We need to accept Jesus as our Savior, ask Him for forgiveness and live forgiven and redeemed lives.

His Grace

We live and move and have our being in the loving, unmerited grace of the Lord Jesus Christ toward us. The Book of Mormon tells us:

2 Nephi 1:71 RCE, 2 Nephi 2:6 LDS:

Wherefore, redemption cometh in and through the Holy Messiah, <u>For He is full of grace and truth;</u> (Emphasis added)

2 Nephi 1:73-75 RCE, 2 Nephi 2:8 LDS:

Wherefore, how great the importance to make these things known unto the inhabitants of the earth, that they may know that there is no flesh that can dwell in the presence of God, save it be through the merits, and mercy, and <u>grace of the Holy Messiah,</u> Which layeth down His life, according to the flesh, and taketh it again, by the power of the Spirit, That He may bring to pass the resurrection of the dead, being the first that should rise. (Emphasis added)

2 Nephi 6:19 RCE, 2 Nephi 9:8 LDS:

O the wisdom of God, <u>His mercy and grace!</u> (Emphasis added)

2 Nephi 8:11-12 RCE, 2 Nephi 11:5-6 LDS:

Yea, my soul delighteth in <u>His grace</u> and His justice and power and mercy, In the great and eternal <u>plan of deliverance</u> from death. And my soul delighteth in proving unto my people that save Christ should come, all men must perish;... (Emphasis added)

Alma 5:4 RCE, Alma 7:3 LDS:

And behold, I have come having great hopes and much desire that I should find that ye had humbled yourselves before God, and that ye had <u>continued in the supplicating of His grace,</u> that I should find that ye were blameless before him,... (Emphasis added)

Alma 7:40 RCE, Alma 9:26 LDS:

And not many days hence, the Son of God shall come in His glory; And His glory shall be the glory of the Only Begotten of the Father, <u>Full of grace</u>, equity and truth, Full of patience, mercy and long suffering, Quick to hear the cries of His people, and to answer their prayers. (Emphasis added)

Helaman 4:70-72 RCE, Helaman 12:23-25 LDS:

Therefore, blessed are they who will repent, and hearken unto the voice of the Lord their God, For these are they that shall be saved; **And may God grant in His great fullness that men might be brought unto repentance and good works,** <u>*That they might be restored unto grace for grace*</u> *according to their works. And I would that all men might be saved;...* (Emphasis added)

Ether 5:27-28 RCE, Ether 12:26-27 LDS:

...the Lord spake unto me, saying: "Fools mock, but they shall mourn; And <u>My grace is sufficient for the meek</u> that they shall take no advantage of your weakness; And if men come unto Me, I will show unto them their weakness; I give unto men weakness that they may be humble, And <u>My grace is sufficient for all men that humble themselves</u> before Me; For if they humble themselves before Me, and have faith in Me, then will I make weak things become strong unto them...." (Emphasis added)

Moroni 9:28 RCE, Moroni 9:26 LDS:

And may the <u>grace of God the Father</u>, whose throne is high in the heavens, and our Lord Jesus Christ, who sitteth on the right hand of His power until all things shall become subject unto him, <u>be and abide with you forever</u>. Amen. (Emphasis added)

Moroni 10:29-30 RCE, Moroni 10:32-33:

Yea, come unto Christ, and be perfected in Him and deny yourselves of all ungodliness, And if ye shall deny yourselves of all ungodliness and love God with all your might, mind and strength, Then is <u>His grace sufficient for you</u>, that <u>by his grace</u> ye may be perfect in Christ; And if <u>by the grace of God</u> ye are perfect in Christ, ye can in no wise deny the power of God. And again, if ye by the <u>grace of God</u> are perfect in Christ and deny not his power, Then are ye sanctified in Christ by the grace of God <u>through the shedding of the blood of Christ</u>, Which is in the covenant of the Father unto the remission of your sins, that ye become holy without spot. (Emphasis added)

His Plan For Our Redemption And Salvation

Alma 9:42 RCE, Alma 12:25 LDS:

Now if it had not been for the <u>plan of redemption which was laid from the foundation of the world</u>, there could have been no resurrection of the dead. (Emphasis added)

Alma 9:44-45 RCE, Alma 12:26 LDS:

And now behold, if it were possible that our first parents could have gone forth and partaken of the tree of life, they would have been forever miserable, having no preparatory state; And thus the <u>plan of redemption would have been frustrated.</u> And the word of God would have been void, taking none effect. (Emphasis added)

Alma 9:49 RCE, Alma 12:30

And they began from that time forth to call on His name. "Therefore, God conversed with men and made known unto them the <u>plan of redemption which had been prepared from the foundation of the world;...</u> "(Emphasis added)

Alma 9:52-53 RCE, Alma 12:32 LDS:

Therefore, God gave unto them commandments, after having made known unto them the <u>plan of redemption</u>, that they <u>should not do evil</u>, The penalty thereof being a second death which was an everlasting death as to things pertaining unto righteousness, For <u>on such the plan of redemption could have no power</u>, for the works of justice could not be destroyed according to the supreme goodness of God. (Emphasis added)

Alma 9: 54 RCE, Alma 12:33 LDS:

*But God did call on men in the name of His Son, this being the <u>plan of redemption</u> which was laid, saying: "If ye will repent and harden not your hearts, then will I have mercy upon you through Mine only Begotten Son;..." *(Emphasis added)

Alma 12:119 RCE, Alma 18:39 LDS:

But this is not all—For he [Ammon] expounded unto them the <u>plan of redemption</u>, which was prepared from the foundation of the world;... (Emphasis added)

Alma13:45 RCE, Alma 22:13 LDS:

And Aaron did expound unto him the scriptures from the creation of Adam, Laying the fall of man before him, and their carnal state, And also the <u>plan of redemption</u> which was prepared from the foundation of *the world through Christ for all whosoever would believe on His name;...* (Emphasis added)

Alma 15:53 RCE, Alma 29:2 LDS:

Yea, I would declare unto every soul, as with the voice of thunder, repentance and the <u>plan of redemption</u>, That they should repent and come unto our God, That <u>there might be no more sorrow</u> upon all the face of the earth. (Emphasis added)

Alma 16:217-218 RCE, Alma 34:16-18 LDS:

...Therefore, <u>only unto him that hath faith unto repentance is brought about the great and eternal plan of redemption</u>. Therefore, may God grant unto you, my brethren, that ye might begin to exercise your faith unto repentance, That ye begin to call upon His holy name that he would have mercy upon you; Yea, cry unto Him for mercy, for He is mighty to save;... (Emphasis added)

Alma 16:227-228 RCE, Alma 34:31-32 LDS:

Yea, I would that ye would come forth and harden not your hearts any longer; For behold, now is the time, and the day of your salvation; And therefore, if ye will repent and harden not your hearts, <u>Immediately</u> shall the great <u>plan of redemption</u> be brought about unto you; For behold, this life is the time for men to prepare to meet God;... (Emphasis added)

Alma 19:26 RCE, Alma 39:18 LDS:

Is it not as necessary that the plan of redemption should be made known unto this people, as well as unto their children? (Emphasis added)

As in all things spiritual, God's plan of redemption is received through faith.

Alma 16:217 RCE, Alma 34:16 LDS:

...Therefore, only unto him that hath faith unto repentance is brought about the great and eternal <u>plan of redemption</u>.... (Emphasis added)

Alma 19:92 RCE, Alma 42:11 LDS:

And now remember, my son, if it were not for the <u>plan of redemption</u>--laying it aside--As soon as they were dead, their souls were miserable, being cut off from the presence of the Lord. (Emphasis added)

Alma 14:38 RCE, Alma 24:14 LDS:

Yea, and He hath made these things known unto us beforehand because He loveth our souls, as well as He loveth our children; Therefore, in His mercy He doth visit us by His angels, that the <u>plan of salvation</u> might be

made known unto us, as well as unto future generations; O how merciful is our God! (Emphasis added)

Jarom 1:3-4 RCE, Jarom 1:2 LDS:

For what could I write more than my fathers have written? For have not they revealed the <u>plan of salvation</u>? (Emphasis added)

Alma 19:85-86 RCE, Alma 42:5 LDS:

For behold, if Adam had put forth his hand immediately, and partook of the tree of life, he would have lived forever, according to the word of God, having no space for repentance; Yea, and also the word of God would have been void, And the <u>great plan of salvation would have been frustrated</u>. (Emphasis added)

1 Nephi 4:20 RCE, 1 Nephi 15:15 LDS:

And then at that day will they not rejoice and give praise unto <u>their everlasting God, their rock and their salvation</u>? (Emphasis added)

Alma 10:95-100 RCE, Alma 15:6-11 LDS:

And it came to pass that Alma said unto him, taking him by the hand: "Believest thou in <u>the power of Christ unto salvation</u>?" And he answered and said: "Yea, I believe all the words that thou hast taught." And Alma saith: "<u>If thou believest in the redemption of Christ, thou canst be healed</u>." And he saith: "Yea, I believe according to thy words." And then Alma cried unto the Lord, saying: "O Lord our God, have mercy on this man and heal him according to his faith which is in Christ!" And it came to pass that when Alma had said these words, that Zeezrom leaped upon his feet, and began to walk. (Emphasis added)

Even if a person can only believe a little bit, Alma says:

Alma 16:203-204 RCE, Alma 34:4-6 LDS:

Yea, even that ye would have so much faith as even to plant the word in your hearts, that ye may try the experiment of its goodness. And we have beheld that the great question which is in your minds is whether the word be in the Son of God, or whether there shall be no Christ. And ye also beheld that my brother hath proven unto you in many instances that <u>the word is in Christ unto salvation</u>;... (Emphasis added)

1 Nephi 3:185-186 RCE, 1 Nephi 13:35-36 LDS:

*...Behold, these things [The Book of Mormon] shall be hid up to come forth unto the Gentiles by the gift and power of the Lamb; **And <u>in them shall be</u>***

written My gospel, *saith the Lamb, and My rock and My salvation.*
(Emphasis added)

1 Nephi 5:256 RCE, 1 Nephi 19:17 LDS:

"Yea, and all the earth shall <u>see the salvation of the Lord</u>," saith the prophet. (Emphasis added)

2 Nephi 1:63 RCE, 2 Nephi 2:3 LDS:

Wherefore, I know that thou art redeemed because of the righteousness of thy Redeemer, For thou hast beheld that in the fullness of time He cometh to bring salvation unto men,… (Emphasis added)

2 Nephi 1:65-66 RCE, 2 Nephi 2:4 LDS:

For the Spirit is the same yesterday, to-day and for-ever; And <u>the way is prepared</u> from the fall of man, <u>and salvation is free</u>;… (Emphasis added)

2 Nephi 3:50 RCE, 2 Nephi 4:30 LDS

Rejoice, O my heart! and cry unto the Lord and say, O Lord, I will praise Thee forever! Yea, my soul will rejoice in Thee, My God, and the <u>Rock of my salvation</u>. (Emphasis added)

2 Nephi 9:133-134 RCE, 2 Nephi 22:2-3 LDS:

Behold, <u>God is my salvation</u>, I will trust and not be afraid; For the Lord Jehovah is my strength and my song; <u>He also is become my salvation</u>. Therefore, with joy shall ye draw water out of the wells of salvation;…
(Emphasis added)

Omni 1:45-47 RCE, Omni 1:25-26 LDS:

For there is nothing which is good, save it comes from the Lord; And that which is evil cometh from the devil. And now my beloved brethren, <u>I would that ye should come unto Christ</u>, which is the Holy One of Israel, <u>and partake of His salvation</u> and the power of his redemption; Yea, come unto Him, and offer your whole souls as an offering unto Him, and continue in fasting and praying, and endure to the end; And as the Lord liveth, ye will be saved. (Emphasis added)

Mosiah 2:8-10,12 RCE, Mosiah 4:5-6,8 LDS:

For behold, that if the knowledge of the goodness of God at this time hath awakened you to a sense of your nothingness and your worthlessness and fallen state, I say unto you, that if ye have come to a knowledge of the goodness of God and His matchless power and His wisdom and His patience and His longsuffering toward the children of men, And also the atonement which hath been prepared from the foundation of the world, *that thereby <u>salvation might come to him that should put his trust in the Lord</u>,... And <u>there is none other salvation</u> save this which hath been spoken of; Neither are there any conditions whereby man can be saved, except the conditions which I have told you:...* (Emphasis added)

Mosiah 3:11 RCE, Mosiah 5:8 LDS:

There is <u>no other name given whereby salvation cometh</u>; Therefore, I would that ye should take upon you the name of Christ--all you that have entered into the covenant with God—that ye should be obedient unto the end of your lives. (Emphasis added)

2 Nephi 11:39 RCE, 2 Nephi 25:20 LDS:

Yea, behold I say unto you, that as these things are true, And as the Lord God liveth, There is none other name given under heaven, save it be this Jesus Christ of which I have spoken, whereby man can be saved. (Emphasis added)

2 Nephi 15:15 RCE, 2 Nephi 33:12 LDS:

And I pray the Father in the name of Christ that many of us, if not all, <u>may be saved in his kingdom at that great and last day</u>. (Emphasis added)

In conclusion, may we say that the gospel is simple, but our pride and intellectual arrogance often get in the way. Did you notice how The Book of Mormon people rejoiced in their gift of salvation? If we will accept, that joy is there for us too. Sometimes we suppose we don't need any help, but look at what The Book of Mormon advises:

2 Nephi 6:58-61 RCE, 2 Nephi 9:28-29 LDS:

O the vainness and the frailties and the foolishness of men! When they are learned, they think they are wise and they harken not unto the counsel of God, For they set it aside, supposing they know of themselves; Wherefore, their wisdom is foolishness and it profiteth them not; Wherefore, they shall perish; But to be learned is good, if it so be that they hearken unto the counsels of God.

CHAPTER 8

WHAT DO THE BIBLE AND BOOK OF MORMON TEACH ABOUT THE GIFTS OF THE SPIRIT?

If we look at the conditions in the world today, it certainly seems that we are living in what Christians call "the end times." I think that the coming of Christ is near and that we need to prepare quickly for Him. Therefore, we must take advantage of the gifts and power available through the Holy Spirit. Moroni gives us the complete list:

Moroni 10:10-12 RCE. Moroni 10:9-17:

> *For behold, to one is given by the Spirit of God, that he may teach the <u>word of wisdom</u>; And to another that he may teach the word of <u>knowledge</u> by the same Spirit; And to another, exceeding great <u>faith</u>; And to another, the gifts of <u>healing</u> by the same Spirit; And again, to another. that he may work mighty <u>miracles</u>; And again, to another, that he may <u>prophesy</u> concerning all things; And again, to another, the <u>beholding of angels</u> and ministering spirits; And again, to another, all kinds of <u>tongues</u>; And again, to another, the <u>interpretation</u> of languages and of divers kinds of tongues. And all these gifts come by the Spirit of Christ; And they come unto every man severally, according as He will.* (Emphasis added)

We need to take these gifts seriously, and we can have them whenever we choose to ask for them, for we are either the remnant of the Twelve Tribes of Israel or can be the adopted children of Christ.

In a book of limited size, we cannot explore all of the gifts in depth, so let's explore "speaking in tongues," since many people have an interest in that subject. We will find that both the Bible and The Book of Mormon are consistent in their testimony, concerning this.

Speaking In Tongues

The first experience mentioned in the New Testament gives us a good illustration of what happened to the twelve apostles after Jesus ascended into heaven:

Acts 2:1-8:

And when the day of Pentecost was fully come, they were all with one accord in one place. And suddenly there came a sound from heaven as of a rushing mighty wind, and it filled all the house where they were sitting. And there appeared unto them cloven tongues like as of fire, and it sat upon each of them. And they were all filled with the Holy Ghost, and began to speak with <u>other tongues</u>, as the Spirit gave them utterance. And there were dwelling at Jerusalem Jews, devout men, out of every nation under heaven. Now when this was noised abroad, the multitude came together, and were confounded, because that every man <u>heard them speak in his own language</u>. And they were all amazed and marveled, saying one to another, Behold, are not all these which speak Galilaeans? And how hear we every man in our own tongue, wherein we were born.
(Emphasis added)

The Holy Ghost came down upon the apostles with such great power that their preaching, which was spoken in their own native tongue, was heard in multiple languages by the people listening from various countries, so all the people understood the preaching. In this example, the languages were interpreted by the Spirit. This type of experience is promised to each of us.

Speaking in tongues is one of the gifts of the Holy Spirit. It is referenced in the following two quotes:

Mark 16:17-18

And these signs shall follow them that believe; In my name they shall cast out devils; <u>They shall speak with new tongues</u>....(Emphasis added)

The word "new" means a language the speakers have never learned, or in other words, it is "new" to them. Does speaking in tongues always mean using an existing language? Some people believe that, but it is said differently in the following scripture:

Romans 8:26:

Likewise the Spirit also helpeth our infirmities: for we know not what we should pray for as we ought: <u>but the Spirit itself maketh intercession for us with groanings which cannot be uttered</u>. (Emphasis added)

I believe when a person experiences these "groanings," these are words of request, intercession, praise and adoration that are prayed through us by the Holy Ghost and cannot be understood by anyone except God Himself. These are called "the tongue of angels" in The Book of Mormon and follow what is called "the baptism of fire." The Book of Mormon richly adds to our perception of this concept.

2 Nephi 13:17-18 RCE, 2 Nephi 31:13-14 LDS:

Yea, then cometh the baptism of fire and of the Holy Ghost, And then can ye speak with the tongue of angels and shout praises unto the Holy One of Israel. But behold, my beloved brethren, thus came the voice of the Son unto me, saying: 'After that ye have repented of your sins, And witnessed unto the Father that ye are willing to keep My commandments by the baptism of water, And have received the baptism of fire and of the Holy Ghost, And can speak with a new tongue, yea, even with the tongue of angels—And after this should deny Me, It would have been better for you that ye had not known Me.' (Emphasis added)

2 Nephi 13:27-28 RCE, 2 Nephi 31:19 LDS:

And now my beloved brethren, after that ye have got into this strait and narrow path, I would ask if all is done? Behold, I say unto you, Nay; For ye have not come thus far save it were by the <u>word of Christ</u>, with unshaken faith in Him, Relying wholly upon the merits of Him who is mighty to save. (Emphasis added)

In thinking about the following quotes, consider what is the meaning of the "***word of Christ***"? And what does it mean to speak with the "***tongue of angels***"? Are they the same? Nephi gives us the answers:

2 Nephi 14:2-4 RCE, 2 Nephi 32:2-3 LDS:

But behold, why do ye ponder these things in your hearts? Do ye not remember that I said unto you that after that ye have received the <u>Holy Ghost</u>, ye could speak with the <u>tongue of angels</u>? And now, how could ye speak with the <u>tongue of angels</u> save it were by the <u>Holy Ghost</u>? Angels speak by the power of the <u>Holy Ghost</u>, wherefore, they speak the <u>words of Christ</u>. Wherefore, I said unto you: Feast upon the words of Christ, For behold, the <u>words of Christ will tell you all things what ye should do</u>. (Emphasis added)

2 Nephi 13:30 RCE, 2 Nephi 31:20 LDS:

Wherefore, if ye shall press forward, feasting upon the word of Christ and endure to the end, 'Behold,' thus saith the Father, 'ye shall have eternal life.' (Emphasis added)

Jacob 4:12-13 RCE, Jacob 6:8 LDS:

Behold, will ye reject these words? Will ye reject the words of the prophets? And will ye reject all the words which have been spoken *concerning Christ, after that so many have spoken concerning Him? And deny the good <u>word of Christ</u> and <u>the power of God</u> and the gift of the <u>Holy Ghost</u>? And quench the <u>Holy Spirit</u> and make mock of the great plan of redemption which hath been laid for you?* (Emphasis added)

<u>Alma 17:79-80 RCE, Alma 34:44-45 LDS</u>

For behold, it is as easy to give heed to the <u>word of Christ</u>, which will point to you a strait course to eternal bliss, As it was for our fathers to give heed to this compass, which would point unto them a strait course to the Promised Land. And now I say, is there not a type in this thing? For just assuredly as this director did bring our fathers, by following its course, to the Promised Land, Shall the <u>word of Christ</u>, if we follow its course, carry us beyond this vale of sorrow into a far better Land of Promise. (Emphasis added)

<u>3 Nephi 13:45-47 RCE, 3 Nephi 28:33-35</u>

And if ye had all the scriptures which give an account of all the marvelous works of Christ, Ye would, according to the <u>words of Christ</u>, know that these things must surely come to pass; And wo be unto him that will not hearken unto the <u>words of Jesus</u>, and also to them which He hath chosen and sent among them! For whoso receiveth not the <u>words of Jesus</u>, and the <u>words of them which He hath sent</u>, receiveth not Him; And therefore, He will not receive them at the last day; And it would be better for them if they had not been born;... (Emphasis added)

<u>Nephi 13:60 RCE, 3Nephi 29:7 LDS:</u>

Yea, and wo unto him that shall say at that day that there can be no miracle wrought by Jesus Christ, for to get gain! For he that doeth this shall become like unto the son of perdition for whom there was no mercy, according to the <u>words of Christ</u>. (Emphasis added)

<u>2 Nephi 13:26 RCE, 2 Nephi 31:18LDS:</u>

And ye have received the Holy Ghost which witnesses of the Father and the Son unto the fulfilling of the promise which He hath made, that if ye entered in by the way ye should receive.

We are counseled by the scriptures to feast upon the words of Christ. I believe there are two ways of doing that: one is to speak under the influence of the Holy Spirit so that you are speaking by inspiration, with the *tongue of angels which*, according to The Book of Mormon, *are the words of Christ*. The second way is to study the scriptures with full intent of heart, asking Him for the understanding of His words and a witness as to their validity.

If you do, with a contrite heart, ready to hear His answer, then He will give you that witness through His Holy Spirit, and you will receive insight about how to live your life.

Personal Reflections

The words of Christ are the words of eternal life. But, what if a person says, "I have tried, but I am not receiving the confirmation I need." The scripture below tells us that those who fail to understand will perish in the dark:

2 Nephi 14:5 RCE, 2 Nephi 33:4 LDS:

> *Wherefore, now after that I have spoken these words, <u>If ye cannot understand</u> them, it will be <u>because ye ask not, neither do ye knock;</u> Wherefore, ye are not brought into the light, but must perish in the dark.* (Emphasis added)

We need to be sure that we are not trying to tell God what the answer to our prayers should be. If we are, He cannot answer because we have already decided and are not willing to allow Him to guide us. Remember, satan wants us to fail. He wants us to stop praying, to give up, so he can claim our souls and torment us forever:

2 Nephi 14:11 RCE, 2 Nephi 32:8 LDS:

> *For if ye would harken unto the Spirit which teacheth a man to pray, ye would know that ye must pray, For the <u>evil spirit teacheth not a man to pray</u>, but teacheth him that he must not pray.* (Emphasis added)

Therefore, we must always pray, especially before doing anything for the Lord, and if we do His work, giving Him the credit, and not ourselves, then He will consecrate our work for the welfare of our souls and the souls of others.

2 Nephi 14:12 RCE, 2 Nephi 32:9 LDS:

> *But behold, I say unto you that ye must pray always and not faint, That ye must not perform anything unto the Lord save in the first place ye shall pray unto the Father in the name of Christ, That He will consecrate thy performance unto thee, that thy performance may be for the welfare of thy soul.* (Emphasis added)

We may pray through our native language or our prayer language. When studying His scriptures, we pray for Christ to give us clarity of thought so we can understand His words. If we do these things, The Holy Spirit will confirm their truthfulness.

May I ask, are you a born-again child of God? You are certainly not compelled to be. You have the right to choose. Unfortunately, the one thing the Lord cannot deliver you from is your own pride. He gives you your agency. We often think that we do not need

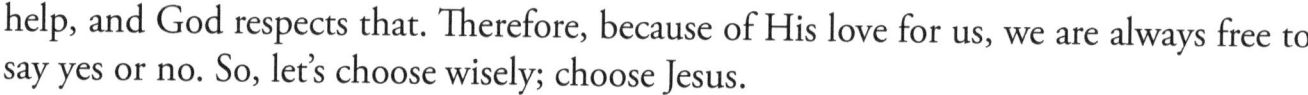

help, and God respects that. Therefore, because of His love for us, we are always free to say yes or no. So, let's choose wisely; choose Jesus.

2 Nephi 15:11-13 RCE, 2 Nephi 33:10-11 LDS:

And now my beloved brethren, and also Jew and all ye ends of the earth, Hearken unto these words and believe in Christ; <u>And if ye believe not in these words, believe in Christ; And if ye shall believe in Christ, ye will believe in these words, for they are the words of Christ and He hath given them unto me;</u> And they teach all men that they should do good.

And if they are not the words of Christ, judge ye, <u>For Christ will show unto you with power and great glory that they are His words at the last day;</u>... (Emphasis added)

Even if you refuse to believe the words of Christ in this life, He will remind you of them in the next life. He will ask, "Why did you refuse to accept the words of My Holy Scriptures, and why did you not listen to My holy prophets?" It is better not to wait. We must acknowledge our imperfections, humble ourselves and repent. We must accept Christ as our Savior and be baptized with the teachableness of a child. If you are willing to receive and have asked Jesus into your heart, He will provide you with the affirmation you are seeking. If you have a problem with these words, look at what The Book of Mormon says:

2 Nephi 15:6 RCE, 2 Nephi LDS:

And it [The Holy Spirit] speaketh harsh against sin, according to the plainness of the truth; Wherefore, no man will be angry at the words which I have written, save he shall be of the spirit of the devil. (Emphasis added)

Although we are not compelled to believe, look at the promises for those who do and those who don't (See also Revelations 6:1-17.):

2 Nephi 5:34-39 RCE, 2 Nephi 6:13-15 LDS:

"...And the people of the Lord shall not be ashamed, For the people of the Lord are they which wait for Him, For they still wait for the coming of the Messiah." And behold, according to the words of the prophet, the Messiah will set Himself again the second time to recover them; Wherefore, He will manifest Himself unto them in power and great glory, unto the destruction of their enemies, when that day cometh when they shall believe in Him; And none will He destroy that believeth in Him. And they that believe not in Him shall be destroyed--both by fire and by

tempest, and by earthquakes and by bloodsheds, and by pestilence and by famine. (Emphasis added)

As I've said, all the gifts of the spirit are meant to edify and equip us for service to our Lord Jesus Christ. Moroni tells us:

Moroni 10:14 RCE, Moroni 10:19 LDS:

And I would exhort you, my beloved brethren, that ye remember that He is the same yesterday, today and forever, And that all these gifts of which I have spoken, which are spiritual, never will be done away, even as long as the world shall stand, only according to the unbelief of the children of men.

Therefore, we are not to take the gifts of the Spirit lightly. God has a severe warning for those who would seek to put an end to them:

Moroni 10:21-25 RCE, Moroni 10:26-28 LDS:

And wo unto them which shall do these things away and die! For they die in their sins, And they cannot be saved in the kingdom of God; And I speak it according to the <u>words of Christ</u>; And I lie not. And I exhort you to remember these things! For the time speedily cometh that ye shall know that I lie not, For ye shall see me at the bar of God, And the Lord God will say unto you: "Did I not declare My words unto you which were written by this man, like as one crying from the dead? Yea, even as one speaking from the dust? I declare these things unto the fulfilling of the prophecies; And behold, they shall proceed forth out of the mouth of the Everlasting God; And His word shall hiss forth from generation to generation; (Emphasis added)

Finally, Jesus, Himself, gives us these sobering words:

Mark 8:38:

Whosoever therefore shall be ashamed of me and of my words in this adulterous and sinful generation; of him also shall the Son of man be ashamed, when He cometh in the glory of His Father with the holy angels.

As Christians we know that we are to *"Ask and it shall be given you, seek and ye shall find; knock and it shall be opened unto you"* (Luke 11:9). Christ will provide you with the witness you desire if you will ask, seek and knock. However, it is important to remember that, if after receiving these things, we deny Christ, if we put him to an open shame, it would have been better that we never knew Him.

CHAPTER 9

WHAT ARE TWO MAIN OBJECTIONS TO THE BOOK OF MORMON?

Joseph Smith Being A Prophet

Joseph Smith started the Restoration Movement because God told him that many "plain and precious" things had been removed from the full, original gospel of Christ. The consequence of his response was that he was much maligned in his lifetime and eventually assassinated in 1844. One might ask how this could have happened in a free country that believes in freedom of religion. The answer is worth investigating. However, for the moment, let's just say that he was a very misunderstood individual. Some people claim that he could not have been a prophet of God because of all the unrest he created. But think about it. Many prophets were surrounded with hate and discontent, so much so that many were killed by the people they prophesied to. This is also true about Jesus Christ Himself. Joseph Smith, like many other righteous men mentioned in the Bible, was killed because of his beliefs; and even today, more than a century and a half after his death, the mention of his name may cause an otherwise calm and collected minister to become angry. Why? The Apostle John explains:

John 4:44:

> *For Jesus Himself testified, that a prophet hath no honour in his own country.*

In light of the above scripture, it is understandable why Joseph Smith might not receive the honor or the respect he deserves, and you certainly have the right to say that he was not chosen of God. However, I ask you to reserve judgment, consider the evidence, and then ask God, through His Holy Spirit, what the truth is. Don't just rely on human wisdom: after all, just look at what He did with a donkey!

Numbers 22:28-31:

> *And the LORD opened the mouth of the ass, and she said unto Balaam, What have I done unto thee, that thou hast smitten me these three times? And Balaam said unto the ass, Because thou hast mocked me: I would*

there were a sword in mine hand, for now would I kill thee. And the ass said unto Balaam, Am not I thine ass, upon which thou hast ridden ever since I was thine unto this day? Was I ever wont to do so unto thee? And he said Nay. Then the LORD opened the eyes of Balaam, and he saw the angel of the LORD standing in the way, and his sword drawn in his hand: and he bowed down his head, and fell flat on his face.

Is it not obvious that God can use anyone, or anything, to accomplish His purposes, even an uneducated and unlikely person like Joseph Smith or an educated but unlikely person like Joseph DeBarthe, or even you? Like Joseph Smith, we would simply have to have:

1. accepted Charist as our Savior,
2. demonstrated our willingness to accept Him by being baptized, as Christ,
3. prayed, asking the Lord through His Holy Spirit to direct our paths, and
4. asked God a direct question, and been willing to accept any answer He gave.

If we have done that, then God is free to use us in whatever way He chooses. While we may not have the calling of a prophet, I am only saying that God used Joseph Smith because of his willingness to ask in faith and to believe what the Holy Spirit told him. We have the same promise that he found in James:

James 1:5:

If any of you lack wisdom, let him ask of God, that giveth to all men liberally, and upbraideth not; and it shall be given him.

Let's see what Joseph Smith said about his experience with Jesus and God and the circumstances that led up to it. The following is quoted from *History of the Reorganized Church of Jesus Christ of Latter Day Saints*:

I was at this time in my fifteenth year. My father's family was proselyted to the Presbyterian faith, and four of them joined that church; namely, my mother Lucy, brothers Hyrum, Samuel Harrison, and my sister Sophronia.

During this time of great excitement my mind was called up to serious reflection and great uneasiness; but though my feelings were deep and often pungent, still I kept myself aloof from all those parties, though I attended their several meetings as often as occasion would permit; but in process of time my mind became somewhat partial to the Methodist sect, and I felt some desire to be united with them, but so great was the confusion and strife among the different denominations that it was impossible for a person young as I was and so unacquainted with men and things to come to any certain conclusion who was right, and who was wrong. My mind at different times was greatly excited, the cry and tumult was so great and incessant. The Presbyterians were most decided against the Baptists and Methodists, and used all their powers of either reason or sophistry to prove their errors, or at least to make the people to think they were in error; on the other hand the Baptists and the Methodists in their turn were equally zealous to establish their own tenets, and disprove all others. In the midst of this war of words and tumult of opinions, I often said to myself, What is to be done? Who of all these parties are right? Or, are they all wrong together? If any one of them be right, which is it, and how shall I know it?

While I was laboring under the extreme difficulties caused by the contest of these parties of religionists, I was one day reading the epistle of James, first chapter and fifth verse, which reads: 'If any of you lack wisdom, let him ask of God, that giveth to all men liberally, and upbraideth not; and it shall be given unto him.' Never did any passage of scripture come with more power to the heart of man than this did at this time to mine. It seemed to enter with great force into every feeling of my heart. I reflected on it again and again, knowing that if any person needed wisdom from God I did, for how to act I did not know, and unless I could get more wisdom than I then had I would never know; for the teachers of religion of the different sects understood the same passage so differently as to destroy all confidence in settling the question by an appeal to the Bible. At length I came to the conclusion that I must either remain in darkness and confusion, or else I must do as James directs; that is, ask of God. I at length came to the determination to 'ask of God,' concluding that if He gave wisdom to them that lacked wisdom and would give liberally, and not upbraid, I might venture. So in accordance with this my determination, to ask of God, I retired to the woods to make the attempt. It was on the morning of a beautiful clear day, early in the spring of eighteen hundred and twenty. It was the first time in my life that I made such an attempt, for amidst all my anxieties I had never as yet made the attempt to pray vocally.

After I had retired into the place I had previously designed to go, having looked around me and finding myself alone, I kneeled down and began to offer up the desires of my heart to God. I had scarcely done so when immediately I was seized upon by some power which entirely overcame me, and had such astonishing influence over me as to bind my tongue so that I could not speak. Thick darkness gathered around me, and it seemed to me for a time as if I were doomed to sudden destruction. But exerting all my powers to call upon God to deliver me out of the power of this enemy which had seized upon me, and at the very moment when I was ready to sink into despair and abandon myself to destruction, (not an imaginary ruin but to the power of some actual being from the unseen world who had such a marvelous power as I had never before felt in my being,) just at this moment of great alarm, I saw a pillar of light exactly over my head, above the brightness of the sun; which descended gradually until it fell upon me. It no sooner appeared than I found myself delivered from the enemy which held me bound. When the light rested upon me I saw two personages (whose brightness and glory defy all description) standing above me in the air. One of them spake unto me, calling me by name, and said (pointing to the other), 'This is my beloved Son, hear him.'

My object in going to inquire of the Lord was to know which of all the sects was right, that I might know which to join. No sooner therefore did I get possession of myself, so as to be able to speak, than I asked the personages who stood above me in the light, which of all the sects was right, (for at this time it had never entered into my heart that all were wrong) and which I should join. I was answered that I must join none of them, for they were all wrong, and the personage who addressed me said that all their creeds were an abomination in His sight; that those professors were all corrupt; "they draw near to me with their lips, but their hearts are far from me; they teach for doctrine the commandments of men, having a form of godliness, but they deny the power thereof." He again forbade me to join with any of them: and many other things did He say unto me which I cannot write at this time. When I came to myself again I found myself lying on my back, looking up into heaven. (7-10)

Remember, Joseph was only fifteen at this time, and it was a life-changing event for him; I know it would be for me if God were to provide me with that kind of experience. Even at sixty-one, it would have an impact upon me for the rest of my life. No amount of anger, ridicule, or persecution would ever cause me to change my testimony. If you're honest with yourself, neither would you and neither did Joseph Smith. He suffered greatly for his beliefs, even unto death. No other prophet brought forth as much scripture that teaches the everlasting gospel, speaks of the ministry Christ, verifies the Bible's authenticity and is foretold by biblical prophecy. You and I know that the great leaders of the Old Testament (Abraham, Isaac, Jacob, Moses, David and Solomon) were imperfect

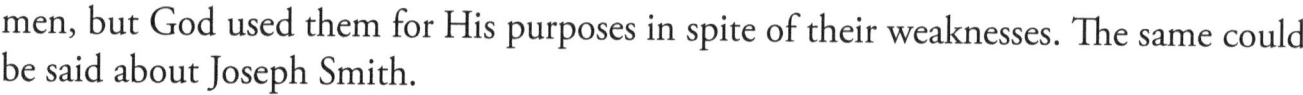

men, but God used them for His purposes in spite of their weaknesses. The same could be said about Joseph Smith.

Nevertheless, independent of your personal opinion of Joseph Smith does the Bible tell us about a man like Joseph Smith? Look at Isaiah 29:

Isaiah 29:11-12, 14:

> *And the vision of all is become unto you as the <u>words of a book</u> that is <u>sealed</u>, which <u>men deliver</u> to <u>one that is learned</u>, saying, <u>Read this</u>, I pray thee: and he saith, <u>I cannot; for it is sealed</u>:*
>
> *And the book is delivered to him that is <u>not learned</u>, saying, <u>Read this</u>, I pray thee: and he saith, <u>I am not learned</u>*
>
> *Therefore, behold, <u>I will</u> proceed to do a <u>marvelous work</u> among this people, even a <u>marvelous work and a wonder</u>: for the wisdom of the wise men shall perish, and the understanding of their prudent men shall be hid.* (Emphasis added)

For those of you who still think that the New Testament is the Stick of Joseph, consider the following questions:

1. Whereas, I believe that the book mentioned above is The Book of Mormon, you believe it is the New Testament. Is that right?

2. The above scripture tells us that the book will be sealed. What part of the New Testament was sealed? We know from testimony that part of the gold plates of The Book of Mormon were, in fact, sealed.

3. This scripture also tells us that the book was taken to a learned man. In reference to the New Testament, who would that learned man be? We know that a part of The Book of Mormon manuscript was taken to Professor Anton in New York to get the translation verified. He refused to validate Joseph Smith's translation because he could not see the whole book. He said, *"I cannot; for it is sealed."*

4. This scripture then tells us that it was given to an uneducated man. With respect to the New Testament, who was that unlearned man? In reference to The Book of Mormon, we know that man was Joseph Smith.

5. So then God said, in effect, I will do it Myself (*"a marvelous work and a wonder"*) through the unlearned man. What was the marvelous work and a wonder that happened in connection to the *writing* of the New Testament?

Not one of Isaiah's requirements for the Stick of Joseph was fulfilled by the New Testament, but every one of them was by the bringing forth of The Book of Mormon. Would you prefer to deny words of Isaiah rather than accept that God could have used Joseph Smith for His purposes? Yes, Joseph was an imperfect man, but so were many of God's favored servants. Remember, Abraham committed adultery; Jacob also, plus polygamy; Moses committed murder and other sins; Solomon had 700 wives and last but not least, King David not only committed adultery but also murder to cover it up. Yet God did not remove any of them from their positions, but used them in spite of their failures. The same thing can also be said about Joseph Smith, Jr. He was not a perfect man, but God used him too.

I know we have briefly looked at this before, but let's look more closely at Ezekiel. What does the Bible says about that second witness.

Ezekiel 37: 16-17

Moreover, thou son of man, take thee one stick, and write upon it, for Judah, and for the children of Israel his companions: then take another stick, and write upon it, for Joseph, the stick of Ephraim, and for all the house of Israel his companions: And join them one to another into one stick; and they shall become one in thine hand. (Emphasis added)

Most people would agree that the *Bible is the stick of Judah*. Some say the New Testament is the stick of Joseph, but it cannot be! Show me one instance that refers to any of the Ten Tribes (the House of Israel) in the timeframe of the writing of the New Testament. You can't. It is just not there! They are not mentioned again after their dispersion or scattering. They just flatly disappear from the Bible. Therefore, the record of Joseph, must be about some of the descendants of Joseph, the son of Israel, one of the lost tribes. Ezekiel 37 states that the stick of Joseph is a completely separate book from the Bible. The New Testament does not meet that requirement, but the Book of Mormon does.

To continue, let's look at "Time Stamping." It occurs when a prophet of God prophesies that after a certain event transpires, a second specific event will happen. As an example, at the birth of Christ, we are told that a new star would appear. So we know that when the new star appeared, the Christ child has already been born. In this next verse, there is a time stamp given:

Isaiah 29:17-18:

Is it not yet a very little while, and Lebanon shall be turned into a fruitful field, and the fruitful field shall be esteemed as a forest? And in that day shall the deaf hear the words of the book, and the eyes of the blind shall see out of obscurity, and out of darkness. (Emphasis added)

This scripture is part of the same Isaiah prophecy discussed on the previous page. It explains that this predicted book would be brought forth shortly before Lebanon becomes a fruitful field. Roy Weldon tells us:

In 1830 there were very few Jews in Palestine, and the country itself was desolate. The restoration of the Jews involves more than people. It involves land also.

An old encyclopedia gives us the situation in Palestine in the early part of the eighteenth century.

Eighteen centuries of war, ruin and neglect have passed over it. Its valleys have been cropped for ages without the least attempt at fertilization. Its terraced walls have been allowed to crumble, and its soil has washed down its ravines, leaving the hillsides rocky and sterile. Its trees have been cut down and never replaced. Its fields have been desolate. Its structures pillaged and all its improvements ruthlessly destroyed. A land of ruins without man or beast. Everywhere, on plain or mountain, in rocky desert, or on beetling cliff the spoilers hand has rested. (80)

The Jews started returning to Lebanon after 1830; by 1889 there were 50 thousand: by 1935 there were 61,541. In 1958 there were two million. In about 1850, irrigation and fertilization were introduced into the fields of Lebanon, and they became productive for the first time in centuries. The Book of Mormon was translated in 1830, just a few years before Lebanon became "*a fruitful field*," thus fulfilling this prophecy. (80)

To put this in perspective, when was the canon of the New Testament created? The King James Version was compiled in 1611 A.D., but the earliest version of The New Testament was the Latin Vulgate in 380 A.D. God's "very little while" could easily be 20 to 45 years, but not likely many centuries (1611 to 1850 =) 239 years or (380 to 1850=) 1,470 years before Lebanon became a fruitful field. So the New Testament does not fulfill the above prophecy, but The Book of Mormon does.

Let's now look further into these words of Isaiah. The next part of the scripture points out that the deaf will hear, and the blind will see. What do you think this means? I believe that this prophetic word was also fulfilled, in 1825. How do blind people see and deaf people hear? Think about it: the sightless can see by reading braille, and the deaf can hear by watching sign language. Various forms of sign language have been around since the sixth century, but braille was invented by Louis Braille in 1825. So the prophetic statement that the "***deaf hear the words of the book, and the eyes of the blind shall see out of obscurity, and out of darkness***" was fulfilled in 1825 and the book was printed in 1830. As I see it, this prophecy has been completely fulfilled with two time stamps and a third circumstance (Lebanon becoming fruitful, Braille and sign language), which verify that the book prophesized about is The Book of Mormon.

May I also bring to your attention this curious prophetic word?

Revelation 14:6:

And I saw another angel fly in the midst of heaven, having the everlasting gospel to preach unto them that dwell on the earth, and to every nation, and kindred, and tongue, and people.

I am convinced that these words of John were fulfilled through Joseph Smith and The Book of Mormon. Most people believe that the Bible contains the everlasting Gospel. But if that is so, then why does the angel bring the everlasting gospel to the earth in the last days? The fulfillment of this angel message was predicted to occur well after the Bible became available to man.

How could this imperfect man give us so much scripture? Because he asked and then listened to God when, it seems, no one else would. The Lord took the initiative and Joseph received the gold plates and the gift and power to use the Urim and Thummim[1] to translate them. Therefore, the book did not come by the knowledge of man or by his skill. As a result, the face of Christianity has been forever changed.

A Racist Book

In keeping with our intention to answer objections about The Book of Mormon, I am paraphrasing information taken from an unpublished article by Ralph Williston and used with his permission. Although some people claim that The Book of Mormon is racist, Williston maintains that that is not true. But, at the outset, let's first establish what we can agree on. I think we can agree that the scriptures teach that all are created in the image of God and are equal in His sight. Consider the following:

Genesis 1:27:

So God created man in His own image, in the image of God created He him; male and female created He them.

Genesis 5:1:

This is the book of the generations of Adam. In the day that God created man, in the likeness of God made He him;... (Emphasis added)

Galatians 3:28:

...neither Jew nor Greek, there is neither bond nor free, there is neither male nor female: for ye are all one in Christ Jesus.

---

1 Urim and Thummim, Objects not specifically described, perhaps stones, placed in the breastplate of the high priest: by which he ascertained the will of God in any important matter affecting the nation (Exodus 28:30; Leviticus 8:8). The New Compact Dictionary, Zondervan Publishing House, Grand Rapids, Michigan 1967 (597).

2 Nephi 11:114-115 RCE, 2 Nephi 26:33:

And He denieth none that come unto Him--black and white, bond and free, male and female; And He remembereth the heathen; And all are alike unto God--both Jew and Gentile.

Romans 10:12-13:

For there is no difference between the Jew and the Greek: for the same Lord over all is rich unto all that call upon him. For whosoever shall call upon the name of the Lord shall be saved.

While the scriptures teach that all are alike unto God, nevertheless, God did select a group of people in the Bible commonly known as "the chosen people." As we know, they were chosen for a special purpose. They were to be:

Deuteronomy. 7:6:

...above all people that are upon the face of the earth,...

I believe that God also chose another group of people found in The Book of Mormon who were called the Nephites. They also considered themselves to be:

Helaman 5:90 RCE, Helaman15:3 LDS:

... a chosen people of the Lord;...

The most severe consequence for rebellion in the Bible was for a person to be "shut out from the presence of the Lord" (2 Thessalonians 1:9 NIV). Similarly, Nephi was told:

1 Nephi 1:55,57 RCE, 1 Nephi 2:21,23 LDS:

And inasmuch as thy brethren shall rebel against thee, they shall be <u>cut off from the presence of the Lord</u>.

For behold, in that day that they shall rebel against Me, I will curse them even with a sore curse, And they shall have no power over thy seed except they shall rebel against Me also;... (Emphasis added)

In the following case, some mark or skin color change was made. By way of comparison, in the Bible, this was for protection or to distinguish a people (Genesis 4:15). In The Book of Mormon, the intent is slightly different:

Alma 1:104 RCE, Alma 3:6 LDS:

And the skins of the Lamanites were dark, according to <u>the mark</u> which was set upon their fathers, Which was a <u>curse upon them</u> because of their transgression and their rebellion against their brethren which consisted of Nephi, Jacob and Joseph and Sam, which were just and holy men. (Emphasis added)

As we see from the above scripture, with those who were set apart, there was some reference to skin mark or color change. (Also found in 2 Nephi 4:35 RCE, 2 Nephi 5:21 LDS; Jacob 2:60 RCE, Jacob 3:9 LDS; Alma 1:104-117 RCE, Alma 3:6-18 LDS)

Only The Book of Mormon explains that when a disobedient group repented, not only did God's Spirit return to them, but also their skin color or "stain" disappeared:

<u>Helaman 2:163 RCE, Helaman 6:36 LDS:</u>

> *...the Lord began to pour out His Spirit upon the Lamanite because of their easiness and willingness to believe in His word.*

<u>Alma 14:33 RCE, Alma 24:11 LDS:</u>

> *And now behold, my brethren, since it has been all that we could do--as we were the most lost of all mankind--to repent of all our sins and the many murders which we have committed and to get God to take them away from our hearts--For it was all we could do to repent sufficiently before God that He would take away our stain.*

For full definitions of racial discrimination, see footnote.

1. **a belief or doctrine that inherent differences among the various human races determine cultural or individual achievement, usually involving the idea that one's own race is superior and has the right to rule others.**
2. **a policy, system of government, etc., based upon or fostering such a doctrine of discrimination.**
3. **hatred or intolerance of another race or other races.**

Racialism: "a doctrine or teaching, without scientific support that claims to find racial differences in character, intelligence, etc., that asserts the superiority of one race over another or others, and that seeks to maintain the supposed purity of a race or races."

Discrimination: "showing of partiality or prejudice in treatment; specific action or polices directed against the welfare of minority groups."

Prejudice: "a judgment or opinion formed before facts are known, preconceived idea, suspicion, intolerance or hatred of other races, creeds, regions, occupations,..."

According to Williston, prejudice in The Book of Mormon, as such and by definition, was found only among the Lamanite culture and had to do with their feelings of being wronged (feelings that went all the way back to their departure from Jerusalem), and not their race (Mosiah 6:46-53 RCE, Mosiah 10:12-17 LDS).

Footnote: These definitions were included with Williston's material.

Racism: any program or practice of racial discrimination; based on racialism.

As previously stated, God had a chosen people in The Book of Mormon. They were not part of the tribe of Judah but were a part of the House of Israel and thus chosen because of their lineage. Jesus *also* identified The Book of Mormon peoples as part of the House of Joseph, and therefore a chosen people because of their lineage:

In speaking to His twelve apostles in Bountiful, Jesus said:

3 Nephi 7:13 RCE, 3 Nephi 15:12 LDS:

> *… 'Ye are My disciples; and ye are a light unto this people, which are a remnant of the house of Joseph.'* (Emphasis added)

While we reaffirm God's love for all people and His provision for them, nevertheless, at least twice in history God has separated out a people because of disobedience--once in the Bible and once in The Book of Mormon.

Genesis 4:15-16:

> *And the Lord, said unto him, Therefore whosoever slayeth Cain, vengeance shall be taken on him sevenfold. And the Lord set a mark upon Cain, lest any finding him should kill him. And Cain went <u>out from the presence of the Lord</u>, and dwelt in the land of Nod, on the east of Eden.* (Emphasis added)

Apparently the life of Cain was in danger of being destroyed ("**vengeance shall be taken on him sevenfold**") because of the murder of his brother Abel, and the Lord wanted to protect him by placing "a mark" on him. Probably the most important thing was not the mark but that Cain was shut "out from the presence of the Lord," or that God withdrew His Spirit from him and his family.

Is this teaching also found in The Book of Mormon? Yes, when the followers of Laman rebelled:

1 Nephi 1:55 RCE, 1 Nephi 2:21 LDS:

> *And inasmuch as thy brethren shall rebel against thee [Nephi], <u>they shall be cut off from the presence of the Lord</u>;…* (Emphasis added)

(See also: 2 Nephi 1:34, 3:9, 4:31-32, 6:14 RCE, 2 Nephi 1:20, 4:4, 5:20, 9:6 LDS; Alma 7:16-18, 17:30, 17:44; 19:88, 19:90, 19:92, 19:96; 22:21 RCE, Alma 9:13-14, 36:30, 37:13; 42:7,9,11,14; 50:20 LDS; Helaman 4:68, 5:70 RCE, Helaman 12:21, 14:16 LDS; Ether 1:41, 4:55 RCE, Ether 2:15, 10:11 LDS.)

But this action was not limited to just the Lamanites:

Helaman 2:162 RCE, Helaman 6:35 LDS:

And thus we see that <u>the Spirit of the Lord began to withdraw from the Nephites</u> because of the wickedness and the hardness of their hearts.
(Emphasis added)

Conversely, as previously stated, when the wicked Lamanites repented:

Helaman 2:163 RCE, Helaman 6:36 LDS:

...that the Lord began to pour out His Spirit upon the Lamanites because of their easiness and willingness to believe in His word.

Let's consider: was dark skin really a curse pronounced on the Lamanites by God? That seems to be the general consensus, but what does The Book of Mormon really say? Speaking to Nephi, the Lord *distinguished* between the *curse* and the *mark*.

Alma 1:113 RCE, Alma 3:14 LDS:

Behold, the <u>Lamanites have I cursed; And I will set a mark upon them</u>, that they and their seed may be separated from thee and thy seed from this time, henceforth and forever, except they repent of their wickedness and turn to Me, that I may have mercy upon them. (Emphasis added)

At the time this promise was given, apparently the curse of separation had already been placed on the Lamanites while the mark was yet to happen. The Lord also told Nephi that others, including his own posterity, who mingled with the Lamanites, would be affected in the same way:

Alma 1:114-115 RCE, Alma 3:15-16 LDS:

And again, I will <u>set a mark</u> upon him that mingleth his seed with thy brethren, that they <u>may be cursed</u> [separated] also. And again, will I <u>set a mark</u> upon him that fighteth against thee and thy seed. (Emphasis added)

Therefore, in connection with the curse of separation, the Lord "set a mark" upon the Lamanites. The purpose of it, according to The Book of Mormon, was to distinguish the Lamanites from the Nephites, so that the Nephites would not intermarry and accept their incorrect beliefs. After Alma led away those who accepted his teachings about Jesus, he wrote:

Alma 1:105-108 RCE, Alma 3:7-10 LDS:

And their brethren sought to destroy them [Nephi, Jacob, Joseph and Sam]; Therefore, they were cursed, And the Lord God <u>set a mark upon them</u>, yea, upon Laman and Lemuel, and also the sons of Ishmael and the Ishmaelitish women; And this was done, <u>that their seed might be</u>

> *distinguished from the seed of their brethren, that thereby the Lord God might preserve His people, that they might not mix and believe in incorrect traditions which would prove their destruction. And it came to pass that whosoever did mingle his seed with that of the Lamanites did bring the same curse upon his seed; Therefore, whomsoever suffered himself to be led away by the Lamanites were called under that head and there was **a mark set** upon him.* (Emphasis added)

So, while many of the Nephites avoided the Lamanites because of the mark on their skin, the Lord was concerned about the sinful nature of their brethren and merely used a physical characteristic to keep others from accepting their wicked ways.

It is interesting that some Nephites, having rejected the Nephite religion, did mingle with the Lamanites, thus bringing "***the same curse upon his seed***" *and having* "***a mark set upon him.***" Again, we see that the curse and the mark, while going together, were two different things. The curse was separation from God. The mark was a stain or a blemish. In reference to the mark, what started as a "skin of blackness"(2 Nephi 4:35 RCE, 2 Nephi 5:21 LDS) became a skin of "darkness"(Jacob 2:60 RCE, Jacob 3:9) then a "red mark" on the skin (Alma 1:104-117 RCE, Alma 3:6-18) and finally, a "stain" on it (Alma 14:33 RCE, Alma 24:11 LDS). Through all of this, only the withdrawal of God's Spirit continued.

When Moroni was searching for a spy to go into the Lamanite camp, he asked for any Lamanite who had joined his army to come forward. Laman responded and went into the enemy camp. So when Laman joined Moroni's army, there apparently was no skin color difference. (See Alma 25:30-35 RCE, Alma 55:4-8 LDS) Therefore, neither the skin color nor the withdrawal of the Lord's Spirit was permanent, so when the Lamanites repented:

3 Nephi 1:52-53 RCE, 3 Nephi 2:15-16:
> *...that those Lamanites which had united with the Nephites were numbered among the Nephites; And their curse was taken from them, and their skin became white like unto the Nephites, And their young men and their daughters became exceeding fair, And they were numbered among the Nephites and were called Nephites;...*

Both the Bible and the Book of Mormon use terms like white or fair or *filthiness* or *delightsome* in reference to people's spirituality and should not be mistaken for a reference to skin color. (Isaiah 1:18, Daniel 11:33-35; Daniel 12:10; 2 Corinthians 7:1 Jacob 2:54,59 RCE, Jacob 3:5,8 LDS; 3 Nephi 9:25 RCE, 3 Nephi 19:25 LDS; Mormon 4:65 RCE, Mormon 9:6 LDS) As you read the following skin-color analogies found in the

Bible and The Book of Mormon, recall Noah Webster's 1928 definition of *white* as being "*purified from sin*":

Genesis 6:2:

...the sons of God saw the daughters of men that they <u>were fair</u>; and they took them wives of all which they chose. (Emphasis added)

Daniel 11:35:

And some of them of understanding shall fall, to try them, and to purge, and <u>to make them white</u>, even to the time of the end: because it is yet for a time appointed. (Emphasis added)

Daniel 12:10:

Many shall be purified, <u>and made white</u>, and tried; but the wicked shall do wickedly: and none of the wicked shall understand; but the wise shall understand." (Emphasis added)

1 Samuel 17:42:

And when the Philistine looked about, and saw David, he disdained him: for he was but a youth, and ruddy, and <u>of a fair countenance</u>. (Emphasis added)

In the vision given to Nephi when he saw the Gentiles coming to his land in the future, we have the following:

1 Nephi 3:151 RCE, 1 Nephi 13:15 LDS:

And I beheld the Spirit of the Lord, that it was upon the Gentiles; that they did prosper and obtain the land for their inheritance; And I beheld that <u>they were white and exceeding fair and beautiful</u>, like unto my people before that they were slain. (Emphasis added)

2 Nephi 4:34-35 RCE, 2 Nephi15:21:

For behold, they had hardened their hearts against Him that they had become like unto a flint; Wherefore, as they were <u>white and exceeding fair and delightsome</u>, That they might not be enticing unto my people, therefore, the Lord God did cause a skin of blackness to come upon them;... (Emphasis added)

2 Nephi 12:82-84 RCE, 2 Nephi 30:5-7 LDS:

And the gospel of Jesus Christ shall be declared among them; Wherefore, they shall be restored unto the knowledge of their fathers, And also to the knowledge of Jesus Christ, which was had among their fathers. And then shall they rejoice, For they shall know that it is a blessing unto them from *the hand of God; And their scales of darkness shall begin to fall from their eyes; And many generations shall not pass away among them, save they shall <u>be a white and a delightsome people</u>.* (Emphasis added)

This is a beautiful example of the proper use for the terms "they shall be a white and delightsome people," and "Their scales of darkness shall begin to fall from their eyes...." Could it be that the best understanding of these terms *is that they refer to a spiritual condition and not skin color?!*

So, let's understand. The following examples actually refer to a change in the spiritual condition of the Lamanites:

3 Nephi 9:25 RCE, 3 Nephi 19:25:

And it came to pass that Jesus beheld them, as they did pray unto Him, and His countenance did smile upon them, And <u>the light of His countenance did shine</u> upon them; And behold, <u>they were as white as the countenance</u>, and also the garments of Jesus;... (Emphasis added)

3 Nephi 9:31 RCE, 3 Nephi 19:30 LDS:

And it came to pass that when Jesus had spake these words, He came again unto His disciples; And behold, they did pray steadfastly without ceasing unto Him; And He did smile upon them again; And <u>behold, they were white even as Jesus</u>. (Emphasis added)

Mormon 4:65 RCE, Mormon 9:6 LDS:

O then ye unbelieving, turn ye unto the Lord! Cry mightily unto the Father in the name of Jesus, that perhaps ye may be found spotless, pure, fair and white, Having been cleansed by the blood of the Lamb at that great and last day. (Emphasis added)

Jacob warned his people, the Nephites, that because they were deep in sin, the Lamanites might become more righteous than they:

Jacob 2:59 RCE, Jacob 3:8 LDS:

O my brethren, I fear, that unless ye shall repent of your sins, <u>that their skins will be whiter than yours</u> when ye shall be brought with them before the throne of God. (Emphasis added)

Again, the use of black and white imagery to typify purity and righteousness is exemplified by Jacob in the phrase "...that their skins will be whiter than yours...."

In the quote below, the fact that the Bible is not referring to skin color but spiritual conditions is obvious in the following symbolism:

John 4:35:

> *...look on the fields; for they are white already to harvest.* (Emphasis added)

By way of illustration, we can now understand the symbolism of what Isaiah meant when he said:

Isaiah 1:18:

> *Come now, and let us reason together, saith the LORD: though your sins be as scarlet, they shall be as white as snow; though they be red like crimson, they shall be as wool.* (Emphasis added)

Thus, we can now interpret what Daniel was saying:

Daniel 12:10:

> *Many shall be purified, and made white, and tried; but the wicked shall do wickedly: and none of the wicked shall understand; but the wise shall understand.* (Emphasis added)

You may want to look at other scriptures that mention "their garments are made white" and consider that God is illustrating the spiritual condition of the people. Here, for example, is another one:

1 Nephi 3:117-119 RCE, 1 Nephi 12:10-11 LDS:

> *And behold, they are righteous forever, For because of their faith in the Lamb of God, their garments are made white in His blood. And the angel saith unto me: "Look!" And I looked and beheld three generations did pass away in righteousness; Their garments were white, even like unto the Lamb of God; And the angel saith unto me: "These are made white in the blood of the Lamb because of their faith in Him."* (Emphasis added)

If all humans are created in the image of God, and alike to Him, is it not probable that terms such as *white, delightsome, fair* and *filthy* refer to a spiritual condition, not a skin color? In other words, the use of such words is not evidence of a racist mindset. Keep in mind, the scriptures should be studied in the context of the times in which they were written. Also remember that our language changes over time as new words are added, archaic ones dropped, and meanings change. According to the 1928 Webster's Dictionary (the one in use during Joseph Smith's day), one definition of white is *"Having the color of purity; pure; clean; free from spot; as white robed innocence, Pure, unblemished, and in a spiritual sense, purified from sin; sanctified. Psalm 51."*

Now let's go back to review what the scriptures actually say about God's perspective. Here are four points:

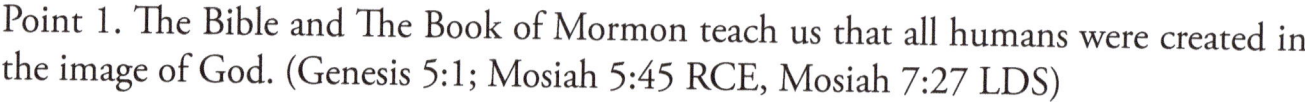

Point 1. The Bible and The Book of Mormon teach us that all humans were created in the image of God. (Genesis 5:1; Mosiah 5:45 RCE, Mosiah 7:27 LDS)

Genesis 1:26:

> *And God said, Let us make man in our image, after our likeness…*

Alma 12:112 RCE, Alma 18:34 LDS:

> *Ammon saith unto him, I am a man; And man in the beginning was created <u>after the image of God</u>;…* (Emphasis added)

Alma 13:44 RCE, Alma 22:12:

> *…reading the scriptures unto the king--How God created man <u>after His own image</u>….* (Emphasis added)

Point 2. The Bible and The Book of Mormon tell us that God accepts all people:

Galatians 3:28:

> *There is neither Jew nor Greek, there is neither bond nor free, there is neither male nor female: for ye are <u>all one in Christ Jesus</u>.* (Emphasis added)

2 Nephi 11:96-97 RCE, 2 Nephi 26:24 LDS:

> *…For He loveth the world, even that He layeth down His own life that He may draw <u>all men</u> unto Him; Wherefore, He commandeth none that they shall not partake of His salvation.* (Emphasis added)

2 Nephi 11:114-115 RCE, 2 Nephi 26:33 LDS:

> *And He denieth none that come unto Him--black and white, bond and free, male and female; And He remembereth the heathen; And <u>all are alike unto God</u>--both Jew and Gentile.* (Emphasis added)

Point 3. Both the books tell us that God would come down among the children of men and take upon Him flesh and blood and go forth upon the face of the earth in order to bring all of us back to Him.

Isaiah 7:14:

> *Therefore the LORD himself shall give you a sign; Behold a virgin shall conceive, and bear a son, and shall call his name Immanuel.*

3 Nephi 12:26, 28 RCE, 3 Nephi 27:14-15 LDS:

> *And My Father sent Me that I might be lifted up upon the cross; And after that I had been lifted up upon the cross, I might draw all men unto Me; And for this cause have I been lifted up; Therefore, according to the power of the Father, I will draw all men unto Me, that they may be judged according to their works.* (Emphasis added)

Point 4. Historically, we see that God has separated out certain groups for His purposes. In the Old Testament, He divided humanity into two groups: Jew and Gentile. He intended for the Jews to be a kingdom that would minister to the Gentile nations; but, instead, for the most part, the Jews became proud of their status and looked down on the Gentiles. However, Jesus will join them together again:

Ephesians 2:14:

> *For He is our peace, who hath made both one, and hath <u>broken down the middle wall of partition between us</u>;...* (Emphasis added)

Within this context, God did select a group that He called for a special purpose:

Deuteronomy 7:6:

> *For thou art <u>an holy people</u> unto the LORD thy God: the Lord thy God hath chosen thee to be <u>a special people</u> unto himself, <u>above all people that are upon the face of the earth</u>.* (Emphasis added)

Deuteronomy 14:2:

> *For thou art an holy people unto the LORD thy God, and the LORD hath chosen thee to be a peculiar people unto himself, above all the nations that are upon the earth.*

In conclusion, can we agree that:

1. Our scriptures teach that all are created in the image of God and all are alike unto Him.

2. In history, God separated out certain groups for His purposes:

a. One group, called "***the chosen people***," were the Twelve Tribes of Israel, who were given a divine task. This action does not reflect racism because God extends His Spirit to everyone.

b. At least twice in history God singled out groups because of their disobedience:

    i. Cain and his family were separated, and called "***cursed***." This action involved two parts: the withdrawing of His Spirit from that family and the placing of a mark to protect that family from others.

    ii. The followers of Laman were also disconnected from the Nephites, and God again withdrew His Spirit and made a temporary skin change. This action was lifted when they repented.

CHAPTER 10

WHAT ARE THE NON-BIBLICAL EVIDENCES THAT THE BOOK OF MORMON WAS TRANSLATED, NOT WRITTEN?

As stated earlier, Joseph Smith had a meager education according to today's standards. He was only twenty-three years old when he translated The Book of Mormon from the gold plates-- and he did it in just eighty days! It is not humanly possible for a person to write a book of that size that quickly. (Just look at this book; it has taken around nine months to write—with a lot of editorial help, and a much higher level of education!)

The Translation Process

The speed of Joseph's deciphering was amazing! He averaged eight pages per day, and on some days ten! Compare that to modern-day translators who normally achieve only one page a day and think that's fast. God had to be involved for Joseph to be able to work so quickly. When interruptions occurred, Joseph never asked for a review of his previous work.

He never inquired: "Now, where were we?" God always directed him to the next pictorial symbol to be converted, and he never used any outside sources as an aid in the process. His wife Emma was very clear on this point. She stated, **"He had neither manuscript nor book to read from, if he had anything of the kind he could not have concealed it from me"** (Maxwell 8). Therefore, The Book of Mormon came *through* Joseph Smith, but not *from* him. Also, he was not a Bible scholar. According to Emma, when she was his scribe for the section that talked about Jerusalem being a walled city, he asked her if the writers of The Book of Mormon were pulling his leg. She confirmed to him that Jerusalem was indeed a walled city (Maxwell 8). She bore witness to the existence of the gold plates since she had touched them through a cloth, but because she had been directed by Joseph, she did not read them.

Oliver Cowdery was the most involved witness to the translation process. Even though he was later disaffected from the church, after a while he humbly returned. On his death bed, he reaffirmed his testimony of the validity of The Book of Mormon. Oliver's half-sister, Lucy

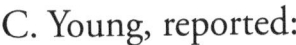

C. Young, reported:

Just before he breathed his last he asked to be raised up in bed so he could talk to the family and friends and he told them to live according to The Book of Mormon, and they would meet him in heaven, then he said lay me down and let me fall asleep in the arms of Jesus, and he fell asleep without a struggle. (Maxwell 11)

How much more of an endorsement do you want?!

One of the authors in *Echoes and Evidences of The Book of Mormon*, Neal A Maxwell, made the following point:

The book's spiritual significance, of course, lies in its capacity for "convincing… the Jew and the Gentile that Jesus is the Christ." This is the very same reason given by the Apostle John concerning some text he wrote: *"But these are written, that ye might believe that Jesus is the Christ, the Son of God; and that in believing ye might have life through his name." (John 20:31)* **This is why prophets write, whether** [it be Matthew, Mark, Luke] **John, Nephi, Mormon or Moroni.** (11) (Emphasis added)

The problem with evidence is that nothing can be proven to an absolute certainty. Does this mean that this is all a pack of lies? Absolutely not! How then does one determine what is true and what is false? The answer is simple: it is by the witness of the Holy Spirit. The Bible clearly states: "*…**Lean not unto thine own understanding.**" (Proverbs 3:5) "…but* [live] ***by every word that proceedeth out of the mouth of God.**" (Matthew 4:4) That also means not to rely on the words of others. That is to say, test the spirit of everything written or spoken by anybody. Ask God what is true because He is the only source you can completely trust to tell you the truth.

Familiarity With The Arabian Peninsula

At the beginning of The Book of Mormon, Nephi described their travels through various landmarks along the way to Bountiful in Arabia. Those remote locations have recently been verified by researchers but would have been totally unknown to anyone during Joseph Smith's lifetime. (Brown 61) Let's look at some specific Book of Mormon clues. Nephi tells us of their journey to their first camp:

<u>1 Nephi 1:33 RCE, 1 Nephi 2:6 LDS:</u>
> *And it came to pass that when he [Lehi] had traveled three days in the wilderness, he pitched his tent in a valley beside a river of water.*

<u>1 Nephi 1:36 RCE 1 Nephi 2:9 LDS:</u>
> *And when my father saw that the waters of the river emptied into the fountain of the Red Sea, he spake unto Laman, saying: "O that thou*

mightest be like unto this river, continually running into the fountain of all righteousness!"

This is amazing! Here is a present-day river that flows from the desert, all year long! Very striking, don't you think? Nephi also said that the valley was impressive:

1 Nephi 1:37 RCE 1 Nephi 2:10 LDS:

And he also spake unto Lemuel, saying: "Oh that thou mightest be like unto this valley, firm and steadfast and immovable in keeping the commandments of the Lord!"

Photographs by George Potter, rights reserved by Nephi Project, www.nephiproject.com

Laman River?   *Valley of Lemuel?*

Historically, it was traditional for newcomers first arriving at a place to give it a name meaningful to them. Therefore Lehi, in naming the river Laman and the valley Lemuel, is in agreement with customs of the area at the time they were at that location. (Brown 61)

Nephi thus gives us some evidence for the location of their first camp. It was in a large valley next to a river that flowed all year round and emptied into the Red Sea. Sounds impossible, but it does exist. The Valley of Lemuel candidate, "wadi Tayyib alism" (valley of the Good Name), was discovered by George Potter in 1995. It is located almost seventy-five miles south of Aqaba by foot and holds a river that flows continually. This river has cut deep into the granite mountains and has "narrow passages and steep sides that rise to about two thousand feet, features that would fit Lehi's description of an impressive valley." (Brown 61) In northern Arabia there are no other streams that continually flow into the Red Sea. Just consider: Joseph Smith did not have any access to information about Arabian geography.

It was at this point that Lehi sent his sons back to Jerusalem to get the brass plates; days later, when they returned:

1 Nephi 1:157 RCE, 1 Nephi 5:9LDS:

And it came to pass that they did rejoice exceedingly and did offer sacrifice [peace offering] *and burnt offerings* [atonement offerings] *unto the Lord;...*

Notwithstanding that Joseph Smith knew very little scripture and absolutely nothing about Hebraic culture or religious practices, The Book of Mormon depicts the correct sacrifice (peace offering) and burnt offerings (atonement offerings) as required by their religious beliefs.

Next, Nephi recorded the second phase of their journey where they:

1 Nephi 5:16-17 RCE, 1 Nephi 16:13-14 LDS:

...traveled for the space of four days nearly a south, southeast direction; And we did pitch our tents again; And we did call the name of the place Shazer. And it came to pass that we did take our bows and our arrows and go forth into the wilderness to slay food for our families,...

Looking at the proposed site of the first campsite and then going south one hundred miles, I would place them at the northern end of the Al-Sarat Mountains. This would have been a good place to hunt for provisions. No one in America could have known this.

Nephi also explained that they traveled:

1 Nephi 5:18 RCE, 1 Nephi 16:14 LDS:

...in the wilderness following the same direction, keeping in the most fertile parts of the wilderness which were in the borders near the Red Sea.

They must have traveled along the side of these mountains, then continued their travels to Nahom. (Brown 79) In Yemen we find the Nihm Tribal area. The consonants used, NHM, apply to both Nahom and Nihm, and would agree with the statement of Nephi about turning directly east upon leaving Nahom. (79) (1 Nephi 5:55 RCE, 1 Nephi 17:1 LDS)

Lehi and his family traveled on to "Bountiful." It is believed by some that the current city of Salalah in Oman is that location. Looking at a map of Oman and Salalah, we find that there are many streams and mountains. According to Brown, the northeastern flow of air currents off the ocean provides massive amounts of moisture that create a tropical rain forest in that area, which would indeed be fruitful (92).

Nephi then told of God directing him to find ore to create tools for building a ship. (1 Nephi 5:72 RCE, 1 Nephi 17:10) Some people have questioned Nephi's ability to build a ship that could take them across the Pacific Ocean. However, they have no problem accepting that the Israelites were fed by God while traveling in the desert. To me, it makes sense that if God can direct and feed three million plus Israelites for forty years, surely He had the capability of giving Nephi the plans to build a ship. Nor do I find it hard to believe that God had the ability to provide a compass to guide them across the land and the ocean to their Promised Land. Well, Nephi answered this criticism for us and for his brothers Laman and Lemuel because they questioned his ability also:

Lehi's Possible Routes to Bountiful

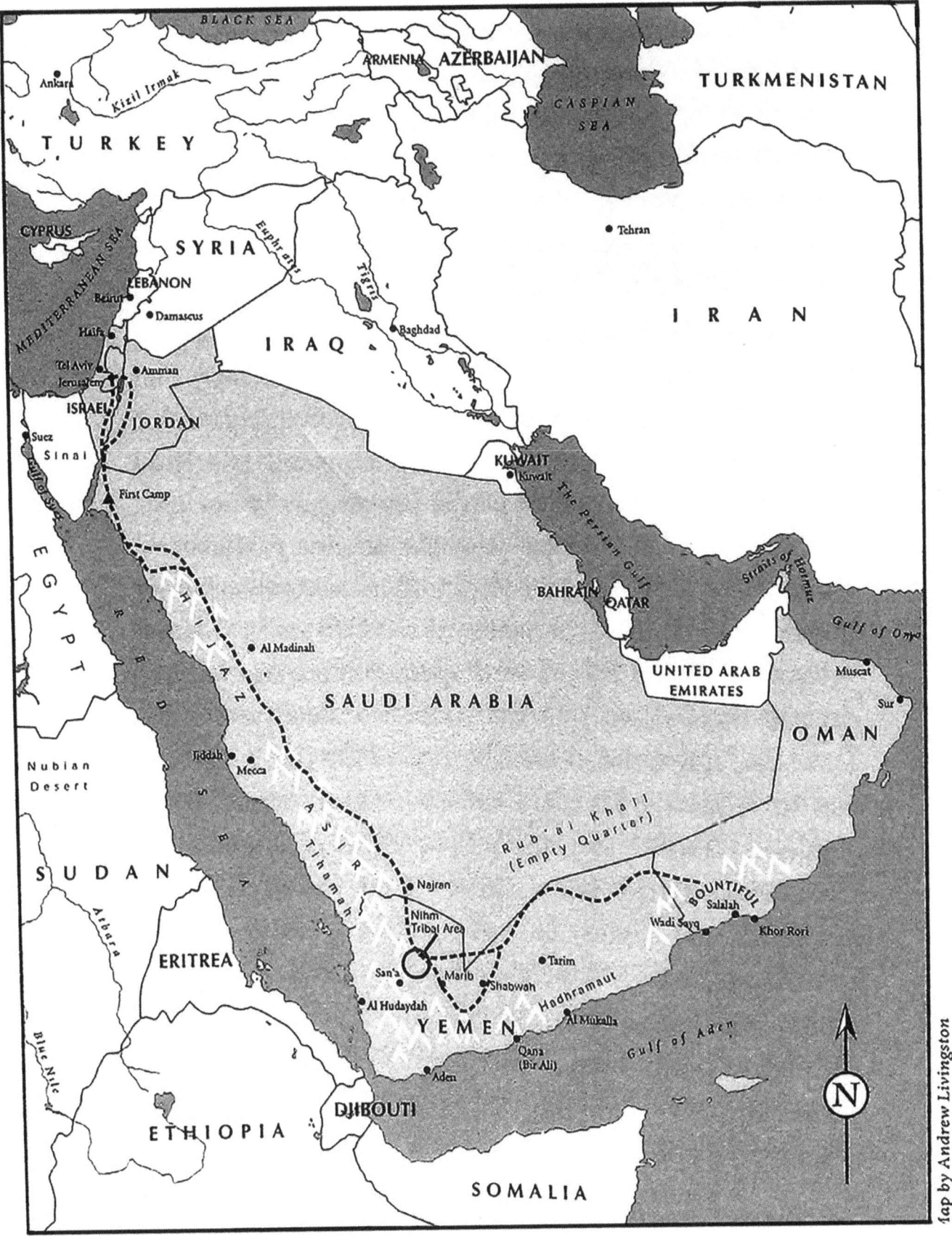

Map from Brown "New Light from Arabia on Lehi's Trail" (58)

1 Nephi 5:159 RCE, 1 Nephi 17:51 LDS:

And now, if the Lord hath such great power and hath wrought so many miracles among the children of men, How is it that He cannot instruct me that I should build a ship?

So Nephi, with the help of his brothers, built a ship over their objections. According to Him, the ship was not built using the techniques of that time:

1 Nephi 5:170-171 RCE, 1 Nephi 18:2 LDS:

Now I, Nephi, did not work the timbers after the manner which was learned by men, Neither did I build the ship after the manner of man, But I did build it after the manner which the Lord had shown unto me; Wherefore, it was not after the manner of men.

(I think it is interesting that the people of Oman were renowned shipbuilders at the time and in the area that Nephi built his ship. Some people have even called them the "Vikings of the Arabian Gulf." They used a shipbuilding technique known as the "Sewn Boat." This technique used 56,000 meters of coconut hair rope. (Reynolds 129) As stated earlier, obviously Nephi did not use that method, because the Lord gave him specific directions for how to build the boat.)

All of these recently proven regional geographical references are things that would be impossible for anyone to know in the 1800s. They would be hard to figure out today, even if you were to go there.

Prophetic Speech Formulas

A similarity between the Bible and The Book of Mormon can be found in what is known as **Prophetic Speech Formulas**. These formulas are

1. Messenger (Thus saith the Lord) Amos 1:3,6; 1 Nephi 6:24 RCE, 1 Nephi 20:17
2. Proclamation (Hear the word of the Lord) 1 Kings 22:19; Jacob 2:36, Jacob 2:27
3. Oath (The Lord God hath sworn) Judges 8:19; 1 Nephi 1:75 RCE, 1 Nephi 3:15 LDS
4. Revelation (The word of the Lord came to…) 1 Samuel 15:10; Helaman 5:4 RCE, Helaman 13:3
5. Woe (Wo unto…) (Parry 169) Isaiah 5:8; 1 Nephi 1:11-12 RCE, 1 Nephi 1:13

It is not by chance that The Book of Mormon contains these formulas, and a writer who wished to imitate the Bible would likely have overlooked them, employed them in improper contexts, or failed to integrate them into the text in a natural manner. (169)

Numbers

To continue, the Hebrew language uses no complex numbers, i.e., *mono, bi, di, uni, tri, multi* and *poly*. It uses only cardinal numbers, i.e., 1, 2, 3 etc., and ordinal numbers, i.e., *first, second, third* etc. It also connects two or more numbers with the conjunction "*and*," like "thirty *and* two kings," rather than "thirty-two kings." The Book of Mormon uses numbers in their true Hebrew form. Unlike the Bible translators, however, Joseph Smith did not add descriptive words to make reading easier. For example, for "ten weight of gold," the Bible adds *shekels* to make it read "ten *shekels* of gold." (Parry 174)

Compound Prepositions

Compound prepositions, or double prepositions, use expressions like: *from before, from behind, and to behind.* (172) These expressions are common in the Old Testament. Here is an example from the Bible:

Judges 11:23:

> *So now the LORD God of Israel hath dispossessed the Amorites <u>from before</u> His people Israel, and shouldest thou possess it? (172)* (Emphasis added)

According to Parry, The Book of Mormon also uses these expressions:

1 Nephi 1:132 RCE, 1 Nephi 4:28 LDS:

> *And they fled from before my presence, For they supposed it was Laban and that he had slain me and had sought to take away their lives also.* <u>(172)</u> (Emphasis added)

1 Nephi 3:51 RCE, 1 Nephi 11:12 LDS:

> *And it came to pass that He said unto me: "Look!" And I looked as if to look upon Him and I saw Him not, for He had gone <u>from before</u> my presence. (172)* (Emphasis added)

2 Nephi 6:20 RCE, 2 Nephi 9:8 LDS:

> *For behold, if the flesh should rise no more, our spirits must become subject to that angel which fell from before the presence of the Eternal God and became the devil, to rise no more;... (172)* (Emphasis added)

And it came to pass

Most readers will recall that one of the most frequent phrases used in the Bible is *And it came to pass.* In the original Hebrew text, this phrase occurs 1,200 times, but in the King James Version, only 727 times. (Parry 163) Given that The Book of Mormon has histories and chronologies that are similar to the Bible, it is not surprising that *And it came to pass* is frequently used to take the reader forward in time.

Word Printing

There are many who, understandably, believe that Joseph Smith wrote The Book of Mormon, so let's examine this scientific technique which relies on the fact that each person uses different words to describe the same or similar topics. Reynolds, quoting Hilton, shares the results of a word printing analysis shown on the chart on the following page and summarized here:

Hilton compared three independent texts of the didactic writings of Nephi and Alma with one another and with the writings of Joseph Smith, Oliver Cowdery, and Solomon Spaulding. The results unambiguously showed that the word prints of Nephi and Alma are distinct and significantly different from each other and from the word prints of Smith, Cowdery and Spaulding. The original findings were therefore confirmed, rendering it, in Hilton's words, as "Statistically indefensible" to claim that Joseph Smith or one of his contemporaries was the author of The Book of Mormon. (Reynolds 135)

In other words, it is a false assumption that Joseph Smith or any of his contemporaries wrote The Book of Mormon. As recent disclosures in this chapter prove, the entire book is Hebrew and not a nineteenth-century American English text. For example, Donald Parry in his article "Hebraisms and Other Ancient Peculiarities in The Book of Mormon" points out that both the Bible and The Book of Mormon use only proper names, no surnames. Also, he informs us that q, x, or w are not used in any proper names, and none of them start with the letter f in either book. (159) This shows the conformity of the Book of Mormon to the Bible.

Parallelisms

In addition, according to E. W. Bullinger, as referenced by Parry, there are seven types of "Parallelisms" found in the Bible. They are *"synonymous, synthetic, antithetic, alternate, repeated alternate, extended alternate and chiasmus"* (160). In one of her papers, Angela Crowell points out one called *staircase* or *climatic* (1). Examples of these same parallelisms also exist in The Book of Mormon. I will illustrate a few of them. All of my examples come from Parry (160- 179) and Crowell (1-4). Let's start with:

Synonymous

This form consists of two sentences where the first is repeated or echoed in the second. (160) Here is one biblical example:

<u>Job 38:16:</u>

> *Have you entered into the springs of the sea? Or hast thou walked in the search of the depth?*

The parallel is entered into – walked in.(160)

WORDPRINTS AND THE BOOK OF MORMON

NUMBER OF REJECTIONS

TESTS		0	1	2	3	4	5	6	7	8	9	10	11	12	13	14	15
Nephi vs. Nephi	3		x	x		x	x										
Alma vs. Alma	3		x	x	x												
Smith vs. Smith	3	x		xx													
Cowdery vs. Cowdery	1		x														
Spaulding vs. Spaulding	1			x													
Nephi vs. Alma	9			x		x	xx	xx	x	x	x	x					
Smith vs. Nephi	6									xx		x	x	x			
Smith vs. Alma	6				xx			xx	xx								
Cowdery vs. Nephi	6							x	x				xx		x	x	
Cowdery vs. Alma	6								xxxx	x	x						
Spaulding vs. Nephi	5											x	x	x		x	x
Spaulding vs. Alma	6							xxx		xx			x	x			

Clearly different author

The higher the number of "rejections," or differences in measurable stylometric elements, the less likely it is that two blocks of text were written by the same author. This chart shows results comparing blocks by the same authors and then by different authors

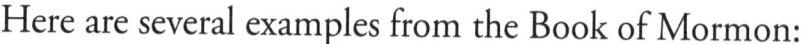

Here are several examples from the Book of Mormon:

2 Nephi 6:103 RCE, 2 Nephi 9:52 LDS:

...Pray unto Him continually by day and give thanks unto His holy name by night.

We see three parallels: Him–His Holy Name, Pray- give thanks, by day-by night. (160)

4 Nephi 11:3 RCE, 2 Nephi 25:2 LDS:

...their works were works of darkness and their doings were doings of abominations.

Parallels: their works- their doings, works of darkness - doings of abominations. (161)

3 Nephi 13:58 RCE, 3 Nephi 29:5 LDS:

Wo unto him that spurneth at the doings of the Lord! Yea, wo unto him that shall deny the Christ and His works!

The parallels here are wo unto him- wo unto him, that spurneth - that shall deny, Lord – Christ, and doings - works. (161)

Antithetic

This form of parallelism shows opposition or contrast of thoughts, where two thoughts are joined together with the words and or but. (161) A biblical example:

Proverbs 17:22:

A merry heart doeth good like a medicine: But a broken spirit drieth the bones. (Emphasis added)

These parallels are merry heart – broken spirit, good like medicine – drieth the bones. Here are several examples from the Book of Mormon:

1 Nephi 5:144 RCE, 1 Nephi 17:45 LDS:

Ye are swift to do iniquity,
but slow to remember the Lord your God;...

The contrasts are apparent: swift – slow, to do iniquity - to remember the Lord. (161)

Alma 3:67 RCE, Alma 5:40 LDS:

For I say unto you that whatsoever is good cometh from God, And whatsoever is evil cometh from the devil.

The opposites are whatsoever is good - whatsoever is evil, cometh from God - cometh from the devil. (162)

Alma 13:37 RCE, Alma 22:6 LDS:

"... *'If ye will repent, ye shall be saved,*

And if ye will not repent, ye shall be cast off at the last Day'?" The parallels are repent ye - ye will not repent, saved - cast off.

Repeated Alternate

This form of parallelism creates an AB, AB, AB pattern. (162-163) Let's start with a biblical example:

Judges 5:24:

A	*Blessed above women shall Jael*
B	*the wife of Heber the Kenite be,*
A	*blessed shall she be above women in the tent.*

Here are several examples from the Book of Mormon:

1 Nephi 5:240-242 RCE, 1 Nephi 19:10 LDS:

A	*...the God of Jacob, yieldeth Himself,*
B	*according to the words of the angel,*
A	*as a man into the hands of wicked men, To be lifted up,*
B	*according to the words of Zenock, And to be crucified, according to the words of Neum,*
A	*And to be buried in a sepulchre,*
B	*according to the words of Zenos...,* (Parry 162)

Alma 16:11 RCE, Alma 30:10 LDS:

A	*But if he murdered,*
B	*he was punished unto death,*
A	*And if he robbed,*
B	*he was also punished, AAnd if he stole,*
B	*he was also punished,*
A	*And if he committed adultery,*
B	*he was also punished;*
A	*Yea, for all this wickedness*
B	*they were punished,... (163)*

Staircase Or Climatic

This is a repetition to climax. (Crowell 1) I changed from the Bible version Angela Crowell used to the King James Version. Here is her biblical example:

Psalm 29:1:

> *Give unto the LORD, O ye mighty,*
> *give unto the LORD, glory and*
> *strength. Give unto the LORD,*
> *the glory due unto His name; worship the LORD, in*
> *the beauty of Holiness. (1)*

Here is her example from the Book of Mormon:

Mosiah 2:13-17 RCE, Mosiah 4:9-10:

> *Believe in God;*
> *Believe that He is*
> *and that He created all things, both in heaven and in*
> *earth; Believe that He hath all wisdom and all power,*
> *both in heaven and in earth;*
> *Believe that man doth not comprehend all the things which the*
> *Lord can comprehend.*
> *And again,*
> *believe that ye must repent of your sins and forsake them,*
> *And humble yourselves before God and ask in sincerity of heart that*
> *He would forgive you;*
> *And now if you believe all these things, See that ye do them! (2)*

Chiasmus

This is **"a sequence of words or ideas that are repeated in reverse order after the center point is reached."** (Crowell 4) The underlined words below illustrate the matching word or words leading to and away from the center point. This is a common Hebrew parallelism that was not recognized until more recent times. Not only sentences, but chapters, and at least one whole book in The Book of Mormon are written in this format. I found the following biblical example as I was researching the scriptures:

Matthew 23:12:

> A   *And whosoever shall <u>exalt</u>*
> B   *<u>himself</u>*
> C   *shall be <u>abased</u>; and*

C'   *he that shall <u>humble</u>*

B'   *<u>himself</u>*

A'   *shall be <u>exalted</u>.*

Here is an example from the Book of Mormon:

1 Nephi 1:1-2 RCE, 1 Nephi 1:1-3 LDS:

A   *...Yea, having had a great knowledge of the goodness and the mysteries of God,*

B   *Therefore, I make a <u>record</u> of my proceedings in my days;*

C   *Yea, I make a record in the <u>language</u> of my father,*

D   *which consists of the <u>learning of the Jews</u>,*

C'   *and the <u>language</u> of the Egyptians;*

B'   *And I know that the <u>record</u> which I make to be true,*

A'   *And I make it with mine own hand, and I make it according to my <u>knowledge</u>. (4)*

Joseph Smith did not have this information or the capability of writing in a Hebrew way; however, The Book of Mormon is filled with all manner of parallelisms, including chiasmus. Therefore, in a literary sense, it would be implausible for him to have written The Book of Mormon.

Prophetic Perfect

The next literary form involves sentence structure. This is **"the use of the past tense or past participle verb forms...when referring to future events"** when expressing a prophetic word (Parry 164). Parry offers the following biblical example:

Isaiah 53:4-8:

Surely He <u>hath born</u> our griefs, and <u>carried</u> our sorrows: yet we did esteem Him <u>stricken</u>, smitten of God, and <u>afflicted</u>. But He <u>was wounded</u> for our transgressions, The chastisement of our peace <u>was upon</u> Him; and with His stripes we are healed. All we like sheep have gone astray; we have turned every one to his own way; and the LORD <u>hath laid</u> on him the iniquity of us all. He <u>was oppressed</u>, and He <u>was afflicted</u>, yet He opened not his mouth: He is brought as a lamb to the slaughter, and as a sheep before the shearers is dumb, so He openeth not His mouth. He was taken from prison and from judgement: and who shall declare His generation? for He <u>was cut off</u> out of the land of the living: for the transgressions of my people <u>was He stricken</u>. (165) (Emphasis added)

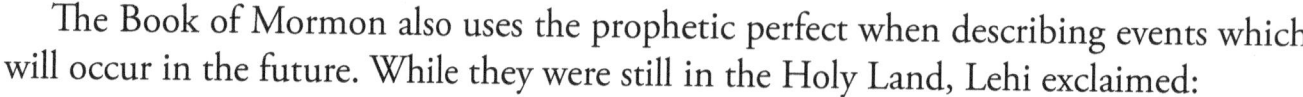

The Book of Mormon also uses the prophetic perfect when describing events which will occur in the future. While they were still in the Holy Land, Lehi exclaimed:

1 Nephi 1:150 RCE, 1 Nephi 5:5 LDS:

> *But behold, I <u>have obtained</u> a land of promise, in the which thing I do rejoice;… (165)*

1 Nephi 3:74 RCE, 1 Nephi 11:27 LDS:

> *And after that He <u>was baptized</u>, I beheld the heavens open and the Holy Ghost <u>come down</u> out of heaven and abode upon Him in the form of a dove;… (165)* (Emphasis added)

2 Nephi 13:10 RCE, 2 Nephi 31:8 LDS:

> *Wherefore, after He <u>was baptized</u> with water, the Holy Ghost <u>descended upon</u> Him in the form of a dove. (165)* (Emphasis added)

Mosiah 8:79 RCE, Mosiah 16:6 LDS:

> *And now, if Christ <u>had not come</u> into the world, speaking of things to come as though <u>they had already come</u>, there could have been no redemption;… (165)* (Emphasis added)

Jarom 1:25 RCE, Jarom 1:11 LDS:

> *Persuading them to look forward unto the Messiah and believe in Him to come as though He already was;… (165)* (Emphasis added)

The Book of Mormon, with its prophetic perfect forms, reads like an ancient scriptural work rather than a nineteenth-century text. (166) This form of writing shows the writer's profound expectations for the future.

Names Of Deity

It is not surprising that The Book of Mormon reflects multiple names for God and Jesus Christ as does the Bible. (Parry 171) Look at this huge list of biblical names for God found at www.smilegod:

Old Testament Names For God

ELOHIM……	Genesis 1:1
meaning "God," a reference to God's power and might	Psalm 19:1
ADONAI……	Malachi 1:6
meaning "Lord," a reference to the Lordship of God	
JEHOVAH--YAHWEH	Genesis 2:4
a reference to God's divine salvation	
JEHOVAH-MACEADDESHEM	Exodus 31:13
meaning "The Lord thy sanctifier"	

JEHOVAH-ROHI   Psalm 23:1

meaning "The Lord my shepherd"

JEHOVAH-SHAMMAH   Ezekiel 48:35

meaning "The Lord who is present"

JEHOVAH-RAPHA   Exodus 15:26

meaning "The Lord our healer"

JEHOVAH-TSIDKENU   Jeremiah 23:6

meaning "The Lord our righteousness"

JEHOVAH-JIREH   Genesis 22:13-14

meaning "The Lord will provide"

JEHOVAH-NISSI   Exodus 17:15

meaning "The Lord our banner"

JEHOVAH-SHALOM   Judges 6:24

meaning "The Lord is peace"

JEHOVAH-SABBAOTH   Isaiah 6:1-3

meaning "The Lord of Hosts"

JEHOVAH-GMOLAH   Jeremiah 51:6

meaning "The God of Recompence"

EL-ELYON   Genesis 14:17-20,

meaning "The most high God"   Isaiah 14:13-14

EL-ROI   Genesis 16:13

meaning "The strong one who sees"

EL-SHADDAI   Genesis 17:1,

meaning "The God of the mountains or God Almighty"   Psalm 91:1

EL-OLAM   Isaiah 40:28-31

meaning "The everlasting God"

More Names Of God From The Old And New Testament

ABBA   Romans 8:15
ADVOCATE   I John 2:1
ALMIGHTY   Genesis 17:1
ALPHA   Revelation 22:13
AMEN   Revelation 3:14
ANCIENT OF DAYS   Daniel 7:9
ANOINTED ONE   Psalm 2:2
APOSTLE   Hebrews 3:1
ARM OF THE LORD   Isaiah 53:1

AUTHOR OF LIFE	Acts 3:15
AUTHOR OF OUR FAITH	Hebrews 12:2
BEGINNING	Revelation 21:6
BLESSED AND HOLY RULER	1 Timothy 6:15
BRANCH	Jeremiah 33:15
BREAD OF GOD	John 6:33
BREAD OF LIFE	John 6:35
BRIDEGROOM	Isaiah 62:5
BRIGHT AND MORNING STAR	Revelation 22:16
BUCKLER	Psalm 18:2,
	Psalm 18:30,
	Proverbs 2:7
CHIEF SHEPHERD	1 Peter 5:4
CHOSEN ONE	Isaiah 42:1
CHRIST	Matthew 22:42
CHRIST OF GOD	Luke 2:11
CHRIST, THE SON OF THE LIVING GOD	Matthew 16:16
COMFORTER	John 14:26
COMMANDER	Isaiah 55:4
CONSOLATION OF ISRAEL	Luke 2:25
CONSUMING FIRE	Deut. 4:24,
	Heb. 12:29
CORNERSTONE	Isaiah 28:16
COUNSELOR	Isaiah 9:6
CREATOR	1 Peter 4:19
DELIVERER	Romans 11:26
DESIRED OF ALL NATIONS	Haggai 2:7
DOOR	John 10:7
END	Revelation 21:6
ETERNAL GOD	Deut. 33:27
EVERLASTING FATHER	Isaiah 9:6
FAITHFUL AND TRUE	Revelation 19:11
FAITHFUL WITNESS	Revelation 1:5
FATHER	Matthew 6:9
FIRSTBORN	Rom.8:29,
	Rev.1:5,
	Col.1:15
FIRSTFRUITS	1 Cor.15:20-23

FOUNDATION	1 Cor. 3:11
FRIEND OF TAX COLLECTORS	Matthew 11:19
GENTLE WHISPER	1 Kings 19:12
GIFT OF GOD	John 4:10
GLORY OF THE LORD	Isaiah 40:5
GOD	Genesis 1:1
GOD ALMIGHTY	Genesis 17:1
GOD OVER ALL	Romans 9:5
GOD WHO SEES ME	Genesis 16:13
GOOD SHEPHERD	John 10:11
GREAT HIGH PRIEST	Hebrews 4:14
GREAT SHEPHERD	Hebrews 13:20
GUIDE	Psalm 48:14
HEAD OF THE BODY	Colossians 1:18
HEAD OF THE CHURCH	Ephesians 5:23
HEIR OF ALL THINGS	Hebrews 1:2
HIGH PRIEST	Hebrews 3:1
HIGH PRIEST FOREVER	Hebrews 6:20
HOLY ONE	Acts 2:27
HOLY ONE OF ISRAEL	Isaiah 49:7
HOLY SPIRIT	John 15:26
HOPE	Titus 2:13
HORN OF SALVATION	Luke 1:69
I AM	Exodus 3:14, John 8:58
IMAGE OF GOD	2 Cor. 4:4
IMAGE OF HIS PERSON	Hebrews 1:3
IMMANUEL	Isaiah 7:14
JEALOUS	Exodus 34:14
JEHOVAH	Psalm 83:18
JESUS	Matthew 1:21
JESUS CHRIST OUR LORD	Romans 6:23
JUDGE	Isaiah 33:22, Acts 10:42
KING	Zechariah 9:9
KING ETERNAL	1 Timothy 1:17
KING OF KINGS	1 Timothy 6:15
KING OF THE AGES	Revelation 15:3

LAMB OF GOD	John 1:29
LAST ADAM	1 Cor. 15:45
LAWGIVER	Isaiah 33:22
LEADER	Isaiah 55:4
LIFE	John 14:6
LIGHT OF THE WORLD	John 8:12
LIKE AN EAGLE	Deut. 32:11
LILY OF THE VALLEYS	Song of Solomon 2:1
LION OF THE TRIBE OF JUDAH	Revelation 5:5
LIVING STONE	1 Peter 2:4
LIVING WATER	John 4:10
LORD	John 13:13
LORD GOD ALMIGHTY	Revelation 15:3
LORD JESUS CHRIST	1 Cor. 15:57
LORD OF ALL	Acts 10:36
LORD OF GLORY	1 Cor. 2:8
LORD OF HOSTS	Haggai 1:5
LORD OF LORDS	1 Tim. 6:15
LORD OUR RIGHTEOUSNESS	Jeremiah 23:6
LOVE	1 John 4:8
MAN OF SORROWS	Isaiah 53:3
MASTER	Luke 5:5
MEDIATOR	1 Timothy 2:5
MERCIFUL GOD	Jeremiah 3:12
MESSENGER OF THE COVENANT	Malachi 3:1
MESSIAH	John 4:25
MIGHTY GOD	Isaiah 9:6
MIGHTY ONE	Isaiah 60:16
NAZARENE	Matthew 2:23
OFFSPRING OF DAVID	Revelation 22:16
OMEGA	Revelation 22:13
ONLY BEGOTTEN SON	John 1:18
OUR PASSOVER LAMB	1 Cor. 5:7
OUR PEACE	Ephesians 2:14
POTTER	Isaiah 64:8
POWER OF GOD	1 Cor. 1:24
PRINCE OF PEACE	Isaiah 9:6
PROPHET	Acts 3:22

PURIFIER	Malachi 3:3
RABBONI (TEACHER)	John 20:16
RADIANCE OF GOD'S GLORY	Heb.1:3
REDEEMER	Job 19:25
REFINER'S FIRE	Malachi 3:2
RESURRECTION	John 11:25
RIGHTEOUS ONE	1 John 2:1
ROCK	1 Cor.10:4
ROOT OF DAVID	Rev. 22:16
ROSE OF SHARON	Song 2:1
RULER OF GOD'S CREATION	Rev. 3:14
RULER OVER KINGS OF EARTH	Rev 1:5
RULER OVER ISRAEL	Micah 5:2
SAVIOR	Luke 2:11
SCEPTER OUT OF ISRAEL	Numbers 24:17
SEED	Genesis 3:15
SERVANT	Isaiah 42:1
SHEPHERD OF OUR SOULS	1Peter 2:25
SHIELD	Genesis 15:1
SON OF DAVID	Matthew 1:1
SON OF GOD	Matthew 27:54
SON OF MAN	Matthew 8:20
SON OF THE MOST HIGH	Luke 1:32
SOURCE	Hebrews 5:9
SPIRIT OF GOD	Genesis 1:2
STAR OUT OF JACOB	Numbers 24:17
STONE	1 Peter 2:8
STRONG TOWER	Proverbs 18:10
SUN OF RIGHTEOUSNESS	Malachi 4:2
TEACHER	John 13:13
TRUE LIGHT	John 1:9
TRUE WITNESS	Revelation 3:14
TRUTH	John 14:6
VINE	John 15:5
WAY	John 14:6
WISDOM OF GOD	1 Cor. 1:24
WITNESS	Isaiah 55:4
WONDERFUL	Isaiah 9:6

WORD
WORD OF GOD

John 1:1
Revelation 19:13

Book Of Mormon Names For God Or Christ

According to Book of Mormon scholar Susan Easton Black (Parry 171), The Book of Mormon has 101 epithets for Christ. This list includes:

NAME	APPEARS
Redeemer of Israel	1 time
Son of the living God	1 time
Lord God Omnipotent	1 time
True Messiah	2 times
Great Creator	2 times
Stone	2 times
Lamb of God	10 or more times
Lord Jesus Christ	10 or more times
Holy One of Israel	10 or more times
God	100 or more times
Jesus	100 or more times
Lord	100 or more times
Lord God	100 or more times
Christ	100 or more times

Black provides further evidence for the book's testimony:

…on average, a name or title of Christ appears once every 1.7 verses. The frequent occurrence and variety of deific names and titles in The Book of Mormon distinguish the book from religious works created in the nineteenth century and place it squarely within the tradition of ancient religious text. (Parry 172)

Plural Amplifications

This is a literary device in which more contemporary English authors would have used a singular noun, but the ancient Hebrew writers used a plural noun. In the King James Version, the plural nouns are translated back into singular ones. Here are some examples from Parry's list (173):

Genesis 4:10:

And He [the Lord] *said, What hast thou done? the voice of thy brother's blood crieth unto me from the ground.* (173) (Emphasis added)

In this verse, the original *bloods* from the Hebrew text was translated as <u>blood</u> to make it conform to English norms.

Isaiah 33:6:

And wisdom and knowledge shall be the stability of thy times, and strength of <u>salvation</u>: the fear of the LORD is His treasure. (173) (Emphasis added)

Here, *salvations* was translated as *salvation*.

Psalm 94:1:

Oh LORD God, to whom <u>vengeance</u> belongeth; O God, to whom <u>vengeance</u> belongeth, shew thyself. (173) (Emphasis added)

Once again, in this verse, *vengeances* from the Hebrew text was translated as *vengeance*. The Book of Mormon also uses plural amplification, but Joseph Smith translated the words correctly using the plural form Look at the following Book of Mormon examples from Parry (173):

2 Nephi 1:25 RCE, 2 Nephi 1:12 LDS:

Yea, as one generation passeth to another, there shall be <u>bloodsheds</u> and great visitations among them. (173) (Emphasis added)

Jacob 3:8 RCE, Jacob 4:7 LDS:

Nevertheless, the Lord God showeth us our weakness, that we may know that it is by His Grace and His great <u>condescensions</u> unto the children of men that we have power to do these things. (173) (Emphasis added)

Jacob 3:140 RCE, Jacob 5:72 LDS:

And it came to pass that the servants did go to it and labor with their <u>mights</u>, And the Lord of the vineyard labored also with them, And they did obey the commandments of the Lord of the vineyard in all things;... (173) (Emphasis added)

Mosiah 5:85 RCE, Mosiah 8:20 LDS:

Yea, and how blind and impenetrable are the <u>understandings</u> of the children of men! (173) (Emphasis added)

Because this is an important evidence showing that Joseph Smith did not plagiarize from the Bible, here are six additional quotations: 1 Nephi 3:99 RCE, 1 Nephi 12:2 LDS (slaughters); Mormon 1:20 RCE, Mormon 1:19 LDS (magics); Alma 12:196 RCE, Alma 20:13 LDS (lyings); 1 Nephi 4:6 RCE, 1 Nephi 15:5 LDS (afflictions); 1 Nephi 1:39 RCE, 1 Nephi 2:11 LDS (imaginations) (173).

Again, if Joseph Smith were copying from the Bible, he probably would have made the same "corrections" that the King James translators made. But *he did not make those mistakes.* This provides an additional evidence that he was translating from an original Hebrew text.

Repetition Of The

Parry continues. He indicates that scribes writing in Hebrew, unlike English, repeat the definite article *the* for every noun in a sentence. For example, we would say, "We did observe to keep *the* judgments, statutes, and commandments of the Lord" while Parry says that Hebrew writers would write (176):

2 Nephi 4:14 RCE, 2 Nephi 5:10 LDS:

And we did observe to keep <u>the</u> judgments and <u>the</u> statutes and <u>the</u> commandments of the Lord in all things, according to the law of Moses. (176) (Emphasis added)

Frequent Use Of And

Many times Hebrew writers repeat the word *and*. In *Echoes and Evidences of The Book of Mormon*, Parry (177) gives these two biblical examples:

1 Samuel 17:34-35:

*<u>And</u> David said unto Saul, Thy servant kept his father's sheep, <u>and</u> there came a lion, <u>and</u> a bear, <u>and</u> took a lamb out of the flock: <u>And</u> I went out after him, <u>and</u> smote him, <u>and</u> delivered it out of his mouth: <u>and</u> when he arose against me, I caught him by his beard, <u>and</u> smote him, <u>and</u> slew him. (177) (*Emphasis added)

Joshua 7:24:

<u>And</u> Joshua, <u>and</u> all of Israel with him, took Achan the son of Zerah, <u>and</u> the silver, <u>and</u> the garment, <u>and</u> the wedge of gold, <u>and</u> his sons, <u>and</u> his daughters, <u>and</u> his oxen, <u>and</u> his asses, <u>and</u> his sheep, <u>and</u> his tent, <u>and</u> all that he had: <u>and</u> they brought them unto the valley of Achor. (178) (Emphasis added)

In The Book of Mormon, I found this quote that uses the repetition of and:

1 Nephi 3:70-87 RCE, 1 Nephi 11:26-33 LDS:

<u>And</u> the angel said unto me again: "Look <u>and</u> behold the Condescension of God!" <u>And</u> I looked <u>and</u> beheld the Redeemer of the world of which my father had spoken; <u>And</u> I also beheld the prophet which should prepare the way before Him; <u>And</u> the Lamb of God went forth and was baptized

of him; And after that He was baptized, I beheld the heavens open and the Holy Ghost come down out of heaven and abode upon Him in the form of a dove; And I beheld that He went forth ministering unto the people in power and great glory; And the multitudes were gathered together to hear Him; And I beheld that they cast Him out from among them; And I also beheld twelve others following Him; And it came to pass that they were carried away in the Spirit from before my face, that I saw them not. And it came to pass that the angel spake unto me, saying: "Look!" And I looked and I beheld the heavens open again; And I saw angels descending upon the children of men, And they did minister unto them. And he spake unto me again, saying: "Look!" And I looked and I beheld the Lamb of God going forth among the children of men; And I beheld multitudes of people which were sick and which were afflicted of all manner of diseases and with devils and unclean spirits; And the angel spake and showed all these things unto me; And they were healed by the power of the Lamb of God, And the devils and the unclean spirits were cast out. And it came to pass that the angel spake unto me again, saying: "Look!" And I looked and beheld the Lamb of God, that He was taken by the people, Yea, the Everlasting God was judged of the world; And I saw and bear record; And I, Nephi, saw that He was lifted up upon the cross and slain for the sins of the world;... (Emphasis added)

There are thirty-seven instances of the use of the word *and* in the above quote. This frequent usage of *and* appears throughout The Book of Mormon. If Joseph Smith had written the book he would have used *and* like we do, not like the Hebrew authors.

Cognate Accusative

This is the use of a verb form with a related noun. Biblical examples would be (Parry 176-177):

Genesis 37:5:

And Joseph dreamed a dream, and he told it his brethren: and they hated him yet the more. (176) (Emphasis added)

This is written in contrast to "Joseph had a dream."

Isaiah 35:2:

It shall blossom abundantly, and rejoice even with joy and singing: The glory of Lebanon shall be given unto it,... (177) (Emphasis added)

The above Hebrew phrase would be written in English as follows: "It shall blossom abundantly and there shall be **great joy** and singing."

The Book of Mormon also contains such cognate accusative writings:

1 Nephi 1:57 RCE, 1 Nephi 2:23 LDS:

For behold, in that day that they shall rebel against Me, I will <u>curse them even with a sore curse</u>,... (177) (Emphasis added)

We would say, "I will severely curse them."

1 Nephi 1:60 RCE, 1 Nephi 3:2 LDS:

And it came to pass that he spake unto me, saying: "Behold, I have <u>dreamed a dream</u> in the which the Lord hath commanded me that thou and thy brethren shall return to Jerusalem,..." (177) (Emphasis added)

In English we would probably say, "I have had a dream," or "I have had a vision." I found the following example:

Mosiah 5:20 RCE, Mosiah 7:415 LDS:

For behold, we are in bondage to the Lamanites and are <u>taxed with a tax</u> which is grievous to be borne. (Emphasis added)

In English we would probably say, "We have been heavily taxed." There are a great many more instances; see how many you can find.

Possessive Pronouns

In Hebrew these are repeated frequently, e.g., their, our, your, thy, his and her. The following biblical examples are taken from Parry (179):

Exodus 10:9:

And Moses said, We will go with <u>our</u> young and with <u>our</u> old, with <u>our</u> sons and with <u>our</u> daughters, with <u>our</u> flocks and with <u>our</u> herds will we go; for we must hold a feast unto the LORD. (179) (Emphasis added)

The word *our* is used six times in that verse. This is a convention uncommon in English. Other examples include:

Deuteronomy 26:7:

And when we cried unto the LORD God of <u>our</u> fathers, the LORD heard <u>our</u> voice, and looked on <u>our</u> affliction, and our labor, and our oppression:... (179) (Emphasis added)

The word *our* is used five times in this one sentence.

Exodus 12:11:

And thus shall ye eat it; with <u>your</u> loins girded, <u>your</u> shoes on <u>your</u> feet, and <u>your</u> staff in <u>your</u> hand; and ye shall eat it in haste: it is the LORD's Passover. (179) (Emphasis added)

Here, the word your is used five times. Many examples of the same usage appear in The Book of Mormon. For instance, in the following verses your is used twelve times, and and is used fourteen times:

3 Nephi 14:2-3 RCE, 3 Nephi 30:2 LDS:

Turn, all ye Gentiles, from <u>your</u> wicked ways! <u>And</u> repent of <u>your</u> evil doings— of <u>your</u> lyings <u>and</u> deceivings, <u>and your</u> whoredoms, <u>and of your</u> secret abominations, <u>and your</u> Idolatries, <u>and of your</u> murders, <u>and your</u> priestcrafts, and your envyings, and your strifes, and from all your wickedness and abominations— <u>And</u> come unto Me <u>and</u> be baptized in My name! That ye may receive a remission of <u>your</u> sins and be filled with the Holy Ghost, That ye may be numbered with My people which are of the house of Israel. (179) (Emphasis added)

In the following, *their* is used eight times:

Mosiah 7:6 RCE, Mosiah 11:3 LDS:

And he laid a tax of one fifth part of all they possessed: A fifth part of <u>their</u> gold and of <u>their</u> silver, And a fifth part of <u>their</u> ziff and of <u>their</u> copper and of <u>their</u> brass and of <u>their</u> iron, And a fifth part of <u>their</u> fatlings, And also a fifth part of all their grain;... (180) (Emphasis added)

There are, of course, many other places in the Bible and The Book of Mormon that use the possessive pronoun repetition.

Emphatic Pronouns

Emphatic pronouns are another distinction between the Hebrew way of writing and the English way. The following biblical examples were taken from Parry (180):

Genesis 6:17:

And behold, <u>I, even</u> I, do bring a flood of waters upon the earth, to destroy all flesh,... (Emphasis added)

Genesis 27:38:

And Esau said unto his father, Hast thou but one blessing, my father? <u>bless me, even me</u> also, Oh my father. And Esau lifted up his voice, and wept. (Emphasis added)

There are many such instances in The Book of Mormon. Here is one:

Mosiah 1:62 RCE, Mosiah 2:26 LDS

> And <u>*I, even*</u> *I whom ye call your king, am no better than ye yourselves are, for I am also of the dust.* (Emphasis added)

This ends our brief discussion about Hebrew linguistics. Obviously, Joseph Smith did not have the knowledge or resources to write a book that included any such array of Hebrew literary devices. These stylistics features provide solid evidence that he had to have translated The Book of Mormon from an ancient Hebrew text, as he claimed.

CHAPTER 11

WHAT ARE SOME RECENT HISTORIC, SCIENTIFIC AND ARCHEOLOGICAL DISCOVERIES THAT CONFIRM THE BOOK OF MORMON?

Historical Evidence

In a broad historical sense, it is true that many things related to The Book of Mormon were simply unknown in 1830. Consequently, we can agree with John Clark that *"what Joseph Smith knew and understood about the book ought to be research questions rather than presumptions* (84)." Thanks in large part to his critics, it has become increasingly clear that, as Clark says, *"Joseph Smith did not fully understand the geography, scope, historical scale, literary form, or cultural content of the book"* (85). We know that Joseph Smith had no access to large libraries or other specialized sources of information in Palmyra before 1830; however, in the July 15 Times and Seasons of 1842, twelve years after the publication of The Book of Mormon, he tells us about his orientation to those ancient peoples:

> *I was also informed concerning the aboriginal inhabitants of this country* [America] *and shown who they were, and from whence they came; a brief sketch of their origin, progress, civilization, laws, governments, of their righteousness and iniquity, and the blessings of God being finally withdrawn from them as a people was [also] made known unto me.* (860)

Later that same year (1842), in one of his articles on The Book of Mormon, while he was still editor of the *Times and Seasons*, he declared:

> *If men, in their research into the history of this country, would notice the mounds, fortifications, statues, architecture, implements of war, of husbandry, and ornaments of silver, brass,--were to examine The Book of Mormon, their conjectures would be removed, and their opinions altered; uncertainty and doubt would be changed into certainty and facts; and they would find that those things that they are anxiously prying into were matters of history, unfolded in that book. They would find their conjectures were more than realized--that a great and a mighty people*

had inhabited this continent and that, arts, sciences and religion, had prevailed to a very great extent. There were cities on this continent as great as on the continent of Asia. Babylon, Nineveh, nor any of the ruins of the Levant could boast of more perfect sculpture, better architectural designs, and more imperishable ruins, than what are found on this continent. Stephens and Catherwood's research in Central America abundantly testifies of this. There are stupendous ruins, elegant sculptures as well as magnificent ruins in Guatemala, and other countries. These corroborate the above statement, and provide evidence that a great and mighty people,--men with great minds, high intellect, bright genius, and comprehensive building designs, inhabited this continent. Their ruins speak of their greatness, and The Book of Mormon tells us their story.
(Smith 862)

By way of anecdote, Lucy Mack Smith, from her book The History of Joseph Smith offered this comment about her son:

In the course of our evening conversations, Joseph gave us some of the most amusing recitals which could be imagined. He would describe the ancient inhabitants of this continent, their dress, their manner of traveling, the animals which they rode, the cities that they built, and the structure of their buildings with every particular, their mode of warfare, and their religious worship as specifically as though he had spent his life with them. (31)

Since there is no mention of a specific geographical location in her description, it would seem that that was not one of those things revealed to the Prophet.

To point out the historical data concerning Joseph Smith's time and circumstances:

1. Joseph Smith became aware of Stephens and Catherwood's discoveries in Central America in 1841, eleven years after The Book of Mormon was published.
2. He and his close associates were very interested in those discoveries and felt that they were important and should be broadcast. In his view, they corresponded with and supported The Book of Mormon.
3. Joseph Smith was the editor of the *Times & Seasons* from about February 15 to October 15, 1842. The press was destroyed by a mob in 1843, and he was killed in 1844.
4. Between March and October, 1842, the only men said to be working in the printing office were Joseph Smith, John Taylor and Wilford Woodruff.
5. Five articles about The Book of Mormon endorsing the discoveries of Stephens and Catherwood were published while Joseph Smith was editor.

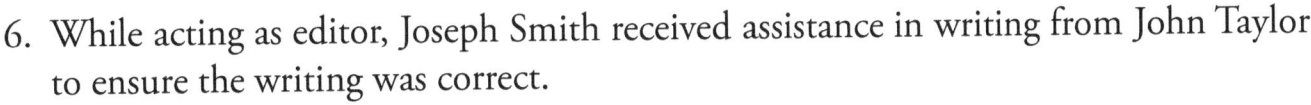

6. While acting as editor, Joseph Smith received assistance in writing from John Taylor to ensure the writing was correct.

Scientific Evidence

For lack of space, we cannot explore all the scientific resources possible. Let's just look at three: DNA, Hebrew Epigraphy and Carbon-14 dating as they relate to The Book of Mormon. Rupe states:

> **Although these types of discoveries are stunning,** [they do] **not "prove" the Book of Mormon is true.** [They do]**, however, demonstrate that the basic story of the Book of Mormon—that Jewish immigrants came to the New World—is perfectly plausible.** (78)

DNA And The Book Of Mormon

In his book *The Book of Mormon An Inconvenient Truth*, author Richard E. Rupe refers to Joseph Smith as a "practically illiterate youth" (69), which agrees with the statements made by numerous other references.

Rupe dedicates a chapter to the subject of DNA. In discussing the ramifications of DNA in connection with The Book of Mormon, Rupe first introduces the reader to a detractor, Simon Southerton, who claimed that The Book of Mormon is false because the DNA of the American Indians studied showed an Asian, not a Middle Eastern, ancestry (69-70). Rupe says that although Southerton ignored many of the facts available and refuted The Book of Mormon's authenticity, he did explain why there could have been no evidence:

> **In 600 B.C. there were probably several million American Indians living in the Americas. If a small group of Israelites, say less than thirty, entered such a massive population, it would be very hard to detect their genes today.** (71)

Southerton also forgot to mention that The Book of Mormon chronicled the Jaredite civilization that arrived in the Americas around 3000 B.C. This group came from the Great Tower (Ether 1:5 RCE, Ether 1:5 LDS) and traveled north and presumably east, staying in various places as they crossed the continent of Asia. They were directed by God *"...into a quarter where there never had man been"* (Ether 1:26 RCE Ether 2:5 LDS). In other words, they were the first to inhabit the area since the end of the Ice Age. I believe that some people probably decided not to continue the journey, and their descendants would make up part of the Asian population of today, so an Asian DNA connection actually provides more evidence for the validity of The Book of Mormon, not the other way around. (74)

Then Rupe introduces the reader to the Central Band of Cherokee. This is such an interesting case that he has allowed me to quote it in its entirety:

> *Perhaps having the potential to directly affect the DNA discussion above, I recently came across an item of interest concerning two Cherokee Indian groups in Lawrence County, Tennessee. Their story is a fascinating one. The information below is a small tribal information excerpt from their web site:*

> *There are two main settlements in Lawrence County, TN that were here before "The Trail of Tears." There was no gold known in this area, thus the U.S. Army did not bother to round us up for the "Death March" to Oklahoma.*

> *The Penningtons (Wind Clan) were the first legal settlers in Lawrence County with land grants. These decedents of Chief Tuttle and "Poker Hunter" set roots in Heneryville [sic], TN pronounced (Hen-er-vull) and still reside and prosper in the area.*

> *The other Main Group are decedents of Chief Van Glass and his tribe that fled Muscle Shoals, AL to Steadman Ridge in Lawrence County. The U.S. Army based in Nashville, TN went through the Blue Water Area to kill all of the Cherokee at Muscle Shoals. The Cherokee did an excellent flanking movement to save all of the children, women and elderly.*

> *As a result, many other Cherokee friends and family found Lawrence County to be a good place to live and raise their families. The Cherokee have been in Lawrence County, TN for over 200 years. (72)*

Rupe continues:

> *On their web site, I read this from their press release concerning how the Cherokee first realized, through DNA testing, their Jewish heritage: (72)*

> *During the Cherokee Snowy Moon, Dec 11ᵗʰ, we received a phone call from our Little Sister, Maryland Two Moons Rising Childress from Lynchburg, VA. She had been helping a friend with his DNA test results, and noticed an obscure work printed several times on his Haplogroup, the word Ashkenazi.*

I quote from Rupe's footnote:

(The name Ashkenazi was applied in the Middle Ages to Jews living along the Rhine River in northern France and Western Germany. The center of Ashkenazi Jews later spread to Poland-Lithuania and now there are Ashkenazi settlements all over the world. The term 'Ashkenazi' became identified primarily with German customs and descendants of German Jews. Quoted from Shira Schoenberg, February 10, 2008 (72). See http://www.jewish virtuallibrary.org/jsource/Judaism/ Ashkenazim. html/

She [Childress] did not understand the word but looked it up, and found it to be a scientific DNA term used for the race of Jew. She immediately had Chief Joe Sitting Owl White with her discovery [sic].

After the phone conversation we started pulling DNA files we had in various places that contained DNA results from Family Tree DNA. All our DNA Results proved that the Cherokee are Ashkenazi Jews. After making several phone conversations, and email contacts <u>All other tested Cherokee proved to be Ashkenazi Jew, and the Chief had two hits as</u> <u>Levite</u>. All this information has been sitting in front of our nose for over three years and we did not understand it. (72) (Emphasis added)

Rupe concludes:

The Ashkenazi Jew Test Results, scientifically proves James Adair's, 1775 research of the Cherokee Culture, and his "23 Arguments as to why the Cherokee are Hebrew," and a "Lost tribe of Israel", published in London under the title of "A History of the American Indian". (73)

To offer furtheAr support, Rupe went directly to the Cherokee website, the "**Announcements**" section, which has been moved to<http://www.cbcherokee.org>.

O'SIYO BROTHERS, AND SISTERS,
THE CHEROKEE OF LAWRENCE COUNTY, TN IS PLEASED TO ANNOUNCE THAT WE HAVE SCIENTIFICALLY, WITH DNA, PROVEN THAT THE CHEROKEE ARE HEBREW (JEWS).
THIS IS THE ONLY WAY WE COULDPROVE THE HISTORICAL CULTURE OF THE CHEROKEE.
CURRENTLY WE ARE LOOKING AT 141 POSITIVE FOR ASHKENAZI JEW, AND 0 NEGATIVE.

GAY GEY YOU E,
JOE SITTING OWL

WHITE
PRINCIPLE
CHIEF CHEROKEE OF LAWRENCE
COUNTY, TN

After reading the above with great interest, I [Rupe] sent an email to the group as follows:

> *Hello June,*
>
> *My name is Richard Rupe. I read with interest the email about the Cherokee not having haplogroups of A,B,C or D. The email mentioned something about the remainder of the results being available by August of 2007. Do you have any new update about this? If so, I would sure appreciate knowing what you have found.*
>
> *A question I have is whether you are associated with LDS church or not. That is not a bad thing but it would be good to know.*
>
> *Thanks,*
> *Richard Rupe*

The following is my reply from the chief:

> *O'Siyo Richard,*
> *June is out of pocket for a few weeks, so I am answering your email.*
> *The Central Band of Cherokee have all denominations represented in the Tribe, including LDS.*
> *The results of the most recent DNA Group Test is that the Cherokee do not have A, B, C, or D, confirming the first test on the mtDNA side of the test. We have not received the Y-12 test results.*
> *Wado for your interest.*
>
> *Sitting Owl*(73)

This is great news for Book of Mormon believers because we now have very strong evidence that some Israelites came to the Americas just as claimed by The Book of Mormon. As a point of clarification: calling those of German descent "Jews" or "Ashkenazi Jew" is a misnomer. They are not, in fact, from the House of Judah, but rather from the Ten Lost Tribes. Therefore, Cherokee Indians are also from the House of Israel, which is part of the Twelve Tribes of Israel and the Ten Lost Tribes of Israel, but not the House of Judah [Jews]. That means they should be called Israelites, not Jews.

Hebrew Epigraphy

The following is controversial and there are educated people on both sides of the argument. I choose to accept these as factual, you decide for yourself.

Rupe next informs us about the Bat Creek Stone found in Eastern Tennessee by the Smithsonian's Mound Survey project, originally excavated in 1889, and the Los Lunas Decalogue found in Los Lunas, New Mexico. Rupe states:

> **The late Semitic languages scholar Cyrus Gordon (1971) confirmed that it** [the Bat Creek Stone] **is Semitic, and specifically Paleo-Hebrew of approximately first or second century A. D. According to him, the five letters...read, from right to left, LYHWD, or "for Judea." He noted that the broken letter on the far left is consistent with mem, in which case this word would instead read LYHWD[M], or "for the Judeans." (75)**

קץ ליהוד

He then educates us about the Los Lunas Decalogue stone found in New Mexico. On this carved stone is a copy of the Ten Commandments written in a modified form of Hebrew used in about 600 B.C.

Los Lunas Decalogue   Translation of stone

The modern-day English translation follows:

I am Jehovah your God who has taken you out of the land of Egypt, from the house of slaves. There must be no other gods before My face. You must not make any idol. You must not take the name of Jehovah in vain. Remember the sabbath day and keep it holy. Honour your father and your mother so that your days may be long in the land that Jehovah your God has given you. You must not murder. You must not commit adultery. You must not steal. You must not give false witness against your neighbor. You must not desire the wife of your neighbor nor anything that is his. (76)

This is one more proof that some of the people of Israel came to America. For verification of the Decalogue's authenticity, Rupe sent an email to Douglas R. Jones, founder of the Epigraphic Society of New Mexico. Here is his reply:

Dear Mr. Rupe,

Having researched Hidden Mountain for the past 20 years, as it is close to where I live, I am confident that the inscription is very authentic.

It is actually not Hebrew, but Paleo Hebraic. This is a language that latter [sic] the Hebrews and Greeks along with the Etruscans used as the basic foundation for their languages. Based on the form and structure of the inscription, and the word forms used there is no doubt of its ancient origins.

Along with other facts, not only including astrological data that support the time frame for this inscription. [sic] I, as the founder of the Epigraphic Society of New Mexico have spent all my life examining <u>many</u> <u>sites here where there are other such inscriptions</u>. We do not publish the majority of them. The fragile nature, and the unfortunate nature of people to disturb them always leads us to document them respecting the current land owners rights, the value to latter generations, and above all, the protection of these sites. We reveal our information, when deemed appropriate, to specific agencies for the protection of all artifacts found, and their inclusion into preservation programs. (Emphasis added)

Sincerely,
Douglas R. Jones
The Epigraphic Society of New Mexico (77-78)

This is most interesting: he states that there exist many such sites just like the Los Lunas Decalogue! And he gives a very strong statement about its authenticity.

Carbon-14 Dating

In considering Carbon-14 dating, I refer you to "How Accurate Are Carbon-14 and Other Radioactive Dating Methods?" (www.christiananswers.net) and also "Implications of Radiocarbon Dating for the Credibility of The Book of Mormon and the Validity of Book of Mormon Geography Models," by Ted D. Stoddard. These explain that radiocarbon measurements have long been relied upon for a precise way of dating fossils and other materials. However, the measurements are based upon a faulty premise that the levels and ratios of Carbon-14 to Carbon-12 are consistent. This just isn't so. The amount of cosmic rays in our atmosphere, the activity of the sun, and the magnetism of the earth and our solar system impact the Carbon-14 levels. The overall result is that there is more Carbon-14 being produced today than there was a long time ago. Without considering this change, scientists are dating objects as being older than they actually are. The writer of the following article continues under the heading "Other factors affecting Carbon dating," and briefs us:

> **Also, the Genesis flood would have greatly upset the Carbon balance. The flood buried a huge amount of Carbon, which became coal, oil, etc., thus lowering the total 12C in the biosphere (including the atmosphere—plants re-growing after the flood absorbed CO2, which was not replaced by the decay of the buried vegetation). Total 14C is also proportionately lowered at this time, but whereas no terrestrial process generates any more 12C,**

14C is continually being produced, and at a rate which does not depend on Carbon levels (it comes from nitrogen). Therefore, the 14C/12C ratio in plants/animals/the atmosphere before the flood had to be lower than what it is now. (christiananswers)

The author continues:

Unless this effect (which is additional to the magnetic field issue just discussed) were corrected for, Carbon dating of fossils formed in the flood would give ages much older than the true ages. ...Also, volcanoes emit much CO_2 depleted in Carbon-14. (christiananswers)

The results of these problems and inaccuracies with respect to The Book of Mormon are that they open the door to discrepancies in dating. Thus, the reliability of Carbon dating has to be taken in context with other scientific methods.

Archeology

When we look at the archeological record, we find some interesting leads. Let's look at just one case as an example. In David Palmer's book In *Search of Cumorah* (printed with permission), He reports that:

The knowledge of [this] use of cement in Mesoamerica has not been around for [that] many decades. In 1929, Heber J. Grant, a former president of The Church of Jesus Christ of Latter-day Saints, made the following statement in general conference:

"...I have often said, and desire to repeat here that when I was a young unmarried man, another young man who had received a doctor's degree ridiculed me for believing in The Book of Mormon. He said he could point out two lies in that book. One was that the people had built their homes out of cement and that they were very skillful in the use of cement. He said there had never been found and never would be found a house built of cement by the ancient inhabitants of this country, because the people in that early age knew nothing about cement. He said that should be enough to make one disbelieve the book. I said: That does not affect my faith one particle. I read The Book of Mormon prayerfully and supplicated God for a testimony in my heart and soul of the divinity of it, and I have accepted it and believe it with all my heart." I also said to him, "If my children do not find cement houses, I expect that my grandchildren will." He said, "Well,

what is the good of talking with a fool like that? (April 1929 Conference Reports, p128ff)" (121-122)

Teotihuacan ancient cement

Helaman tells us about cement use by those who traveled into the northern areas:

Helaman 2:7 RCE, Helaman 3:7 LDS:

And there being but little timber upon the face of the land, Nevertheless, the people which went forth became exceeding expert in the working of cement; Therefore, they did build houses of cement in which they did dwell.

Palmer continues:

...the use of cement and concrete spread throughout Mesoamerica in a time span from at least as early as 100 B.C. through A.D. 400. The tourist sees it in great abundance at Teotihuacan [near Mexico City]. At Kaminaljuyu [Guatemala City] the concrete mix was similar. Tiny pieces of volcanic stone, 0.5 to 2 millimeters in diameter were mixed with clay and

lime. After drying, a very smooth and durable surface is formed. An early manifestation of the use of cement is at Chiapa DeCorzo [Chiapas], where it was used to surface the temple known as Mound 1. This can also be seen at Monte Alban [Oaxaca]. (1)

John (Jack) Welch has written that when asked where Book of Mormon lands are, his answer is that it has to be a place where there is evidence of expert workmanship in cement structures. This would identify the Nephite lands. (2)

The documentation of use of cement in Mesoamerica is now so overwhelming and obvious that President Grant's statement stands out as prophecy now fulfilled. (2).

Agriculture

Linda Schele, lecturing at Malone College in Ohio in the spring of 1988, stated that until the 1990s, archeologists believed that the ancient Central Americans used the slash-and-burn method to provide food for their communities. This would mean the Book of Mormon was false because that system could not have supported the large populations that the book described. More recently, it was discovered that the Maya had diverse and sophisticated methods of food production. It was formerly believed that shifting cultivation (swidden) agriculture provided most of their food, but it is now thought that permanent raised fields, terracing, forest gardens, managed fallows, and wild harvesting were also crucial to supporting the large populations of the Clasic period in some areas. Roy Weldon also informs us that:

The Book of Mormon gives numerous instances of proficiency in cultivation of all kinds of agriculture products. (Mosiah 4:9, RCE, Mosiah 6:7 LDS; Enos 1:34 RCE, Enos 1:21 LDS) (92)

[Although not in Central America], Archaeologists have found that to reclaim a single acre of mountainside land in Peru involved the laying of approximately seven hundred perches of stone and the transportation of nearly five thousand tons of soil. The staircase farms built by pre- historic man in Peru involved the moving of millions of tons of earth and the cutting and transportation of millions of perches of stone. (92)

This would mean that they could have, indeed, supported millions. Today, in Central and South America, after this discovery, some people are returning to these more productive ways of producing food.

Time Periods

As pointed out earlier, three groups came to the Americas. The Jaredites came from the Great Tower and were the earliest Book of Mormon settlers. These people crossed Asia and eventually arrived at the ocean where they built barges and crossed the Pacific. It is believed that they arrived in the Americas sometime between 3114 and 3000 B.C. This date coincides with the Popol Vuh creation date, or you could say, the beginning of their civilization. According to archeologists, the earliest pottery discovered in Mesoamerica, at Puerto Marques, dates to around 2900 B.C. Without regard to The Book of Mormon, archeologists recognize that the Olmec civilization started and ended in the same time frame as the Jaredites (3114 B.C. to 200 B.C.) and in the same location. (Heater, centerfold) The second group that The Book of Mormon tells us about is Lehi and his family that left Jerusalem around 600 B. C.:

I Nephi 3:4 RCE, I Nephi 10:4 LDS:

Yea, even six hundred years from the time that my father left Jerusalem, a Prophet would the Lord God raise up among the Jews, Yea, even a Messiah, or in other words, a Savior of the World.

The book also reports that the third group was led away from Jerusalem about 586 B.C. Omni gives us the details:

Omni 1:26-27 RCE, Omni 1:15-16 LDS:

Behold, it came to pass that Mosiah discovered that the people of Zarahemla came out from Jerusalem at the time that Zedekiah, king of Judah, was carried away captive into Babylon; And they journeyed in the wilderness and were brought by the hand of the Lord across the Great Waters into the land where Mosiah discovered them; And they had dwelt there from that time forth;

Crossing the Atlantic Ocean, these people arrived about the same time as the Nephites, but landed on the *eastern* side of Central America.

Based on Carbon-14 dating, archeologists also tell us that civilizations began to appear in the Guatemala highlands on the Pacific side and also in the lowlands on the Gulf coast around 600 B.C. (Because of difficulties with Carbon-14 dating, those dates could be off as much as fifty years. This means that these groups could have arrived as late as 550 B.C. This would allow sufficient time for both to travel to Central America.) We are also told by archeologists that around that same year, Mayan cities first appeared and that there is documentation of a population explosion then (Heater centerfold).

Following the population shifts within The Book of Mormon can be challenging. In one instance, it narrated an event about a group of Lamanites who converted to Nephite

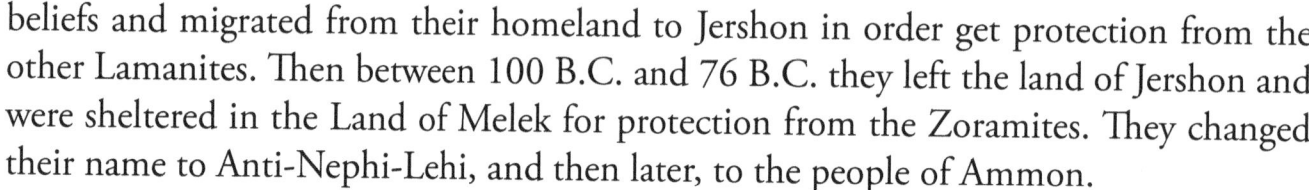

beliefs and migrated from their homeland to Jershon in order get protection from the other Lamanites. Then between 100 B.C. and 76 B.C. they left the land of Jershon and were sheltered in the Land of Melek for protection from the Zoramites. They changed their name to Anti-Nephi-Lehi, and then later, to the people of Ammon.

Alma 15:29-30 RCE, Alma 27:26-27 LDS:

And it came to pass that they went down into the Land of Jershon and took possession of the Land of Jershon. And they were called by the Nephites, the people of Ammon, Therefore, they were distinguished by that name ever after;...

Alma 16:254 RCE, Alma 35:13 LDS:

And the people of Ammon departed out of the land of Jershon and came over into the Land of Melek, And gave place in the land of Jershon for the armies of the Nephites, that they might contend with the armies of the Lamanites and the armies of the Zoramites.

As one example of this shifting, archeologists tell us that a migration to Barton Raimie and Lamanai in Belize from Chalchuapa in El Salvador occurred between 100 B.C. and 76 B.C. (Heater centerfold). Could these be the same people who migrated to Jershon and then to Melek?

To explore another lead, let's talk about the star that guided the Wise Men. As we know, they followed a new star to *"where the young child was"*:

Matthew 2:2:

Saying, Where is He that is born King of the Jews? For we have seen His star in the east, and are come to worship Him.

Matthew 2:9:

...and, lo, the star, which they saw in the east, went before them, till it came and stood over where the young child was.

According to The Book of Mormon, when Jesus was born, a new star appeared in the sky after a night without darkness:

3 Nephi 1:17,21,24 RCE, 3 Nephi 1:15,19, 21 LDS:

For he beheld at the going down of the sun there was no darkness, And the people began to be astonished because there was no darkness when the night came.

And it came to pass that there was no darkness in all that night, but it was as light as though it was midday.

And it came to pass also that a new star did appear according to the word.

Mesoamerican legends tell of a new star occurring at the time period of Jesus' birth. (Heater centerfold)

By the same token, at the time of Christ's death, the Book of Mormon testifies that there was great destruction. In fact, there was such a great amount of havoc in the Americas, that, I believe, it was felt in Israel. Why? Because the Bible also talks about the darkness and the earth quaking. I believe the whole earth was literally shaken by His death--the earth itself mourned.

3 Nephi 4:6-16 RCE, 3 Nephi 8:5 LDS:

And it came to pass that in the thirty and fourth year, in the first month, in the fourth day of the month, There arose a great storm, such an one as never had been known in all the land; And there was also a great and terrible tempest; And there was terrible thunder, insomuch that it did shake the whole earth as if it was about to divide asunder; And there were exceeding sharp lightnings, such as never had been known in all the land. And the City of Zarahemla did take fire; And the City of Moroni did sink into the depths of the sea and the inhabitants thereof were drowned; And the earth was carried up upon the City of Moronihah, that in the place of the city thereof there became a great mountain; And there was a great and terrible destruction in the Land Southward. But behold, there was a more great and terrible destruction in the Land Northward; For behold, the whole face of the land was changed because of the tempests and the whirlwinds and the thundering and the lightnings and the exceeding great quaking of the whole earth; And the highways were broken up, And the level roads were spoiled, And many smooth places became rough, And many great and notable cities were sunk, And many were burned, And many were shook till the buildings thereof had fallen to the earth, And the inhabitants thereof were slain, And the places were left desolate. And there were some cities which remained, but the damage thereof was exceeding great, And there were many in them which were slain; And there were some which were carried away in the whirlwind, And whither they went, no man knoweth, save they know that they were carried away. And the face of the whole earth became deformed because of the tempests and the thundering and the lightnings and the quaking of the earth; And behold, the rocks were rent in twain, yea, they were broken up upon the face of the whole earth, Insomuch that they were found in broken fragments and in seams and in cracks upon all the face of the land. And it came to pass that when the thundering and the lightnings and the storm and the tempest and the quaking of the earth did cease--For behold, they did last for about the space of three hours, And it was said by some that the time was greater;...

Archeological remains confirm that there are many remnants of cities throughout Mesoamerica, some under the water of oceans, some at the bottom of lakes, plus many above ground, some of which were covered by earth. In addition, many were abandoned and later covered by foliage and earth. Scientists today also tell us that an eruption of volcanoes causes furious storms in the areas around them, just as depicted. The above reference is an astoundingly correct description of what happens during a flare-up, something that even most people today do not know.

The Book of Mormon recounts that the Lamanites had a king around 330 A.D. and that all the people had become wicked:

Mormon 1:30-31 RCE, Mormon 2:8-9 LDS:

Therefore there was blood and carnage spread throughout all the face of the land--Both on the part of the Nephites, and also on the part of the Lamanites; And it was one complete revolution throughout all the face of the land. And now the Lamanites had a king and his name was Aaron, And he came against us with an army of forty and four thousand;

Archaeological discoveries reveal that around 300 A.D., in the Maya Classic era, kings appeared (Heater centerfold).

The Book of Mormon also tells us there were a great number of people in Mesoamerica around 321 A.D.:

Mormon 1:7 RCE, Mormon 1:6 LDS:

And it came to pass that I, being eleven years old, was carried by my father into the Land Southward, even to the Land of Zarahemla--The whole face of the land having become covered with buildings, And the people were as numerous almost as it were the sand of the sea.

Roy Weldon recounts that just prior to the final destruction of the Nephites, the Lord helped them arrange a truce with the Lamanites for ten years. (Mormon 1:63) But the Nephites refused to repent. (23)

Roy then states:

> **From the account in Bancroft's *Native Races* we find a similar story. Unable to resist the formidable army, the Toltec king was compelled to send ambassadors bearing rich presents to sue for peace. ...A truce... was concluded...to the effect that the Toltecs should not be molested for ten years. (Vol. 5 279)**

Final Destruction

Finally, The Book of Mormon reports that between 320 and 384 A.D., the Nephites were in a constant state of warfare with the Lamanites:

Mormon 3:6 RCE, Mormon 6:5 LDS:

And when three hundred and eighty four years had passed away, we had gathered in all the remainder of our people unto the land Cumorah.

They gathered for the last battle in the year 384. Before Mormon died, he described how all but twenty-four Nephites were killed and it was probably the last battle he observed. (Mormon 3:16 RCE, Mormon 6:15 LDS)

Mormon 4:7-8 RCE, Mormon 8:6-7 LDS:

Behold, four hundred years have passed since the coming of our Lord and Savior. And behold, the Lamanites have hunted my people the Nephites down from city to city and from place to place, even until they are no more, And great has been their fall, Yea, great and marvelous is the destruction of my people the Nephites;

Mormon's son Moroni wrote the last chapter of Mormon's book:

Mormon 4:10 RCE, Mormon 8:8 LDS:

And behold also, the Lamanites are at war one with another; And the whole face of this land is one continual round of murder and bloodshed; And no one knoweth the end of the war.

As a personal observation, I fear that the same destruction brought upon the Nephites because of their iniquity is about to fall upon America for the same reason. If we are not fearful about the evils happening around us, we should be, and we must be repentant. We all need to pray for our country, our leaders, and for the will of God to triumph.

What I have included here represents only a few of the many archeological evidences that agree with The Book of Mormon. Undoubtedly, no one knew this information in the early 1800s.

CHAPTER 12

WORDS SPOKEN BY JESUS CHRIST (IN RED) IN THE BOOK OF MORMON DURING HIS VISIT TO THE AMERICAS

The Third Book of
Nephi

The Son of Nephi Which was the Son of Helaman

3 Nephi 5:

1. And now it came to pass that there were a great multitude gathered together of the people of Nephi, round about the temple which was in the Land Bountiful [in the Americas];

2. And they were marveling and wondering one with another and were showing one to another the great and marvelous change which had taken place;

3. And they were also conversing about this Jesus Christ of which the sign had been given concerning His death.

4. And it came to pass that while they were thus conversing one with another, They heard a voice as if it came out of heaven; And they cast their eyes round about, for they understood not the voice which they heard;

5. And it was not a harsh voice, neither was it a loud voice, Nevertheless, and not withstanding it being a small voice, it did pierce them that did hear to the center, Insomuch that there was no part of their frame that it did not cause to quake; Yea, it did pierce them to the very soul and did cause their hearts to burn.

6. And it came to pass that again they heard the voice and they understood it not; And again the third time they did hear the voice and did open their ears to hear it;

7. And their eyes were toward the sound thereof; And they did look steadfastly toward heaven from whence the sound came. And behold, the third time they did understand the voice which they heard,

8. And it saith unto them: "Behold My beloved Son in whom I am well pleased, in whom I have glorified My name-Hear ye Him!"

9. And it came to pass as they understood, they cast their eyes up again toward heaven; And behold, they saw a Man descending out of heaven;

10. And He was clothed in a white robe, And He came down and stood in the midst of them; And the eyes of the whole multitude were turned upon Him, And they durst not open their mouths, even one to another; And they wist not what it meant, for they thought it was an angel that had appeared unto them.

11. And it came to pass that He stretched forth His hand and spake unto the people, saying: "Behold, I Am Jesus Christ of which the prophets testified that should come into the world;

12. And behold, I Am the light and the life of the world; And I have drunk out of that bitter cup which the Father hath given Me, And have glorified the Father in taking upon Me the sins of the world, in the which I have suffered the will of the Father in all things from the beginning."

13. And it came to pass that when Jesus had spake these words, the whole multitude fell to the earth, For they remembered that it had been prophesied among them that Christ should show Himself unto them after His ascension into heaven.

14. And it came to pass that the Lord spake unto them, saying: "Arise and come forth unto Me, That ye may thrust your hands into My side, And also that ye may feel the prints of the nails in My hands and in My feet, That ye may know that I Am the God of Israel and the God of the whole earth and have been slain for the sins of the world."

15. And it came to pass that the multitude went forth and did thrust their hands into His side and did feel the prints of the nails in His hands and in His feet;

16. And this they did do, going forth one by one, Until they had all gone forth, and did see with their eyes, and did feel with their hands, and did know of a surety, and did bear record, That it

was He of whom it was written by the prophets that should come.

17. And it came to pass that when they had all gone forth and had witnessed for themselves, they did cry out with one accord, saying: "Hosanna! Blessed be the name of the Most High God!" And they did fall down at the feet of Jesus and did worship Him.

18. And it came to pass that He spake unto Nephi- for Nephi was among the multitude-and commanded him that he should come forth;

19. And Nephi arose and went forth and bowed himself before the Lord and he did kiss His feet;

20. And the Lord commanded him that he should arise, And he arose and stood before Him.

21. And the Lord said unto him: "I give unto you power that ye shall baptize this people when I am again ascended into heaven."

22. And again the Lord called others and said unto them likewise; And He gave unto them power to baptize.

23. And He saith unto them: "On this wise shall ye baptize-and there shall be no disputations among you-

24. Verily I say unto you, that whosoever repenteth of his sins through your words and desireth to be baptized in My name, On this wise shall ye baptize them: Behold, ye shall go down and stand in the water and in My name shall ye baptize them.

25. "And now behold, these are the words which ye shall say, calling them by name, saying, 'Having authority given me of Jesus Christ, I baptize you in the name of the Father and of the Son and of the Holy Ghost. Amen.'

26. "And then shall ye immerse them in the water and come forth again out of the water.

27. "And after this manner shall ye baptize in My name. "For behold, verily I say unto you that the Father and the Son and the Holy Ghost are one; And I Am in the Father and the Father in Me and the Father and I are one;

28. And according as I have commanded you, thus shall ye baptize;

29. And there shall be no disputations among you as there hath hitherto been, Neither shall there be disputations among you concerning the points of My doctrine as there hath hitherto been;

30. For verily, verily I say unto you, he that hath the spirit of contention is not of Me, but is of the devil which is the father of contention, And he stirreth up the hearts of men to contend with anger one with another.

31. "Behold, this is not My doctrine-to stir up the hearts of men to anger against one another; But this is My doctrine-that such things should be done away.

32. "Behold, verily, verily I say unto you, I will declare unto you My doctrine; And this is My doctrine and it is the doctrine which the Father hath given unto Me-

33. And I bear record of the Father, And the Father beareth record of Me, And the Holy Ghost beareth record of the Father and Me-And I bear record that the Father commandeth all men everywhere to repent and believe in Me;

34. And whoso believeth in Me and is baptized, the same shall be saved, And they are they which shall inherit the kingdom of God;

35. And whoso believeth not in Me and is not baptized shall be damned!

36. "Verily, verily I say unto you that this is My doctrine, And I bear record of it from the Father; And whoso believeth in Me, believeth in the Father also;

37. And unto him will the Father bear record of Me, For He will visit him with fire and with the Holy Ghost;

38. And thus will the Father bear record of Me; And the Holy Ghost will bear record unto him of the Father and Me, For the Father and I and the Holy Ghost are one.

39. "And again I say unto you, Ye must repent, and become as a little child, and be baptized in My name, Or ye can in no wise receive these things!

40. "And again I say unto you, Ye must repent, and be baptized in My name, and become as a little child, Or ye can in nowise inherit the kingdom of God!

41. "Verily, verily I say unto you that this is My doctrine; And whoso buildeth upon this, buildeth upon My rock, And the gates of hell shall not prevail against them.

42. "And whoso shall declare more or less than this and establish it for My doctrine, The same cometh of evil and is not built upon My rock; But he buildeth upon a sandy foundation, And

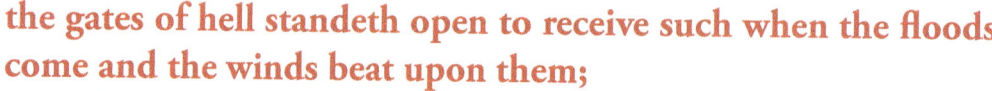

the gates of hell standeth open to receive such when the floods come and the winds beat upon them;

43. Therefore, go forth unto this people and declare the words which I have spoken unto the ends of the earth."

44. And it came to pass that when Jesus had spake these words unto Nephi and to those which had been called-now the number of them which had been called and received power and authority to baptize were twelve-

45. And behold, He stretched forth His hand unto the multitude and cried unto them, saying: "Blessed are ye if ye shall give heed unto the words of these twelve which I have chosen from among you to minister unto you and to be your servants;

46. And unto them I have given power that they may baptize you with water; And after that ye are baptized with water, Behold, I will baptize you with fire and with the Holy Ghost.

47. "Therefore, blessed are ye if ye shall believe in Me and be baptized after that ye have seen Me and know that I Am.

48. "And again, more blessed are they which shall believe in your words because that ye shall testify that ye have seen Me and that ye know that I Am;

49. Yea, blessed are they which shall believe in your words and come down into the depths of humility and be baptized, For they shall be visited with fire and with the Holy Ghost and shall receive a remission of their sins.

50. "Yea, blessed are the poor in spirit which cometh unto Me, for theirs is the kingdom of heaven.

51. "And again, blessed are all they that mourn, for they shall be comforted.

52. "And blessed are the meek, for they shall inherit the earth.

53. "And blessed are all they which do hunger and thirst after righteousness, for they shall be filled with the Holy Ghost.

54. "And blessed are the merciful, for they shall obtain mercy.

55. "And blessed are all the pure in heart, for they shall see God.

56. "And blessed are all the peacemakers, for they shall be called the children of God.

57. "And blessed are all they which are persecuted for My name's sake, for theirs is the kingdom of heaven.

58. "And blessed are ye when men shall revile you and persecute you and shall say all manner of evil against you falsely for My sake,

59. for ye shall have great joy and be exceeding glad, for great shall be your reward in heaven; For so persecuted they the prophets which were before you.

60. "Verily, verily I say unto you, and I give unto you to be the salt of the earth, But if the salt shall lose its savor, wherewith shall the earth be salted? The salt shall be thenceforth good for nothing, but to be cast out and to be trodden underfoot of men.

61. "Verily, verily I say unto you, I give unto you to be the light of this people; A city that is set on a hill cannot be hid;

62. Behold, do men light a candle and put it under a bushel? Nay, but on a candlestick and it giveth light to all that are in the house;

63. Therefore, let your light so shine before this people, that they may see your good works and glorify your Father which is in heaven.

64. "Think not that I am come to destroy the law or the prophets; I am not come to destroy, but to fulfill;

65. For verily I say unto you, one jot nor one tittle hath not passed away from the law, but in Me it hath all been fulfilled.

66. "And behold, I have given unto you the law and the commandments of My Father, that ye shall believe in Me, And that ye shall repent of your sins and come unto Me with a broken heart and a contrite spirit;

67. Behold, ye have the commandments before you and the law is fulfilled, Therefore, come unto Me and be ye saved;

68. For verily I say unto you, that except ye shall keep My commandments which I have commanded you at this time, Ye shall in no case enter into the kingdom of heaven.

69. "Ye have heard that it hath been said by them of old time-and it is also written before you-that, 'Thou shalt not kill and whosoever shall kill shall be in danger of the judgment of God';

70. But I say unto you, that whosoever is angry with his brother shall be in danger of His judgment; And whosoever shall say to his brother, 'Raca!' shall be in danger of the council; And whosoever shall say, 'Thou fool!' shall be in danger of hell fire;

71. Therefore, if ye shall come unto Me, or shall desire to come unto Me, and rememberest that thy brother hath aught against thee,

72. Go thy way unto thy brother and first be reconciled to thy brother and then come unto Me with full purpose of heart and I will receive you.

73. "Agree with thine adversary quickly while thou art in the way with him, lest at any time he shall get thee and thou shalt be cast into prison;

74. Verily I say unto thee, thou shalt by no means come out thence until thou hast paid the uttermost senine;

75. And while ye are in prison, can ye pay even one senine? Verily, verily I say unto you, Nay.

76. "Behold, it is written by them of old time that, 'Thou shalt not commit adultery';

77. But I say unto you that whosoever looketh on a woman to lust after her hath committed adultery already in his heart.

78. "Behold, I give unto you a commandment that ye suffer none of these things to enter into your heart, For it is better that ye should deny yourselves of these things, wherein ye will take up your cross, than that ye should be cast into hell.

79. "It hath been written that, 'Whosoever shall put away his wife, let him give her a writing of divorcement';

80. Verily, verily I say unto you that whosoever shall put away his wife, saving for the cause of fornication, causeth her to commit adultery, And whoso shall marry her who is divorced committeth adultery.

81. "And again, it is written, 'Thou shalt not forswear thyself but shalt perform unto the Lord thine oaths';

82. But verily I say unto you, swear not at all- neither by heaven, for it is God's throne, nor by the earth, for it is His footstool, Neither shalt thou swear by thy head, because thou canst not make one hair black or white;

83. But let your communication be, 'Yea, yea'; 'Nay, nay'; For whatsoever cometh of more than these are evil.

84. "And behold, it is written, 'An eye for an eye and a tooth for a tooth';

85. But I say unto you that ye shall not resist evil, But whosoever shall smite thee on thy right cheek, turn to him the other also;

86. And if any man will sue thee at the law and take away thy coat, let him have thy cloak also;

87. And whosoever shall compel thee to go a mile, go with him twain;

88. Give to him that asketh thee, And to him that would borrow of thee, turn thou not away.

89. "And behold, it is written also that, 'Thou shalt love thy neighbor and hate thine enemy';

90. But behold, I say unto you, love your enemies, bless them that curse you, do good to them that hate you; And pray for them which despitefully use you and persecute you,

91. that ye may be the children of your Father which is in heaven, For He maketh His sun to rise on the evil and on the good. "Therefore, those things which were of old time, which were under the law in Me, are all fulfilled;

92. Old things are done away and all things have become new, Therefore, I would that ye should be perfect even as I or your Father which is in heaven is perfect.

93. "Verily, verily I say that I would that ye should do alms unto the poor; But take heed that ye do not your alms before men to be seen of them, Otherwise ye have no reward of your Father which is in heaven;

94. Therefore, when ye shall do your alms, do not sound a trumpet before you as will hypocrites do in the synagogues and in the streets, that they may have glory of men; Verily I say unto you, they have their reward;

95. But when thou doest alms, let not thy left hand know what thy right hand doeth,

96. that thine alms may be in secret; And thy Father which seeth in secret, Himself shall reward thee openly.

97. "And when thou prayest, thou shalt not do as the hypocrites, For they love to pray standing in the synagogues and in the corners of the streets, that they may be seen of men; Verily I say unto you, they have their reward;

98. But thou, when thou prayest, enter into thy closet, And when thou hast shut thy door, pray to thy Father which is in secret, And thy Father, which seeth in secret, shall reward thee openly;

99. But when ye pray, use not vain repetitions as the heathen, For they think that they shall be heard for their much speaking;

100. Be not ye therefore like unto them, for your Father knoweth what things ye have need of before ye ask Him.

101. "After this manner, therefore, pray ye:

102. 'Our Father which art in heaven, Hallowed be Thy name.

103. Thy will be done in earth, as it is in heaven.

104. And forgive us our debts, as we forgive our debtors.

105. And lead us not into temptation, But deliver us from evil.

106. For Thine is the kingdom and the power and the glory forever! Amen.'

107. "For if ye forgive men their trespasses, your heavenly Father will also forgive you, But if ye forgive not men their trespasses, neither will your Father forgive your trespasses.

108. "Moreover, when ye fast, be not as the hypocrites, of a sad countenance, For they disfigure their faces that they may appear unto men to fast; Verily I say unto you, they have their reward;

109. But thou, when thou fasteth, anoint thy head and wash thy face, That thou appear not unto men to fast, but unto thy Father, which is in secret, And thy Father, which seeth in secret, shall reward thee openly.

110. "Lay not up for yourselves treasures upon earth, where moth and rust doth corrupt and thieves break through and steal,

111. But lay up for yourselves treasures in heaven, where neither moth nor rust doth corrupt and where thieves do not break through nor steal;

112. For where your treasure is there will your heart be also.

113. "The light of the body is the eye; If therefore thine eye be single, thy whole body shall be full of light;

114. But if thine eye be evil, thy whole body shall be full of darkness; If therefore the light that is in thee be darkness, how great is that darkness!

115. "No man can serve two masters, Or either he will hate the one and love the other, Or else he will hold to the one and despise the other; Ye cannot serve God and mammon."

3 Nephi 6

1. And now it came to pass that when Jesus had spoken these words, He looked upon the twelve whom He had chosen and saith unto them: "Remember the words which I have spoken,

2. For behold, ye are they which I have chosen to minister unto this people.

3. "Therefore I say unto you, take no thought for your life, what ye shall eat or what ye shall drink, Nor yet for your body, what ye shall put on; Is not the life more than meat and the body than raiment?

4. Behold the fowls of the air, for they sow not, neither do they reap, nor gather into barns, Yet your heavenly Father feedeth them; Are ye not much better than they?

5. "Which of you by taking thought can add one cubit unto his stature?

6. And why take ye thought for raiment? Consider the lilies of the field, how they grow- they toil not, neither do they spin-

7. And yet I say unto you that even Solomon in all his glory was not arrayed like one of these;

8. Wherefore, if God so clothe the grass of the field, which today is, and tomorrow is cast into the oven, Even so will He clothe you, if ye are not of little faith.

9. "Therefore, take no thought, saying, 'What shall we eat?' or 'What shall we drink?' or 'Wherewithal shall we be clothed?'

10. For your heavenly Father knoweth that ye have need of all these things;

11. But seek ye first the kingdom of God and His righteousness, And all these things shall be added unto you;

12. Take, therefore, no thought for the morrow, For the morrow shall take thought for the things of itself; Sufficient is the day unto the evil thereof."

13. **And now it came to pass that when Jesus had spoken these words, He turned again to the multitude and He did open His mouth unto them again, saying:** "Verily, verily I say unto you, judge not that ye be not judged;

14. For with what judgment ye judge, ye shall be judged, And with what measure ye mete, it shall be measured to you again;

15. And why beholdest thou the mote that is in thy brother's eye, But considerest not the beam that is in thine own eye?

16. Or how wilt thou say to thy brother, 'Let me pull out the mote out of thine eye,' and behold, a beam is in thine own eye?

17. Thou hypocrite! First cast out the beam out of thine own eye, And then shalt thou see clearly to cast out the mote out of thy brother's eye.

18. "Give not that which is holy unto the dogs, Neither cast ye your pearls before swine, lest they trample them under their feet and turn again and rend you.

19. "Ask, and it shall be given unto you, Seek, and ye shall find, Knock, and it shall be opened unto you;

20. For everyone that asketh, receiveth, And he that seeketh, findeth, And to him that knocketh, it shall be opened.

21. "Or what man is there of you who, if his son ask bread, will he give him a stone?

22. Or if he ask a fish, will he give him a serpent?

23. If ye then, being evil, know how to give good gifts unto your children, How much more shall your Father which is in heaven give good things to them that ask Him!

24. Therefore, all things whatsoever ye would that men should do to you, do ye even so to them, For this is the law and the prophets.

25. "Enter ye in at the strait gate, For wide is the gate and broad is the way that leadeth to destruction, And many there be which go in thereat;

26. Because strait is the gate and narrow is the way which leadeth unto life, And few there be that find it.

27. "Beware of false prophets which come to you in sheep's clothing, but inwardly they are ravening wolves;

28. Ye shall know them by their fruits- Do men gather grapes of thorns, or figs of thistles?

29. Even so, every good tree bringeth forth good fruit, but a corrupt tree bringeth forth evil fruit;

30. A good tree cannot bring forth evil fruit, neither a corrupt tree bring forth good fruit;

31. Every tree that bringeth not forth good fruit is hewn down and cast into the fire;

32. Wherefore, by their fruits ye shall know them.

33. "Not everyone that saith unto Me, 'Lord, Lord,' shall enter into the kingdom of heaven, but he that doeth the will of My Father which is in heaven;

34. Many will say to Me in that day, 'Lord, Lord, have we not prophesied in Thy name? And in Thy name have cast out devils? And in Thy name done many wonderful works?'

35. And then will I profess unto them, 'I never knew you; Depart from Me, ye that work iniquity.'

36. "Therefore, whoso heareth these sayings of Mine and doeth them, I will liken him unto a wise man which built his house upon a rock- And the rain descended and the floods came, And the winds blew and beat upon that house, And it fell not, for it was founded upon a rock;

37. And everyone that heareth these sayings of Mine and doeth them not shall be likened unto a foolish man which built his house upon the sand- And the rain descended and the floods came, And the winds blew and beat upon that house, And it fell and great was the fall of it."

3 Nephi 7

1. And now it came to pass that when Jesus had ended these sayings, He cast His eyes round about on the multitude and saith unto them: "Behold, ye have heard the things which I have taught before I ascended to My Father;

2. Therefore, whoso remembereth these sayings of Mine and doeth them, him will I raise up at the last day."

3. And it came to pass that when Jesus had said these words, He perceived that there were some among them which marveled and wondered what He would concerning the law of Moses, For they understood not the saying that old things had passed away and that all things had become new;

4. And He saith unto them: "Marvel not that I said unto you that old things had passed away and that all things had become new-

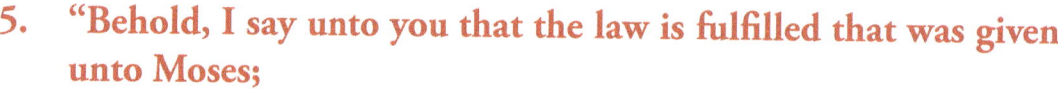

5. "Behold, I say unto you that the law is fulfilled that was given unto Moses;

6. Behold, I Am He that gave the law, And I Am He which covenanted with My people Israel; Therefore, the law in Me is fulfilled, For I have come to fulfill the law, Therefore, it hath an end.

7. "Behold, I do not destroy the prophets, For as many as have not been fulfilled in Me, verily I say unto you, shall all be fulfilled;

8. And because I said unto you that old things hath passed away, I do not destroy that which hath been spoken concerning things which are to come;

9. For behold, the covenants which I have made with My people is not all fulfilled, But the law which was given unto Moses hath an end in Me.

10. "Behold, I Am the law and the light; Look unto Me and endure to the end and ye shall live, For unto him that endureth to the end will I give eternal life.

11. "Behold, I have given unto you the commandments, Therefore, keep My commandments-

12. And this is the law and the prophets, for they truly testify of Me."

13. **And now it came to pass that when Jesus had spoken these words, He said unto those twelve whom He had chosen:** "Ye are My disciples and ye are a light unto this people, which are a remnant of the house of Joseph;

14. And behold, this is the land of your inheritance and the Father hath given it unto you;

15. And not at any time hath the Father given Me commandment that I should tell it unto your brethren at Jerusalem, Neither at any time hath the Father given Me commandment that I should tell unto them concerning the other tribes of the house of Israel which the Father hath led away out of the land.

16. "This much did the Father command Me that I should tell unto them- That other sheep I have which are not of this fold; Them also I must bring, And they shall hear My voice, And there shall be one fold and one Shepherd.

17. "And now because of stiff-neckedness and unbelief, they understood not My word, Therefore, I was commanded to say no more of the Father concerning this thing unto them;

18. But verily I say unto you that the Father hath commanded Me, and I tell it unto you, that ye were separated from among them because of their iniquity; Therefore, it is because of their iniquity that they know not of you.

19. "And verily I say unto you again, that the other tribes hath the Father separated from them, And it is because of their iniquity that they know not of them.

20. "And verily I say unto you that ye are they of which I said: 'Other sheep I have which are not of this fold; Them also I must bring, And they shall hear My voice, And there shall be one fold and one Shepherd'-

21. And they understood Me not; For they supposed it had been the Gentiles, For they understood not that the Gentiles should be converted through their preaching;

22. And they understood Me not, that I said they shall hear My voice; And they understood Me not, that the Gentiles should not at any time hear My voice, That I should not manifest Myself unto them, save it were by the Holy Ghost.

23. "But behold, ye have both heard My voice and seen Me, And ye are My sheep, And ye are numbered among them which the Father hath given Me;

24. And verily, verily I say unto you that I have other sheep which are not of this land, Neither of the Land of Jerusalem, Neither in any parts of that land round about whither I have been to minister;

25. For they of which I speak are they which have not as yet heard My voice, Neither have I at any time manifested Myself unto them,

26. But I have received a commandment of the Father that I should go unto them, And that they shall hear My voice and shall be numbered among My sheep, that there may be one fold and one Shepherd; Therefore, I go to show Myself unto them.

27. "And I command you that ye shall write these things after that I am gone, That if it so be that My people at Jerusalem-they which have seen Me and been with Me in My ministry- Do not ask the Father in My name that they may receive a knowledge of you by the Holy Ghost, and also of the other tribes which they know not of,

28. That these sayings which ye shall write shall be kept and shalt be manifested unto the Gentiles, That through the fullness of the Gentiles, the remnant of their seed-which shall be scattered forth

upon the face of the earth because of their unbelief- may be brought in, or may be brought to a knowledge of Me, their Redeemer;

29. And then will I gather them in from the four quarters of the earth; And then will I fulfill the covenant which the Father hath made unto all the people of the house of Israel.

30. "And blessed are the Gentiles because of their belief in Me, in and of the Holy Ghost, which witness unto them of Me and of the Father;

31. 'Behold, because of their belief in Me,' saith the Father, 'and because of the unbelief of you, O house of Israel, In the latter day shall the truth come unto the Gentiles, that the fullness of these things shall be made known unto them.

32. 'But wo,' saith the Father, 'unto the unbelieving of the Gentiles!' For notwithstanding that they have come forth upon the face of this land and have scattered My people which are of the house of Israel, And My people which are of the house of Israel have been cast out from among them and have been trodden under feet by them,

33. And because of the mercies of the Father unto the Gentiles, and also the judgments of the Father upon My people which are of the house of Israel- Verily, verily I say unto you that after all this- And I have caused My people which are of the house of Israel to be smitten, and to be afflicted, and to be slain, and to be cast out from among them, and to become hated by them, and to become a hiss and a byword among them-

34. "And thus commandeth the Father that I should say unto you: 'At that day when the Gentiles shall sin against My gospel, And shall reject the fullness of My gospel, And shall be lifted up in the pride of their hearts above all nations and above all the people of the whole earth, And shall be filled with all manner of lyings, and of deceits, and of mischiefs, and all manner of hypocrisy and murders, and priestcrafts and whoredoms, and of secret abominations-

35. And if they shall do all these things, And shall reject the fullness of My gospel, Behold,' saith the Father, 'I will bring the fullness of My gospel from among them;

36. And then will I remember My covenant which I have made unto My people, O house of Israel, And I will bring My gospel unto them;

37. And I will show unto thee, O house of Israel, that the Gentiles shall not have power over you, But I will remember My covenant unto you, O house of Israel, And ye shall come unto the knowledge of the fullness of My gospel.

38. 'But if the Gentiles will repent and return unto Me,' saith the Father, 'Behold, they shall be numbered among My people, O house of Israel;

39. And I will not suffer My people which are of the house of Israel to go through among them and tread them down,' saith the Father;

40. 'But if they will not return unto Me and hearken unto My voice, I will suffer them-yea, I will suffer My people, O house of Israel-that they shall go through among them and shall tread them down,

41. And they shall be as salt that has lost its savor, which is thenceforth good for nothing but to be cast out and to be trodden underfoot of My people, O house of Israel.'

42. "Verily, verily I say unto you, thus hath the Father commanded Me that I should give unto this people this land for their inheritance;

43. And when the words of the prophet Isaiah shall be fulfilled which saith: 'Thy watchmen shall lift up the voice, With the voice together shall they sing; For they shall see eye to eye when the Lord shall bring again Zion.

44. Break forth into joy! Sing together, ye waste places of Jerusalem! For the Lord hath comforted His people, He hath redeemed Jerusalem.

45. The Lord hath made bare His holy arm in the eyes of all the nations; And all the ends of the earth shall see the salvation of God!'"

3 Nephi 8

1. Behold, now it came to pass that when Jesus had spoken these words, He looked round about again on the multitude, And He saith unto them: "Behold, My time is at hand;

2. I perceive that ye are weak, that ye cannot understand all My words which I am commanded of the Father to speak unto you at this time;

3. Therefore, go ye unto your homes and ponder upon the things which I have said, And ask of the Father in My name, that ye may understand and prepare your minds for the morrow; And I come unto you again;

4. But now I go unto the Father, and also to show Myself unto the lost tribes of Israel, For they are not lost unto the Father, for He knoweth whither He hath taken them."

5. And it came to pass that when Jesus had thus spoken, He cast His eyes round about again on the multitude, And behold, they were in tears and did look steadfastly upon Him as if they would ask Him to tarry a little longer with them;

6. And He saith unto them: "Behold, My bowels are filled with compassion toward you- Have ye any that are sick among you? Bring them hither.

7. "Have ye any that are lame or blind or halt or maimed or leprous? Or that are withered? Or that are deaf? Or that are afflicted in any manner? Bring them hither and I will heal them, for I have compassion upon you.

8. "My bowels are filled with mercy, For I perceive that ye desire that I should show unto you what I have done unto your brethren at Jerusalem, For I see that your faith is sufficient that I should heal you."

9. And it came to pass that when He had thus spoken, all the multitude with one accord did go forth with their sick and their afflicted and their lame and with their blind and with their dumb and with all they that were afflicted in any manner; And He did heal them every one as they were brought forth unto Him;

10. And they did all--both they which had been healed and they which were whole- bow down at His feet and did worship Him;

11. And as many as could come, for the multitude, did kiss His feet, insomuch that they did bathe His feet with their tears.

12. And it came to pass that He commanded that their little children should be brought,

13. So they brought their little children and sat them down upon the ground round about Him, And Jesus stood in the midst and the multitude gave way till they had all been brought unto Him.

14. And it came to pass that when they had all been brought and Jesus stood in the midst, He commanded the multitude that they should kneel down upon the ground.

15. And it came to pass that when they had knelt upon the ground, Jesus groaned within Himself and saith: "Father, I am troubled because of the wickedness of the people of the house of Israel."

16. And when He had said these words, He Himself also knelt upon the earth, And behold, He prayed unto the Father, And the things which He prayed cannot be written, And the multitude did bear record which heard Him.

17. And after this manner do they bear record: "The eye hath never seen, neither hath the ear heard before, so great and marvelous things as we saw and heard Jesus speak unto the Father!

18. And no tongue can speak, neither can there be written by any man, Neither can the hearts of men conceive so great and marvelous things as we both saw and heard Jesus speak!

19. And no one can conceive of the joy which filled our souls at the time we heard Him pray for us unto the Father!"

20. And it came to pass that when Jesus had made an end of praying unto the Father, He arose; But so great was the joy of the multitude that they were overcome.

21. And it came to pass that Jesus spake unto them and bade them arise,

22. And they arose from the earth; And He saith unto them: "Blessed are ye because of your faith! And now behold, My joy is full."

23. And when He had said these words, He wept and the multitude bear record of it; And He took their little children, one by one, and blessed them and prayed unto the Father for them.

24. And when He had done this, He wept again; And He spake unto the multitude and saith unto them: "Behold your little ones!"

25. And as they looked to behold, they cast their eyes toward heaven, And they saw the heavens open, And they saw angels descending out of heaven, as it were, in the midst of fire; And they came down and encircled those little ones about,

26. And they were encircled about with fire, And the angels did minister unto them. And the multitude did see and hear and bear record; And they know that their record is true, for they-all of them-did see and hear, every man for himself;

27. And they were in number about two thousand and five hundred souls; And they did consist of men, women and children.

28. And it came to pass that Jesus commanded His disciples that they should bring forth some bread and wine unto Him;

29. And while they were gone for bread and wine, He commanded the multitude that they should sit themselves down upon the earth;

30. And when the disciples had come with bread and wine, He took of the bread and brake and blessed it; And He gave unto the disciples and commanded that they should eat;

31. And when they had eaten and were filled, He commanded that they should give unto the multitude.

32. And when the multitude had eaten and were filled, He saith unto the disciples: "Behold, there shall one be ordained among you, And to him will I give power that he shall break bread and bless it and give it unto the people of My church, unto all they which shall believe and be baptized in My name;

33. And this shall ye always observe to do, even as I have done, even as I have broken bread and blessed it and gave it unto you;

34. And this shall ye do in remembrance of My body which I have shown unto you;

35. And it shall be a testimony unto the Father that ye do always remember Me;

36. And if ye do always remember Me, ye shall have My Spirit to be with you."

37. And it came to pass that when He had said these words, He commanded His disciples that they should take of the wine of the cup and drink of it, And that they should also give unto the multitude that they might drink of it.

38. And it came to pass that they did so and did drink of it and were filled; And they gave unto the multitude and they did drink and they were filled.

39. And when the disciples had done this, Jesus saith unto them: "Blessed are ye for this thing which ye have done, for this is fulfilling My commandments, And this doth witness unto the Father that ye are willing to do that which I have commanded you;

40. And this shall ye always do unto those who repent and are baptized in My name; And ye shall do it in remembrance of My blood which I have shed for you, that ye may witness unto the Father that ye do always remember Me;

41. And if ye do always remember Me, ye shall have My Spirit to be with you.

42. "And I give unto you a commandment that ye shall do these things,

43. And if ye shall always do these things, blessed are ye, for ye are built upon My Rock;

44. But whoso among you shall do more or less than these are not built upon My Rock, but are built upon a sandy foundation;

45. And when the rain descends and the floods come and the winds blow and beat upon them, they shall fall, And the gates of hell are already open to receive them.

46. "Therefore, blessed are ye if ye shall keep My commandments which the Father hath commanded Me that I should give unto you;

47. Verily, verily I say unto you, ye must watch and pray always, lest ye be tempted by the devil and ye are led away captive by him;

48. And as I have prayed among you, even so shall ye pray in My church among My people which do repent and are baptized in My name;

49. Behold, I Am the light- I have set an example before you."

50. **And it came to pass that when Jesus had spake these words unto His disciples, He turned again unto the multitude and saith unto them:** "Behold, verily, verily I say unto you, ye must watch and pray always, lest ye enter into temptation;

51. For Satan desireth to have you, that he may sift you as wheat; Therefore, ye must always pray unto the Father in My name; And whatsoever ye shall ask the Father in My name, which is right, believing that ye shall receive- And behold, it shall be given unto you;

52. Pray in your families unto the Father, always in My name, that your wives and your children may be blessed.

53. "And behold, ye shall meet together oft, And ye shall not forbid any man from coming unto you when ye shall meet together, But suffer them that they may come unto you and forbid them not;

54. But ye shall pray for them and shall not cast them out; And if it so be that they come unto you oft, ye shall pray for them unto the Father in My name. "Therefore, hold up your light that it may shine unto the world;

55. Behold, I Am the light which ye shall hold up. "That which ye have seen Me do-

56. Behold, ye have seen I have prayed unto the Father, And ye all have witnessed and ye see that I have commanded that none of you should go away, But rather have commanded that ye should come unto Me that ye might feel and see-

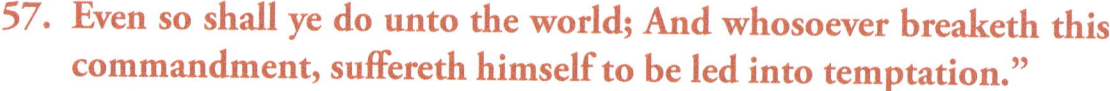

57. Even so shall ye do unto the world; And whosoever breaketh this commandment, suffereth himself to be led into temptation."

58. And now it came to pass that when Jesus had spoken these words, He turned His eyes again upon the disciples whom He had chosen and saith unto them:

59. "Behold, verily, verily I say unto you, I give unto you another commandment, And then I must go unto My Father, that I must fulfill other commandments which He hath given Me.

60. "And now behold, this is the commandment which I give unto you- That ye shall not suffer anyone knowingly to partake of My flesh and blood unworthily when ye shall minister it, For whoso eateth and drinketh My flesh and blood unworthily eateth and drinketh damnation to his soul.

61. "Therefore, if ye know that a man is unworthy to eat and drink of My flesh and blood, ye shall forbid him; Nevertheless, ye shall not cast him out from among you, But ye shall minister unto him and shall pray for him unto the Father in My name;

62. And if it so be that he repenteth and is baptized in My name, then shall ye receive him and shall minister unto him of My flesh and blood;

63. But if he repenteth not, he shall not be numbered among My people, that he may not destroy My people, For behold, I know My sheep and they are numbered;

64. Nevertheless, ye shall not cast him out of your synagogues or your places of worship, For unto such shall ye continue to minister;

65. For ye know not but what they will return and repent and come unto Me with full purpose of heart and I shall heal them, And ye shall be the means of bringing salvation unto them.

66. "Therefore, keep these sayings which I have commanded you, that ye come not under condemnation, For wo unto him whom the Father condemneth!

67. "And I give you these commandments because of the disputations which hath been among you beforetimes,

68. And blessed are ye if ye have no disputations among you.

69. "And now I go unto the Father, because it is expedient that I should go unto the Father for your sakes."

70. And it came to pass that when Jesus had made an end of these sayings, He touched with His hand the disciples whom He had

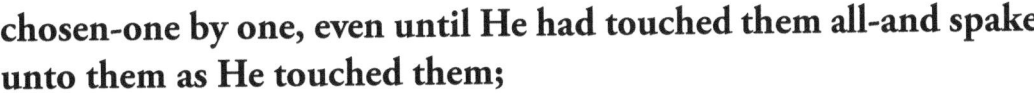

chosen-one by one, even until He had touched them all-and spake unto them as He touched them;

71. And the multitude heard not the words which He spake, Therefore, they did not bear record; But the disciples bear record that He gave them power to give the Holy Ghost,

72. And I will show unto you hereafter that this record is true.

73. And it came to pass that when Jesus had touched them all, there came a cloud and overshadowed the multitude, that they could not see Jesus;

74. And while they were overshadowed, He departed from them and ascended into heaven;

75. And the disciples saw and did bear record that He ascended again into heaven.

3 Nephi 9

1. And now it came to pass that when Jesus had ascended into heaven, the multitude did disperse and every man did take his wife and his children and did return to his own home;

2. And it was noised abroad among the people immediately, before it was yet dark, that the multitude had seen Jesus and that He had ministered unto them and that He would also show Himself on the morrow unto the multitude;

3. Yea, and even all the night it was noised abroad concerning Jesus; And insomuch did they send forth unto the people, that there were many-yea, an exceeding great number did labor exceedingly all that night- That they might be on the morrow in the place where Jesus should show Himself unto the multitude.

4. 4 And it came to pass that on the morrow when the multitude was gathered together, Behold, Nephi and his brother whom he had raised from the dead, whose name was Timothy, and also his son, whose name was Jonas, and also Mathoni and Mathonihah, his brother, and Kumen and Kumenonhi and Jeremiah and Shemnon and Jonas and Zedekiah and Isaiah- Now these were the names of the disciples whom Jesus had chosen-

5. And it came to pass that they went forth and stood in the midst of the multitude;

6. And behold, the multitude was so great that they did cause that they should be separated into twelve bodies,

7. And the twelve did teach the multitude; But behold, they did cause that the multitude should kneel down upon the face of the earth and should pray unto the Father in the name of Jesus,

8. And the disciples did pray unto the Father also in the name of Jesus.

9. And it came to pass that they arose and ministered unto the people;

10. And when they had ministered those same words which Jesus had spoken, nothing varying from the words which Jesus had spoken, Behold, they knelt again and prayed to the Father in the name of Jesus; And they did pray for that which they most desired, And they desired that the Holy Ghost should be given unto them;

11. And when they had thus prayed, they went down unto the water's edge and the multitude followed them.

12. And it came to pass that Nephi went down into the water and was baptized,

13. And he came up out of the water and began to baptize, And he did baptize all they whom Jesus had chosen.

14. And it came to pass when they were all baptized and had come up out of the water, the Holy Ghost did fall upon them, And they were filled with the Holy Ghost and with fire;

15. And behold, they were encircled about as if it were fire; And it came down from heaven and the multitude did witness it and do bear record; And angels did come down out of heaven and did minister unto them.

16. And it came to pass that while the angels were ministering unto the disciples, Behold, Jesus came and stood in the midst and ministered unto them.

17. And it came to pass that He spake unto the multitude and commanded them that they should kneel down again upon the earth, and also that His disciples should kneel down upon the earth.

18. And it came to pass that when they had all knelt down upon the earth, He commanded His disciples that they should pray;

19. And behold, they began to pray, And they did pray unto Jesus, calling Him their Lord and their God.

20. And it came to pass that Jesus departed out of the midst of them and went a little way off from them and bowed Himself to the earth, And He saith: "Father, I thank Thee that Thou hast given the Holy Ghost unto these whom I have chosen, And it is because of their belief in Me that I have chosen them out of the world;

21. Father, I pray Thee that Thou wilt give the Holy Ghost unto all them that shall believe in their words;

22. Father, Thou hast given them the Holy Ghost because they believed in Me, And Thou seest that they believe in Me because Thou hearest them and they pray unto Me; And they pray unto Me because I am with them;

23. And now Father, I pray unto Thee for them, And also for all they which shall believe on their words, that they may believe in Me, that I may be in them as Thou, Father, art in Me, that we may be one."

24. And it came to pass that when Jesus had thus prayed unto the Father, He came unto His disciples, And behold, they did still continue without ceasing to pray unto Him; And they did not multiply many words, for it was given unto them what they should pray, And they were filled with desire.

25. And it came to pass that Jesus beheld them as they did pray unto Him, And His countenance did smile upon them, And the light of His countenance did shine upon them; And behold, they were as white as the countenance and also the garments of Jesus;

26. And behold, the whiteness thereof did exceed all the whiteness- yea, even there could be nothing upon earth so white as the whiteness thereof.

27. And Jesus saith unto them, "Pray on"; Nevertheless, they did not cease to pray.

28. And He turned from them again and went a little way off and bowed Himself to the earth, And He prayed again unto the Father, saying: "Father, I thank Thee that Thou hast purified these which I have chosen because of their faith;

29. And I pray for them, and also for them which shall believe on their words, that they may be purified in Me through faith on their words, even as they are purified in Me;

30. Father, I pray not for the world, But for them which Thou hast given unto Me out of the world because of their faith, that they may be purified in Me, that I may be in them as Thou, Father, art in Me, that we may be one, that I may be glorified in them."

31. And it came to pass that when Jesus had spake these words, He came again unto His disciples; And behold, they did pray steadfastly without ceasing unto Him; And He did smile upon them again; And behold, they were white even as Jesus.

32. And it came to pass that He went again a little way off and prayed unto the Father; And tongue cannot speak the words which He prayed, Neither can be written by man the words which He prayed;

33. And the multitude did hear and do bear record, And their hearts were open, And they did understand in their hearts the words which He prayed;

34. Nevertheless, so great and marvelous were the words which He prayed, that they cannot be written, Neither can they be uttered by man.

35. And it came to pass that when Jesus had made an end of praying, He came again to the disciples and saith unto them: "So great faith have I never seen among all the Jews, Wherefore, I could not show unto them so great miracles because of their unbelief;

36. Verily I say unto you, there are none of them that have seen so great things as ye have seen, Neither have they heard so great things as ye have heard."

37. And it came to pass that He commanded the multitude that they should cease to pray, and also His disciples,

38. And He commanded them that they should not cease to pray in their hearts;

39. And He commanded them that they should arise and stand up upon their feet, And they arose up and stood up upon their feet.

40. And it came to pass that He brake bread again and blessed it and gave to the disciples to eat;

41. And when they had eaten, He commanded them that they should break bread and give unto the multitude;

42. And when they had given unto the multitude, He also gave them wine to drink and commanded them that they should give unto the multitude.

43. Now there had been no bread, neither wine, brought by the disciples, neither by the multitude, But He truly gave unto them bread to eat, and also wine to drink;

44. And He saith unto them: "He that eateth this bread, eateth of My body to their soul, And he that drinketh of this wine, drinketh of My blood to their soul, And their soul shall never hunger nor thirst, but shall be filled."

45. Now when the multitude had all eaten and drank, Behold, they were filled with the Spirit; And they did cry out with one voice and gave glory to Jesus whom they both saw and heard.

46. And it came to pass that when they had all given glory unto Jesus, He saith unto them: "Behold, now I finish the commandment which the Father hath commanded Me concerning this people which are a remnant of the house of Israel.

47. "Ye remember that I spake unto you and said that when the words of Isaiah should be fulfilled- Behold, they are written, Ye have them before you; Therefore, search them-

48. And verily, verily I say unto you that when they shall be fulfilled, Then is the fulfilling of the covenant which the Father hath made unto His people,

49. O house of Israel; And then shall the remnants which shall be scattered abroad upon the face of the earth be gathered in- from the east and from the west, and from the south and from the north; And they shall be brought to the knowledge of the Lord their God who hath redeemed them;

50. And the Father hath commanded Me that I should give unto you this land for your inheritance.

51. "And I say unto you that if the Gentiles do not repent after the blessing which they shall receive after that they have scattered My people, Then shall ye which are a remnant of the house of Jacob go forth among them;

52. And ye shall be in the midst of them, which shall be many; And ye shall be among them, as a lion among the beasts of the forest, and as a young lion among the flocks of sheep, Who, if he goeth through, both treadeth down and teareth in pieces, And none can deliver.

53. Thy hand shall be lifted up upon thine adversaries, And all thine enemies shall be cut off.

54. "And I will gather My people together as a man gathereth his sheaves into the floor, For I will make My people with whom the Father hath covenanted-yea, I will make thy horn iron, And I will make thy hoofs brass;

55. And thou shalt beat in pieces many people; And I will consecrate their gain unto the Lord, And their substance unto the Lord of the whole earth; And behold, I Am He which doeth it.

56. "'And it shall come to pass,' saith the Father, 'that the sword of My justice shalt hang over them at that day; And except they repent, it shall fall upon them,' saith the Father, 'yea, even upon all the nations of the Gentiles.'

57. "And it shall come to pass that I will establish My people, O house of Israel.

58. And behold, this people will I establish in this land, unto the fulfilling of the covenant which I made with your father Jacob, And it shall be a New Jerusalem.

59. And the powers of heaven shall be in the midst of this people, Yea, even I will be in the midst of you.

60. "Behold, I Am He of whom Mosses spake, saying: 'A Prophet shall the Lord your God raise up unto you of your brethren like unto me; Him shall ye hear in all things whatsoever He shall say unto you.

61. And it shall come to pass that every soul which will not hear that Prophet, shall be cut off from among the people.'

62. "Verily I say unto you- Yea, and all the prophets from Samuel and those that follow after, as many as have spoken, have testified of Me-

63. And behold, ye are the children of the prophets; And ye are of the house of Israel; And ye are of the covenant which the Father made with your fathers, saying unto Abraham: 'And in thy Seed shall all the kindreds of the earth be blessed'-

64. The Father having raised Me up unto you first and sent Me to bless you in turning away every one of you from his iniquities, And this because ye are the children of the covenant.

65. "And after that ye were blessed, then fulfilleth the Father the covenant which He made with Abraham saying: 'In thy seed shall all the kindreds of the earth be blessed,' Unto the pouring out of the Holy Ghost through Me upon the Gentiles, Which blessing upon the Gentiles shall make them mighty above all, Unto the scattering of My people, O house of Israel; And they shall be a scourge unto the people of this land.

66. "Nevertheless, when they shall have received the fullness of My gospel, then if they shall harden their hearts against Me, 'I will return their iniquities upon their own heads,' saith the Father;

67. 'And I will remember the covenant which I have made with My people, And I have covenanted with them that I would gather them together in Mine own due time,

68. That I would give unto them again the land of their fathers for their inheritance, Which is the Land of Jerusalem, which is the Promised Land unto them forever,' saith the Father.

69. "And it shall come to pass that the time cometh when the fullness of My gospel be preached unto them, And they shall believe in Me, that I Am Jesus Christ, the Son of God, And shall pray unto the Father in My name.

70. 'Then shall their watchmen lift up their voice, And with the voice together shall they sing; For they shall see eye to eye.

71. Then will the Father gather them together again, And give unto them Jerusalem for the land of their inheritance.

72. Then shall they break forth into joy! Sing together, ye waste places of Jerusalem! For the Father hath comforted His people, He hath redeemed Jerusalem.

73. The Father hath made bare His holy arm in the eyes of all the nations; And all the ends of the earth shall see the salvation of the Father; And the Father and I are one.'

74. "And then shall be brought to pass that which is written: 'Awake! awake again, and put on thy strength, O Zion! Put on thy beautiful garments, O Jerusalem, the holy city! For henceforth there shall no more come into thee the uncircumcised and the unclean.

75. Shake thyself from the dust-arise! Sit down, O Jerusalem! Loose thyself from the bands of thy neck, O captive daughter of Zion!

76. For thus saith the Lord: "Ye have sold yourselves for naught; And ye shall be redeemed without money."

77. 'Verily, verily I say unto you that My people shall know My name-Yea, in that day they shall know that I Am He that doth speak.

78. And then shall they say, "How beautiful upon the mountains are the feet of Him that bringeth good tidings unto them, That publisheth peace, That bringeth good tidings unto them of good, That publisheth salvation, That saith unto Zion, 'Thy God reigneth!'"

79. 'And then shall a cry go forth, Depart ye! Depart ye! Go ye out from thence. Touch not that which is unclean; Go ye out of the midst of her; Be ye clean that bear the vessels of the Lord.

80. For ye shall not go out with haste, nor go by flight; For the Lord will go before you, And the God of Israel shall be your rearward.

81. 'Behold, My Servant shall deal prudently- He shall be exalted and extolled and be very high.

82. As many were astonished at thee; His visage was so marred-more than any man, And His form more than the sons of men;

83. So shall He sprinkle many nations. The kings shall shut their mouths at Him; For that which had not been told them shall they see, And that which they had not heard shall they consider.'

84. "Verily, verily I say unto you, all these things shall surely come, even as the Father hath commanded Me;

85. And then shall this covenant which the Father hath covenanted with His people be fulfilled; And then shall Jerusalem be inhabited again with My people, And it shall be the land of their inheritance.

86. "And verily I say unto you, I give unto you a sign that ye may know the time when these things shall be about to take place, That I shall gather in from their long dispersion My people, O house of Israel, And shall establish again among them My Zion.

87. "And behold, this is the thing which I will give unto you for a sign- "For verily I say unto you, that when these things which I deliver unto you- And which I shall deliver unto you hereafter of Myself and by the power of the Holy Ghost which shall be given unto you of the Father- Shall be made known unto the Gentiles,

88. that they may know concerning this people which are a remnant of the house of Jacob, And concerning this My people which shall be scattered by them-

89. "Verily, verily I say unto you, when these things shall be made known unto them of the Father, And shall come forth of the Father from them unto you- For it is wisdom in the Father that they should be established in this land and be set up as a free people by the power of the Father, That these things might come forth from them unto a remnant of your seed, That the covenant of the Father may be fulfilled which He hath covenanted with His people, O house of Israel-

90. "Therefore, when these works, and the work which shall be wrought among you hereafter, shall come forth from the Gentiles unto your seed, which shall dwindle in unbelief because of iniquity-

91. For thus it behooveth the Father that it should come forth from the Gentiles, That He may show forth His power unto the Gentiles for this cause: That the Gentiles-if they will not harden their hearts- That they may repent and come unto Me and be baptized in My name and know of the true points of My doctrine, That they may be numbered among My people, O house of Israel-

92. "And when these things come to pass- that thy seed shall begin to know these things- It shall be a sign unto them that they may know that the work of the Father hath already commenced, Unto the fulfilling of the covenant which He hath made unto the people which are of the house of Israel.

93. "And when that day shall come, it shall come to pass that kings shall shut their mouths, For that which had not been told them, shall they see, And that which they had not heard, shall they consider;

94. For in that day, for My sake shall the Father work a work which shall be a great and a marvelous work among them; And there shall be among them which will not believe it, although a man shall declare it unto them.

95. "But behold, the life of My servant shall be in My hand; Therefore, they shall not hurt him, although he shall be marred because of them,

96. Yet I will heal him, for I will show unto them that My wisdom is greater than the cunning of the devil.

97. "Therefore, it shall come to pass that whosoever will not believe in My words-which am Jesus Christ- Which the Father shall cause him to bring forth unto the Gentiles, And shall give unto him power that he shall bring them forth unto the Gentiles-it shall be done even as Moses said- They shall be cut off from among My people which are of the covenant.

98. 'And My people which are a remnant of Jacob shall be among the Gentiles, Yea, in the midst of them, as a lion among the beasts of the forest, as a young lion among the flocks of sheep, Who, if he go through, both treadeth down and teareth in pieces, And none can deliver.

99. Their hand shall be lifted up upon their adversaries, And all their enemies shall be cut off.'

100. "Yea, wo be unto the Gentiles, except they repent! 'For it shall come to pass in that day,' saith the Father, 'That I will cut off thy horses out of the midst of thee, And I will destroy thy chariots, And I will cut off the cities of thy land And throw down all thy strongholds.

101. And I will cut off witchcrafts out of thy hand, And thou shalt have no more soothsayers.

102. Thy graven images I will also cut off, And thy standing images out of the midst of thee; And thou shalt no more worship the works of thy hands;

103. And I will pluck up thy groves out of the midst of thee- So will I destroy thy cities.

104. 'And it shall come to pass that all lyings and deceivings and envyings and strifes and priestcrafts and whoredoms shall be done away.

105. For it shall come to pass,' saith the Father, 'that at that day, whosoever will not repent and come unto My beloved Son, Them will I cut off from among My people, O house of Israel, And I will execute vengeance and fury upon them-even as upon the heathen- such as they have not heard!'

3 Nephi 10

1. "But if they will repent, and hearken unto My words, and harden not their hearts, I will establish My church among them; And they shall come in unto the covenant and be numbered among this, the remnant of Jacob, unto whom I have given this land for their inheritance, And they shall assist My people, the remnant of Jacob-

2. And also as many of the house of Israel as shall come- That they may build a city which shall be called the New Jerusalem;

3. And then shall they assist My people that they may be gathered in, which are scattered upon all the face of the land, in unto the New Jerusalem;

4. And then shall the powers of heaven come down among them, And I also will be in the midst; And then shall the work of the Father commence at that day, even when this gospel shall be preached among the remnant of this people.

5. "Verily I say unto you, at that day shall the work of the Father commence among all the dispersed of My people- Yea, even the tribes which have been lost which the Father hath led away out of Jerusalem-

6. Yea, the work shall commence among all the dispersed of My people, with the Father, To prepare the way whereby they may come unto Me, that they may call on the Father in My name.

7. "Yea, and then shall the work commence with the Father among all nations in preparing the way whereby His people may be gathered home to the land of their inheritance;

8. And they shall go out from all nations, And they shall not go out in haste nor go by flight; 'For I will go before them,' saith the Father, 'And I will be their rearward.' "And then shall that which is written come to pass:

9. 'Sing, O barren, thou that didst not bear! Break forth into singing and cry aloud, thou that didst not travail with child! For more are the children of the desolate than the children of the married wife,' saith the Lord.

10. 1'Enlarge the place of thy tent, And let them stretch forth the curtains of thy habitations; Spare not; Lengthen thy cords and strengthen thy stakes.

11. For thou shalt break forth on the right hand and on the left, And thy seed shall inherit the Gentiles, And make the desolate cities to be inhabited.

12. 'Fear not, for thou shalt not be ashamed; Neither be thou confounded, for thou shalt not be put to shame; For thou shalt forget the shame of thy youth, And shalt not remember the reproach of thy widowhood anymore.

13. For thy Maker, thy husband, the Lord of Hosts is His name; And thy Redeemer, the Holy One of Israel, the God of the whole earth shall He be called;

14. For the Lord hath called thee as a woman forsaken and grieved in spirit, And a wife of youth when thou wast refused,' saith thy God.

15. 'For a small moment have I forsaken thee, But with great mercies will I gather thee.

16. In a little wrath I hid My face from thee for a moment; But with everlasting kindness will I have mercy on thee,' saith the Lord thy Redeemer.

17. 'For this, the waters of Noah unto Me, For as I have sworn that the waters of Noah should no more go over the earth, So have I sworn that I would not be wroth with thee.

18. For the mountains shall depart, And the hills be removed, But My kindness shall not depart from thee, Neither shall the covenant of My peace be removed,' saith the Lord that hath mercy on thee.

19. 'O thou afflicted, tossed with tempests and not comforted, Behold, I will lay thy stones with fair colors and lay thy foundations with sapphires.

20. And I will make thy windows of agates and thy gates of carbuncles, And all thy borders of pleasant stones.

21. And all thy children shall be taught of the Lord, And great shall be the peace of thy children.

22. In righteousness shalt thou be established; Thou shalt be far from oppression, for thou shalt not fear; And from terror, for it shall not come near thee.

23. 'Behold, they shall surely gather together against thee, not by Me. Whosoever shall gather together against thee shall fall for thy sake.

24. 'Behold, I have created the smith that bloweth the coals in the fire, And that bringeth forth an instrument for his work; And I have created the waster to destroy.

25. No weapon that is formed against thee shall prosper, And every tongue that shall revile against thee in judgment thou shalt condemn. This is the heritage of the servants of the Lord, And their righteousness is of Me,' saith the Lord.

26. "And now behold, I say unto you that ye had ought to search these things-

27. Yea, a commandment I give unto you that ye search these things diligently, for great are the words of Isaiah,

28. For surely he spake as touching all things concerning My people which are of the house of Israel; Therefore, it must needs be that he must speak also to the Gentiles;

29. And all things that he spake hath been and shall be, even according to the words which he spake.

30. "Therefore, give heed to My words; Write the things which I have told you, And according to the time and the will of the Father, they shall go forth unto the Gentiles;

31. And whosoever will hearken unto My words and repenteth and is baptized, the same shall be saved.

32. "Search the prophets, for many there be that testify of these things."

33. And now it came to pass that when Jesus had said these words, He saith unto them again-after He had expounded all the scriptures unto them which they had received- He saith unto

them: "Behold, other scriptures I would that ye should write that ye have not."

34. And it came to pass that He saith unto Nephi: "Bring forth the records which ye have kept."

35. And when Nephi had brought forth the records and laid them before Him, And He cast His eyes upon them and saith:

36. "Verily I say unto you, I commanded My servant Samuel the Lamanite that he should testify unto this people, That at the day that the Father should glorify His name in Me, That there were many saints which should arise from the dead and should appear unto many and should minister unto them."

37. And He saith unto them, "Were it not so?"

38. And His disciples answered Him and said: "Yea, Lord, Samuel did prophesy according to Thy words, And they were all fulfilled."

39. And Jesus saith unto them: "Howbeit that ye have not written this thing- that many saints did arise and appear unto many and did minister unto them?"

40. And it came to pass that Nephi remembered that this thing had not been written.

41. And it came to pass that Jesus commanded that it should be written, Therefore, it was written according as He commanded.

3 Nephi 11

1. And now it came to pass that when Jesus had expounded all the scriptures in one which they had written, He commanded them that they should teach the things which He had expounded unto them.

2. And it came to pass that He commanded them that they should write the words which the Father had given unto Malachi, which He should tell unto them.

3. And it came to pass that after they were written, He expounded them;

4. And these are the words which He did tell unto them, saying: "Thus said the Father unto Malachi: 'Behold, I will send My messenger, And he shall prepare the way before Me, And the Lord, whom ye seek shall suddenly come to His temple, Even the Messenger of the covenant whom ye delight in- Behold, He shall come,' saith the Lord of Hosts.

5. 'But who may abide the day of His coming? And who shall stand when He appeareth? For He is like a refiner's fire and like fuller's soap.

6. And He shall sit as a refiner and purifier of silver; And He shall purify the sons of Levi and purge them as gold and silver, That they may offer unto the Lord an offering in righteousness.

7. 'Then shall the offering of Judah and Jerusalem be pleasant unto the Lord, As in the days of old, And as in former years.

8. And I will come near to you to judgment; And I will be a swift witness against the sorcerers, And against the adulterers, And against false swearers, And against those that oppress the hireling in his wages, the widow and the fatherless, And that turn aside the stranger and fear not Me,' saith the Lord of Hosts.

9. 'For I Am the Lord, I change not; Therefore, ye sons of Jacob are not consumed.

10. Even from the days of your fathers ye are gone away from Mine ordinances and have not kept them. Return unto Me, and I will return unto you, 'saith the Lord of Hosts. 'But ye say, "Wherein shall we return?"

11. 'Will a man rob God? Yet ye have robbed Me! But ye say, "Wherein have we robbed Thee?" In tithes and offerings.

12. Ye are cursed with a curse, for ye have robbed Me, even this whole nation.

13. 'Bring ye all the tithes into the storehouse, that there may be meat in My house, And prove Me now herewith,' saith the Lord of Hosts, 'If I will not open you the windows of heaven And pour you out a blessing that there shall not be room enough to receive it.

14. 'And I will rebuke the devourer for your sakes- He shall not destroy the fruits of your ground, Neither shall your vine cast her fruit before the time in the field,' saith the Lord of Hosts;

15. 'And all nations shall call you blessed, For ye shall be a delightsome land,' saith the Lord of Hosts.

16. 'Your words have been stout against Me,' saith the Lord, 'Yet ye say, "What have we spoken against Thee?"

17. Ye have said, "It is vain to serve God; And what doth it profit that we have kept His ordinances, And that we have walked mournfully before the Lord of Hosts?

218

18. And now we call the proud happy, Yea, they that work wickedness are set up; Yea, them that tempt God are even delivered."

19. 'Then they that feared the Lord spake often one to another, And the Lord hearkened and heard; And a book of remembrance was written before Him for them that feared the Lord and that thought upon His name.

20. 'And they shall be Mine,' saith the Lord of Hosts, 'In that day when I make up My jewels. And I will spare them as a man spareth his own son that serveth him.

21. Then shall ye return and discern between the righteous and the wicked- Between him that serveth God and him that serveth Him not.

22. 'For behold, the day cometh that shall burn as an oven; And all the proud, yea, and all that do wickedly, shall be stubble. And the day that cometh shall burn them up,' saith the Lord of Hosts, 'That it shall leave them neither root nor branch.

23. 'But unto you that fear My name shall the Son of Righteousness arise with healing in His wings; And ye shall go forth and grow up as calves of the stall.

24. And ye shall tread down the wicked, For they shall be as ashes under the soles of your feet in the day that I shall do this,' saith the Lord of Hosts.

25. 'Remember ye the law of Moses My servant, which I commanded unto him in Horeb for all Israel with the statutes and judgments.

26. Behold, I will send you Elijah the prophet before the coming of the great and dreadful day of the Lord.

27. And he shall turn the heart of the fathers to the children and the heart of the children to their fathers, Lest I come and smite the earth with a curse.'"

28. And now it came to pass that when Jesus had told these things, He expounded them unto the multitude, And He did expound all things unto them, both great and small;

29. And He saith: "These scriptures which ye had not with you, the Father commanded that I should give unto you, For it was wisdom in Him that they should be given unto future generations."

30. And He did expound all things, even from the beginning until the time that He should come in His glory;

31. Yea, even all things which should come upon the face of the earth, even until the elements should melt with fervent heat, And the earth should be wrapped together as a scroll, And the heaven and the earth should pass away;

32. And even unto the great and last day when all people and all kindreds and all nations and tongues shall stand before God to be judged of their works, whether they be good or whether they be evil-

33. If they be good, to the resurrection of everlasting life, And if they be evil, to the resurrection of damnation, Being on a parallel, the one on the one hand, and the other on the other hand- According to the mercy and the justice and the holiness which is in Christ, which was before the world began.

3 Nephi 12

1. And now there cannot be written in this book even an hundredth part of the things which Jesus did truly teach unto the people; But behold, the plates of Nephi do contain the more part of the things which He taught the people;

2. And these things have I written which are a lesser part of the things which He taught the people, And I have written them to the intent that they may be brought again unto this people from the Gentiles according to the words which Jesus hath spoken.

3. And when they shall have received this, which is expedient that they should have first to try their faith, And if it should so be that they shall believe these things, Then shall the greater things be made manifest unto them;

4. And if it so be that they will not believe these things, Then shall the greater things be withheld from them unto their condemnation.

5. Behold, I was about to write them all which were engraven upon the plates of Nephi, But the Lord forbid it, saying, "I will try the faith of My people"; Therefore, I, Mormon, do write the things which have been commanded me of the Lord.

6. And now I, Mormon, make an end of my sayings and proceed to write the things which have been commanded me; Therefore, I would that ye should behold that the Lord truly did teach the people for the space of three days; And after that, He did show Himself unto them oft and did break bread oft and bless it and give it unto them.

7. And it came to pass that He did teach and minister unto the children of the multitude of whom hath been spoken; And He did loose their tongues, And they did speak unto their fathers great and marvelous things-even greater than He had revealed unto the people- And loosed their tongues that they could utter.

8. And it came to pass that after He had ascended into heaven the second time that He showed Himself unto them, And gone unto the Father after having healed all their sick and their lame, And opened the eyes of the blind, And unstopped the ears of the deaf, And even had done all manner of cures among them, And raised a man from the dead, And had shown forth His power unto them, And had ascended unto the Father-

9. Behold, it came to pass on the morrow that the multitude gathered themselves together, And they both saw and heard these children, yea, even babes did open their mouths and utter marvelous things; And the things which they did utter were forbidden that there should not any man write them.

10. And it came to pass that the disciples whom Jesus had chosen began from that time forth to baptize and to teach as many as did come unto them, And as many as were baptized in the name of Jesus were filled with the Holy Ghost;

11. And many of them saw and heard unspeakable things which are not lawful to be written; And they taught and did minister one to another; And they had all things common among them, every man dealing justly one with another.

12. And it came to pass that they did do all things, even as Jesus had commanded them.

13. And they which were baptized in the name of Jesus were called the church of Christ.

14. And it came to pass that as the disciples of Jesus were journeying and were preaching the things which they had both heard and seen and were baptizing in the name of Jesus, It came to pass that the disciples were gathered together and were united in mighty prayer and fasting;

15. And Jesus again showed Himself unto them, for they were praying unto the Father in His name; And Jesus came and stood in the midst of them and saith unto them: "What will ye that I shall give unto you?"

16. And they saith unto Him: "Lord, we will that Thou wouldst tell us the name whereby we shall call this church, For there are disputations among the people concerning this matter."

17. And the Lord said unto them: "Verily, verily I say unto you, why is it that the people should murmur and dispute because of this thing?

18. Have they not read the scriptures which saith, 'Ye must take upon you the name of Christ,' which is My name? For by this name shall ye be called at the last day, And whoso taketh upon him My name and endureth to the end, the same shall be saved at the last day.

19. "Therefore, whatsoever ye shall do, ye shall do it in My name; Therefore, ye shall call the church in My name; And ye shall call upon the Father in My name, that He will bless the church for My sake; And howbeit My church save it be called in My name?

20. For if a church be called in Moses' name, then it be Moses' church; Or if it be called in the name of a man, then it be the church of a man; But if it be called in My name, then it is My church- if it so be that they are built upon My gospel.

21. "Verily I say unto you that ye are built upon My gospel, Therefore, ye shall call whatsoever things ye do call in My name; Therefore, if ye call upon the Father for the church, if it be in My name, the Father will hear you;

22. And if it so be that the church is built upon My gospel, then will the Father show forth His own works in it.

23. "But if it be not built upon My gospel and is built upon the works of man or upon the works of the devil, Verily I say unto you, they have joy in their works for a season; And by and by the end cometh, And they are hewn down and cast into the fire from whence there is no return;

24. For their works do follow them, For it is because of their works that they are hewn down; Therefore, remember the things that I have told you.

25. "Behold, I have given unto you My gospel, And this is the gospel which I have given unto you- That I came into the world to do the will of My Father because My Father sent Me;

26. And My Father sent Me that I might be lifted up upon the cross; And after that I had been lifted up upon the cross, I might draw all men unto Me;

27. That as I have been lifted up by men, even so should men be lifted up by the Father to stand before Me to be judged of their works, whether they be good or whether they be evil;

28. And for this cause have I been lifted up; Therefore, according to the power of the Father, I will draw all men unto Me, that they may be judged according to their works.

29. "And it shall come to pass that whoso repenteth and is baptized in My name shall be filled; And if he endureth to the end, Behold, him will I hold guiltless before My Father at that day when I shall stand to judge the world;

30. And he that endureth not unto the end, The same is he that is also hewn down and cast into the fire from whence they can no more return because of the justice of the Father. "And this is the word which He hath given unto the children of men;

31. And for this cause He fulfilleth the words which He hath given, And He lieth not, but fulfilleth all His words; And no unclean thing can enter into His kingdom;

32. Therefore, nothing entereth into His rest, Save it be those who have washed their garments in My blood because of their faith and the repentance of all their sins and their faithfulness unto the end.

33. "Now this is the commandment: Repent, all ye ends of the earth! and come unto Me! and be baptized in My name! That ye may be sanctified by the reception of the Holy Ghost, That ye may stand spotless before Me at the last day!

34. "Verily, verily I say unto you, this is My gospel. "And ye know the things that ye must do in My church, For the works which ye have seen Me do, that shall ye also do;

35. For that which ye have seen Me do, even that shall ye do; Therefore, if ye do these things, blessed are ye, For ye shall be lifted up at the last day.

3 Nephi 13

1. "Write the things which ye have seen and heard, save it be those which are forbidden; Write the works of this people, which shall be even as hath been written of that which hath been;

2. For behold, out of the books which have been written, and which shall be written, shall this people be judged, For by them should their works be known unto men.

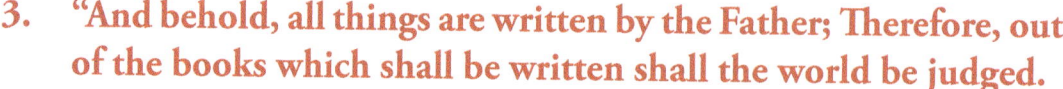

3. "And behold, all things are written by the Father; Therefore, out of the books which shall be written shall the world be judged.

4. "And know ye that ye shall be judges of this people, according to the judgment which I shall give unto you, which shall be just;

5. Therefore, what manner of men had ye ought to be? Verily I say unto you, even as I am. And now I go unto the Father.

6. "And verily I say unto you, whatsoever things ye shall ask the Father in My name, it shall be given unto you; Therefore, ask, and ye shall receive, Knock, and it shall be opened unto you; For he that asketh, receiveth, And unto him that knocketh, it shall be opened.

7. "And now behold, My joy is great, even unto fullness, because of you, and also this generation; Yea, and even the Father rejoiceth, and also all the holy angels, because of you and this generation, For none of them are lost.

8. "Behold, I would that ye should understand- For I mean them which are now alive of this generation; And none of them are lost; And in them I have fullness of joy.

9. "But behold, it sorroweth Me because of the fourth generation from this generation, For they are led away captive by him, even as was the son of perdition; For they will sell Me for silver and for gold, And for that which moth doth corrupt and which thieves can break through and steal;

10. And in that day will I visit them, even in turning their works upon their own heads."

11. And it came to pass that when Jesus had ended these sayings, He saith unto His disciples: "Enter ye in at the strait gate, For strait is the gate and narrow is the way that leads to life, And few there be that find it; But wide is the gate and broad the way which leads to death, And many there be that traveleth therein, until the night cometh wherein no man can work."

12. And it came to pass when Jesus had said these words, He spake unto His disciples one by one, saying unto them: "What is it that ye desire of Me after that I am gone to the Father?"

13. And they all spake, save it were three, saying: "We desire that after we have lived unto the age of man, That our ministry wherein Thou hast called us may have an end, That we may speedily come unto Thee in Thy kingdom."

14. And He saith unto them: "Blessed are ye because ye desire this thing of Me; Therefore, after that ye are seventy and two years old, ye shall come unto Me in My kingdom; And with Me ye shall find rest."

15. And when He had spake unto them, He turned Himself unto the three and said unto them: "What will ye that I should do unto you when I am gone unto the Father?"

16. And they sorrowed in their hearts, for they durst not speak unto Him the thing which they desired.

17. And He saith unto them: "Behold, I know your thoughts; And ye have desired the thing which John My beloved, which was with Me in My ministry before that I was lifted up by the Jews, desired of Me;

18. Therefore, more blessed are ye, for ye shall never taste of death, But ye shall live to behold all the doings of the Father unto the children of men, Even until all things shall be fulfilled according to the will of the Father, when I shall come in My glory with the powers of heaven;

19. And ye shall never endure the pains of death; But when I shall come in My glory, ye shall be changed in the twinkling of an eye from mortality to immortality; And then shall ye be blessed in the kingdom of My Father.

20. "And again, ye shall not have pain while ye shall dwell in the flesh, Neither sorrow, save it be for the sins of the world;

21. And all this will I do because of the thing which ye have desired of Me, For ye have desired that ye might bring the souls of men unto Me while the world shall stand; And for this cause ye shall have fullness of joy and ye shall sit down in the kingdom of My Father;

22. Yea, your joy shall be full, even as the Father hath given Me fullness of joy; And ye shall be even as I am; And I am even as the Father, And the Father and I are one,

23. And the Holy Ghost beareth record of the Father and Me; And the Father giveth the Holy Ghost unto the children of men because of Me."

24. And it came to pass that when Jesus had spake these words, He touched every one of them with His finger, save it were the three which were to tarry; And then He departed.

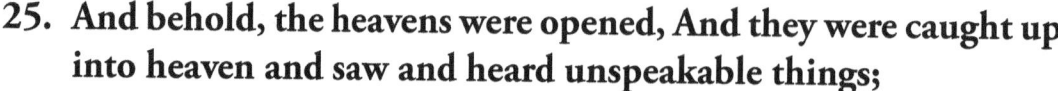

25. And behold, the heavens were opened, And they were caught up into heaven and saw and heard unspeakable things;

26. And it was forbidden them that they should utter, Neither was it given unto them power that they could utter the things which they saw and heard;

27. And whether they were in the body or out of the body, they could not tell; For it did seem unto them like a transfiguration of them, That they were changed from this body of flesh into an immortal state that they could behold the things of God.

28. But it came to pass that they did again minister upon the face of the earth; Nevertheless, they did not minister of the things which they had heard and seen because of the commandment which was given them in heaven.

29. And now whether they were mortal or immortal from the day of their transfiguration, I know not; But this much I know, according to the record which hath been given- They did go forth upon the face of the land and did minister unto all the people, uniting as many to the church as would believe in their preaching, baptizing them,

30. And as many as were baptized did receive the Holy Ghost; And they were cast into prison by them who did not belong to the church,

31. And the prisons could not hold them, for they were rent in twain; And they were cast down into the earth,

32. But they did smite the earth with the word of God, insomuch that by His power they were delivered out of the depths of the earth; And therefore, they could not dig pits sufficiently to hold them;

33. And thrice they were cast into a furnace and received no harm;

34. And twice were they cast into a den of wild beasts, And behold, they did play with the beasts as a child with a suckling lamb and received no harm.

35. And it came to pass that thus they did go forth among all the people of Nephi and did preach the gospel of Christ unto all people upon the face of the land;

36. And they were converted unto the Lord and were united unto the church of Christ; And thus the people of that generation were blessed according to the word of Jesus.

CONCLUSION

We have seen that God's Word tells us that He will provide two or more witnesses to establish the truth of a matter (2 Corinthians 13:1), and He has! The Bible, especially the New Testament, is but one witness from one society, the House of Judah. The Book of Mormon is a clear second witness to the divinity of Jesus Christ. It comes to us from the tribe of Joseph, as prophesied in the Bible. It tells us about a society separated from their brethren and, many believe, brought by God to the Americas. The more a person studies the Book of Mormon, the more improbable it becomes that the nearly illiterate Joseph Smith, Jr., could have invented it.

Now, what do you think? After reading this book, can you find even a small place in your heart to allow for the truth of The Book of Mormon? If so, I would ask you to follow Alma's advice:

Alma 16:151 RCE, Alma 32:27 LDS:

But behold, if ye will awake and arouse your faculties, even to an experiment upon my words, and exercise a particle of faith, Yea, even if ye can no more than desire to believe, let this desire work in you, Even until ye believe in a manner that ye can give place for a portion of my words.

Are you willing to receive the Holy Spirit's confirmation to what you have pondered? If so, then prayerfully read The Book of Mormon, asking God to manifest the truth of it to you. The prophet Moroni explains how to do that:

Moroni 10:4-9 RCE, Moroni 10:4-8 LDS:

And when ye shall receive these things, I would exhort you that ye would ask God the Eternal Father, in the name of Christ, if these things are not true; And if ye shall ask with a sincere heart, with real intent, having faith in Christ, And [then] He will manifest the truth of it unto you by the power of the Holy Ghost; And by the power of the Holy Ghost, ye may know the truth of all things; And whatsoever thing is good, is just and true; Wherefore, nothing that is good denieth the Christ, but acknowledgeth that He is. And ye may know that He is by the power of the Holy Ghost;

Wherefore, I would exhort you that ye deny not the power of God; For He worketh by power according to the faith of the children of men, the same today, tomorrow and forever. And again I exhort you, my brethren, that ye deny not the gifts of God, for they are many and they come from the same God; And there are different ways that these gifts are administered, But it is the same God which worketh all in all; And they are given by the manifestations of the Spirit of God unto men to profit them.

I may not have provided absolute proof that The Book of Mormon is from God, but I believe I have shown a clear preponderance of evidence that it was not by Joseph Smith; indeed, that it was authored by highly literate men upon whom the hand of the Lord rested. Since you need your own testimony as to its validity, I would ask that you put the Book of Mormon to a further test and follow the advice of the Apostle John:

1 John 4:1-2:

"Beloved, believe not every spirit, but try the spirits whether they are of God: because many false prophets are gone out into the world. Hereby know ye the spirit of God: <u>Every spirit that confesseth that Jesus Christ is come in the flesh is of God</u>." (Emphasis added)

In other words, we must be familiar enough with the workings of the Holy Spirit to recognize that still small voice when it speaks to us and tells us the truth. However, please remember, if you ask God to give you a witness, but you have already decided the answer, He will not answer. Why? Because you have already decided. So ask in a spirit of humility, with an open mind.

If you are still having trouble giving God an opportunity to witness that He directed the writers of The Book of Mormon, then allow me to pose a question. Let's consider a hypothetical situation: God sends you one of His holy messengers, Moses for example, and he gives you a book, and he and the Holy Spirit tell you that it is scripture. Now there is no doubt in your mind about whether or not it is. After all, Moses told you and God's Holy Spirit confirmed that the book is scripture.

So now, they have gone, and you sit down to read it. Please answer the following question: **What would you expect to find in this new book?** Before you go on, write your answer. Take as much time as you need and then compare it to what *I think* would be in the book. I am going to make certain assumptions and ask that you use them as you consider your answer:

1. This new book is about a group that left from Jerusalem around the time of its destruction.
2. These people were led by a prophet of God.

3. They had access to all previous scriptures up to the time of their departure.

4. They must at some point travel over a large body of water.

5. They then arrive at their final destination, and that location must have archeological remains proving that someone lived there.

6. There must be prophecies in this new book about the Bible and in the Bible about this book and its people.

7. It must be a strong witness for Jesus Christ.

Here is what I would expect that this scripture would teach:

1. The exodus from Jerusalem and a journey to a new homeland.
2. A history from the exodus until 300 to 400 A.D.
3. God's promises to Abraham about the Twelve Tribes of Israel.
4. God's covenants with the Twelve Tribes of Israel.
5. Extensive quotes from the first five books of Moses.
6. Support for the Bible as scripture.
7. God's love for the Israelites.
8. Teaching about Faith.
9. God's plan for Repentance.
10. Baptism by immersion in water and by the Spirit.
11. The born-again experience.
12. Gifts of the Spirit.
13. The grace of God.
14. God's plan of Redemption.
15. God's plan of Salvation.
16. About the divinity of Jesus Christ.
17. About the atoning blood of Christ.
18. Signs given at the birth of Jesus Christ.
19. Signs that occurred at the death of Jesus Christ.
20. Christ's ministry at their location as promised in Bible (lost sheep).
21. Christ appointing twelve disciples to minister to their people.
22. Prophetic writings about:
    - The virgin conception.
    - Christ's birth.
    - Christ's baptism.
    - Christ's crucifixion.
    - The role of John the Baptist.
    - The last days.

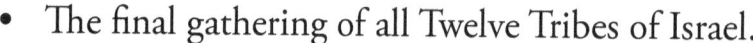
- The final gathering of all Twelve Tribes of Israel.
23   Included in this would be their history.

Well, now that you have seen my list, how does it compare to yours? Does yours include everything on mine? There is no completely right or wrong answer. But what is important is that you get a Book of Mormon and read it through, looking for each of your expectations. I believe that not one of them will be missing. You will see it contains everything that you would expect that a book given to you by Moses would have.

The prophets/writers of The Book of Mormon were men of great faith, and because they literally saw our day, one of them, Moroni, cautioned us with a voice of warning.

Mormon 4:45-47, 52-53 RCE, Mormon 8:34-36, 26-28 LDS:

Behold, the Lord hath shown unto me great and marvelous things concerning that which must shortly come at that day when these things shall come forth among you. Behold, I speak unto you as if ye were present, And yet ye are not; But behold, Jesus Christ hath shown you unto me and I know your doing, And I know that ye do walk in the pride of your hearts. … Why are ye ashamed to take upon you the name of Christ? Why do you not think that greater is the value of an endless happiness than that misery which never dies, because of the praise of the world?

In some ways, I feel that *I* am someone *"speaking out of the dust."* I ask myself, what has happened to our culture? I fear that the same destruction that occurred to the Nephites because of their iniquity and pride is about to fall upon America. We must come together and fight our real enemy, satan. We need to end his influence; this includes, but is not limited to: abortion, illegal discrimination (all laws discriminate in some way), violence, sexual deviancy, abuse, and governmental restrictions on our rights and freedoms, especially our religious freedoms, all of which are so common today. Proverbs tells us that:

Proverbs 14:12:

There is a way which seemeth right unto a man, but the end thereof are the ways of death.

We live in a Christian nation; we are supposed to know what these values are. All of these sins are our joint responsibility, and they fall upon us because we have done little to nothing to end the policies that allow them to prosper. I worry about the horrible consequences of these wrong choices if we do not choose life through the love of God and the guidance of His Holy Spirit. The witness of Deuteronomy is absolutely clear:

<u>Deuteronomy 30:19:</u>

I call heaven and earth to record this day against you, that I have set before you life and death, blessing and cursing: therefore choose life, that both thou and thy seed may live:...

The Book of Mormon is in total agreement and stands on its own merit, independent of any denominational church. Let it speak to us as individuals and as a nation. Let it remind us that we are God's people, a covenant people and a part of the Lost Tribes of Israel who are now scattered over all the face of the earth. We are not better than other people, but we have been given great blessings. Who can doubt that we have received a "double portion."? Therefore, do we not have a greater responsibility? If we now fail to speak out and stand up for what we know is right, then who will?

I pray that you have experienced the urging of God's Holy Spirit as you have read this book. If you read The Book of Mormon and ask God for your own testimony, He will give it to you. He is eager to respond. So open your heart to receive the ministry of His Spirit and accept the answer He gives you. To encourage you, I offer the words of Alma:

<u>Alma 16:143-144 RCE, Alma 32:21-22 LDS:</u>

And now as I said concerning faith, Faith, is not to have a perfect knowledge of things; Therefore, if ye have faith, ye hope for things which are not seen, which are true. And now behold I say unto you, and I would that ye should remember that God is merciful unto all who believe on His name; Therefore, He desireth in the first place that ye should believe, yea, even on His word.

We are not all in the same place spiritually, but nevertheless we are on the same journey, seeking the same God and the same spiritual wholeness. As I said at the beginning, I believe that scripture is whatever the Holy Spirit witnesses that it is. To further clarify that statement, I will close with the following instruction:

Knowing that the Holy Spirit was actively involved in the formation of Scripture through giving of truth (revelation) and the recording of truth (inspiration); and knowing that the Holy Spirit functions today in the role of helping us to understand that truth, which has been revealed and recorded (illumination); we should be driven to spend time reading, memorizing and studying the truth of God's word. (Valley Bible 8)

God bless you; I will be praying for you.

WORKS CITED

Black, Susan Easton. "Names of Christ in the Book of Mormon." *Ensign*. July, 1978: 60-61. Print.

Bancroft, Hubert Howe. *The Native Races*. Vol. 5. San Francisco. The History Co., Publishers 1886: 279. Print.

Board of Publication. *The History of the Reorganized Church of Latter Day Saints*. Vol. 1. Independence: Herald House. 1951: 7-10. Print.

Brown, Kent S. "New Light from Arabia on Lehi's Trail." *Echoes and Evidences of the Book of Mormon*. ed. Parry, Donald W, Daniel C. Peterson, John Welch. Provo: FARMS, 2002: 61, 78. Print.

Clark, John E. "Archaeological Trends and Book of Mormon Origins." *BYU Studies*. 44/4 April, 1944: 84-85. Print.

Crowell, Angela M. "Biblical Hebrew Poetry in the Book of Mormon." Handout. (1,4) Print.

Foster, Lynn. "Handbook to Life in the Ancient Maya World." New York: Oxford University Press. 2002:278. Print.

Hattaway, Paul. "The Heavenly Man." Grand Rapids: Monarch. 2002. Print.

Hamblin, William J. "Sacred Writings on Metal Plates in the Ancient Mediterranean" article 16 pages, Provo Utah, Vol 19 Issue 1. Neal A. Maxwell Institute 2007: 37-54.

<http://maxwellinstitute.byu.edu/publications/ review/?vol=19&num=1&id=637/>. Web. 09/25/2012.

Heater, Shirley. "Mesoamerican & Book of Mormon Timelines Compared: With Selected Old World & Biblical Added" *Quetzal Codex*. Issue 3. 2012: Centerfold. Print.

"How Accurate are Carbon-14 and Other Radioactive Dating Methods?"

<http://www.answering-christianity.com/lost_books.htm. Web. 09/25/2012.

<http://wiki.answers.com/q/When_was_crucifixion_invented>. Web. 09/25/2012.

http://wiki.answers.com/q/When_was_the_Book_of_Psalms_written. Web.09/25/2012.

<http://www.cbcherokee.org>. Web. 23 Jan, 2008. centralbandofcherokee@gmail.com, 931-242-6398, June Lytespirit Hurd email.

<http://www.smilegodlovesyou.org/names.html>. Web. 09/25/2012.

"Israel's Symbols and Heraldry." <http://asis.com/stag/symbols.html>.Web June 3, 2012.

Jessee, Dean C. *Personal Writings of Joseph Smith*. Salt Lake City: Deseret Book. 1984: 243. Print.

Jones, David. "The British (Covenant) Church" 6 pages <http:www.ensignmessage.com/archives/britchurch.html>. Web. 09/25/2012.

Lindsay, Jeff. "Nugget #10: Hiding Sacred Records like the Golden Plates: A Well Established Ancient Practice." *Book of Mormon Nuggets*. <http://www.jefflindsay.com/bme10.shtml>. Web. 09/25/2012.

Maxwell, Neal A. "By the Gift and Power of God." *Echoes and Evidences of the Book of Mormon*.ed. Parry, Donald W, Daniel C. Peterson, John Welch. Provo: FARMS, 2002: 8, 11. Print.

"Mayan Agriculture Diet." <http://www.crystalinks.com/mayanagriculture.html/>. Web. 09/21/2012.

Meakin, John. "Will the United Kingdom Break Apart?" *Tomorrow's World*. Sept.-Oct. 2012: 14. Print.

Noah Webster's 1828 American Dictionary. <http://1828-dictionary.com/d/search/word,white>. Web.

Palmer, David. "Cement in America." *BMAF: 137 Cement in Ancient America*. 15 May 2012. <http://groups.google.com/d/msg/bmaf/-/G1lDqEezuSUJ>. Web. 09/25/2012.

Parry, Donald W. "Hebraisms and Other Ancient Peculiarities in the Book of Mormon." *Echoes and Evidences of the Book of Mormon*. ed. Parry, Donald W, Daniel C. Peterson, John Welch. Provo: FARMS. 2002: 159-80. Print.

Pearse, Colonel R.G. "The Pass of Israel." *The National Message*. 23 Oct. 1937: 676. Print.

Reynolds, Noel B. "By Objective Measures: Old Wine into Old Bottles" *Echoes and Evidences of the Book of Mormon.*ed. Parry, Donald W, Daniel C. Peterson, John Welch. Provo: FARMS. 2002: 128-29, 133,135. Print.

Richardson, Paul. "Lost Books of the Bible" Full Gospel of Christ Fellowship <http://www. icwseminary.org/lostbooks.htm>. Web. 09/25/2012.

Ross, Hugh. "Fulfilled Prophecy: Evidence for the Reliability of the Bible." 08/22/2003. *Reasons to Believe.* http://www. reasons.org/articles/fulfilled-prophecy-evidence-for-the-reliability-of-the-bible/. Web. 09/26/2012.

Rupe, Richard E. *The Book of Mormon: An Inconvenient Truth.* Lamar: Little Eagle Publ. 2009: 71-74. Print.

Smith, Joseph. *Times and Seasons.* 15 Sept. 1842: 862 Print.

Smith, Lucy M. "History of Joseph Smith" 1853: Chapter 18, Page 31.

<http://prophetjosephsmith.org/history/history_mother_menu>. Web. 09/25/2012.

Stoddard, Ted Dee. "Implications of Radiocarbon Dating for the Credibility of the Book of Mormon and the Validity of Book of Mormon Geography Models." *Book of Mormon Archaeological Forum.* <http://www.bmaf.org/node/474>. Web. 2012.

The New Compact Dictionary. Grand Rapids: Zondervan. 1967: 598. Print

"They Went Thattaway: Migrations of the House of Israel." <http://asis.com/users/stag/migratio.html>. Web. 09/25/2012.

Treat, Ray. Summarizing his personal knowledge of the Book of Mormon. Aug. 2012. Personal interview.

Valley Bible Church Theology Studies. "The Work of the Holy Spirit in Relation to Scriptures" http://www.valleybible.net/Adults/ClassNotes/TheologySurvey/HolySpirit/TheHoly Spirit- Scripture.pdf. Web. 09/25/2012.

Weldon, Roy E. *Other Sheep.* Independence: Price Publishing. 1999: 7, 11, 13, 16, 18-19, 23, 37, 57- 58, 80, 92-93. Print.

Wirth, Diane E. "Quetzalcoatl, The Maya God, and Jesus Christ." *Journal of the Book of Mormon Studies.* Vol 11, Issue 1. 2002: 4-15. 009/21/2012.

ORDERING INFORMATION

For questions and comments, please feel free to contact the author at:

Joseph Dean DeBarthe
20 Oak Hill Cluster
Independence, Mo 64057
debarthej@gmail.com

The digital and print version of the book is available at these fine retailers:

Author Reputation Press
Amazon
Barnes and Nobles
Google Books
And other thousands of online retailers

ABOUT THE AUTHOR

Joseph Dean DeBarthe is a fourth-generation member of the Reorganized Church of Jesus Christ of Latter Day Saints, or Community of Christ. He has a Bachelor's Degree in Business Management and Computer Information Systems from Central State University, Warrensburg Mo. Mr. DeBarthe served in the U.S. Navy for eight years nine months and worked as a civilian member of the military for twenty-three years. He retired from government service in 2008. During his employment, Mr. DeBarthe lived in Germany for three years. He travelled throughout Europe Including the following countries: Germany, Holland, The Netherlands France, Spain, Austria, Sweden, Italy and Czechoslovakia. While in the Navy he visited Japan, Korea, The Philippines, Guam and the North Pole. He also visited many Central American countries including Honduras, Mexico, Guatemala and Costa Rica. He currently lives in Independence, Missouri, with his wife, Maria, who is a Registered Nurse of Mayan descent.